T0083503

ELEMENTS OF TIME SERIES ECONOMETRICS: AN APPLIED APPROACH

EVŽEN KOČENDA
ALEXANDR ČERNÝ

CHARLES UNIVERSITY IN PRAGUE
KAROLINUM PRESS 2015

KAROLINUM PRESS
Ovocný trh 3–5
116 36, Prague 1
Czech Republic
www.karolinum.cz

Karolinum Press is the publishing department of Charles University in Prague

Designed by Jan Šerých
Typeset by Studio Lacerta (www.sazba.cz)
Printed in the Czech Republic by Karolinum Press

ISBN 978-80-246-3199-8
ISBN 978-80-246-3198-1 (pdf)

Cataloging-in-Publication Data is available from the National Library of the Czech Republic

The manuscript was reviewed by Jan Kodera (University of Economics, Prague)
and Miloslav Vošvrda (Institute of Information Theory and Automation,
The Czech Academy of Sciences)

CONTENTS

To my mother
(EK)

To Alžběta
(AČ)

INTRODUCTION

This book, in its third edition, presents the numerous tools for the econometric analysis of time series. The text is designed so that it can be used for a semester course on time series econometrics, but by no means is the text meant to be exhaustive on the topic. The major emphasis of the text is on the practical application of theoretical tools. Accordingly, we aim to present material in a way that is easy to understand and we abstract from the rigorous style of theorems and proofs.[1] In many cases we offer an intuitive explanation and understanding of the studied phenomena. Essential concepts are illustrated by clear-cut examples. Readers interested in a more formal approach are advised to consult the appropriate references cited throughout the text.[2]

Many sections of the book refer to influential papers where specific techniques originally appeared. Additionally, we draw the attention of readers to numerous applied works where the use of specific techniques is best illustrated because applications offer a better understanding of the presented techniques. Such applications are chiefly connected with issues of recent economic transition and European integration, and this way we also bring forth the evidence that applied econometric research offers with respect to both of these recent phenomena. The outlined style of presentation makes the book also a rich source of references.

The text is divided into five major sections. The first section, "The Nature of Time Series", gives an introduction to time series analysis. The second section, "Difference Equations", describes briefly the theory of difference equations with an emphasis on results that are important for time series econometrics. The third section, "Univariate Time Series", presents the methods commonly used in univariate time series analysis, the analysis of time series of one single variable. The fourth section, "Multiple Time Series", deals with time series models of multiple interrelated variables. The fifth section "Panel Data and Unit Root Tests", deals with methods known as panel unit root tests that are relevant to issues of convergence. Appendices contain an introduction to simulation techniques and statistical tables.

Photographs, and illustrations based on them, that appear throughout the book are to underline the purpose of the tools described in the book. Photographs, taken by Monika Kočendová, show details and sections of Fresnel lenses used in lighthouses to collimate light into parallel rays so that the light is visible to large distances and guides ships. Tools described in this book are used to process information available in data to deliver results guiding our decisions.

---

1   For rigorous treatment of specific issues Greene (2008) is recommended.
2   Patterson (2000) and Enders (2009) can serve as additional references that deal specifically with time series analysis.

When working on the text we received valuable help from many people and we would like to thank them all. In particular we are grateful for the research assistance provided by Ľuboš Briatka, Juraj Stančík (first edition), and Branka Marković (second edition). We are grateful to the staff of the Karolinum Press. We also thank Professor Jan Kmenta for consenting to our use of the title of his book (Kmenta, 1986) as a part of our title. Special thanks go to Monika (EK) and Alžběta (AČ).

1.

THE NATURE OF TIME SERIES

There are two major types of data sets studied by econometrics: cross-sectional data and time series. Cross-sectional data sets are data collected at one given time across multiple entities such as countries, industries, and companies. A time series is any set of data ordered by time. As our lives pass in time, it is natural for a variable to become a time series. Any variable that registers periodically forms a time series. For example, a yearly gross domestic product (GDP) recorded over several years is a time series. Similarly price level, unemployment, exchange rates of a currency, or profits of a firm can form a time series, if recorded periodically over certain time span. The combination of cross-sectional data and time series creates what economists call a panel data set. Panel data sets can be studied by tools characteristic for panel data econometrics or by tools characteristic for multiple time series analysis.

The fact that time series data are ordered by time implies some of their special properties and also some specific approaches to their analysis. For example, the time ordering enables the estimation of models built upon one variable only – so-called univariate time series models. In such a case a variable is estimated as a function of its past values (lags) and eventually time trends as well. As the variable is regressed on its own past values, such specification is aptly called an autoregressive process, abbreviated as "AR". Because of the time ordering of data, issues of *autocorrelation* gain prominent importance in time series econometrics.

1.1 DESCRIPTION OF TIME SERIES

A set of data ordered by time forms a time series, $\{y_t\}_{t=1}^{T}$. We use the term "time series" for three distinct but closely related objects: a series of random variables, a series of data that are concrete realizations of these variables, and also for the stochastic process that generates these data or random variables.

Example 1.1 The stochastic process that generates the time series can be, for example, described as a simple autoregressive process with one lag: $y_t = 0.5y_{t-1} + \varepsilon_t$ (AR(1) process), where ε_t are normal iid with mean 0 and variance σ^2, which is some positive number. With the initial condition $y_0 = 0$, the sequence of random variables generated by this process is $\varepsilon_1, 0.5\varepsilon_1 + \varepsilon_2, 0.25\varepsilon_1 + 0.5\varepsilon_2 + \varepsilon_3$, etc. Finally, the concrete realizations of these random variables can be the numbers 0.13882, 0.034936, −1.69767, etc. When we say that we estimate a time series, it means that based on the data (concrete realizations) we estimate the underlying process that generated the time series. The specification of the process is also called the model.

The properties *frequency*, *time span*, *mean*, *variance*, and *covariance* are used to give a basic description of time series.

1. *Frequency* is related to the time elapsed between y_t and y_{t+1}. Data can be collected with yearly, quarterly, daily, or even greater frequency. In case of a greater-than-daily frequency we speak about *intra-day data*. For example stock prices may be recorded in minute or even second intervals. The term "frequency" is actually used incorrectly in the context of time series econometrics. When we say daily frequency of the data, we mean in fact that there is one data point recorded per day.
2. *Time span* is the period of time over which the data were collected. If there are no gaps in the data, the time span is equivalent to the number of observations times the frequency. Throughout the text T is reserved to indicate the sample size (the number of observations) unless stated otherwise.
3. The *mean* μ_t is defined as $\mu_t = E(y_t)$. The mean is defined for each element of the time series, so that with T observations there are T means defined.
4. The *variance* is defined as $var(y_t) = E\left[(y_t - \mu_t)^2\right]$. Similarly as with the mean, the variance is defined for each element of the time series.
5. The *covariance* is defined as $cov(y_t, y_{t-s}) = E\left[(y_t - \mu_t)(y_{t-s} - \mu_{t-s})\right]$. The covariance is defined for each time t and for each time difference s, so that in the general case there are $T^2 - T$ covariances defined; however, because of symmetry only half of them are different.

1.2 WHITE NOISE

White noise is a term frequently used in time series econometrics. As the name suggests, white noise is a time series that does not contain any information that would help in estimation (except its variance and higher moments). Residuals from a correctly specified or "true" model that captures fully the data generating process are white noise. In the text, the white noise error process will be usually denoted as ε_t. For example a *series of identically and independently distributed random variables with 0 mean is white noise.*

When we estimate a time series using a correct model as described in sections 1.6 and 3.1 then the remaining inestimable part of the time series (the errors, or residuals) must be white noise. Procedures used to test if a time series is white noise are described in section 3.1.4.

1.3 STATIONARITY

Stationarity is a crucial property of time series. If a time series is stationary, then any shock that occurs in time t has a diminishing effect over time and finally disappears in time $t + s$ as $s \to \infty$. This feature is called *mean reversion*. With a non-stationary time series this is not the case and the effect of a shock either remains present in the same magnitude in all future dates or can be considered as a source behind the "explosion" of the series over time. If the former is the case, then the time series was generated by the so-called *unit root* process. Unit root processes form a special subset of non-stationary processes. Being on the edge between stationary and non-stationary processes, unit root processes play a particularly important role in time series analysis. For more details on stationarity, non-stationarity, and unit root processes see sections 2.4, 2.5, 3.4, and 3.5.

The most frequently used stationarity concept in econometrics is the concept of *covariance stationarity*. Throughout the text, we will for simplicity usually use only the term stationarity instead of covariance stationarity. We say that a time series $\{y_t\}_{t=1}^{T}$ is *covariance stationary* if and only if the following formal conditions are satisfied:

1. $\mu_t = \mu_{t-s} = \mu < \infty$ for all t, s.

2. $var(y_t) = var(y_{t-s}) = \sigma^2 < \infty$ for all t, s.

3. $cov(y_t, y_{t-s}) = cov(y_{t-j}, y_{t-j-s}) = \gamma_s < \infty$ for all t, j, and s.

Translated into plain language the above means that a time series is covariance stationary, if its mean and variance are constant and finite over time and if the covariance depends only on the time distance s between the two elements of the time series but not on the time t itself.

Note that any white noise time series is obviously stationary. However, a stationary time series is not automatically white noise. For white noise we need additional conditions that the mean and all covariances are 0; e.g. $\mu = 0$ and $\gamma_s = 0$ for all s.

Most economic time series are not stationary and specific transformations are needed in order to achieve stationarity. Some useful transformations are described in the next section.

Figure 1.1: Stationary, non-stationary, and unit root time series: a comparison.

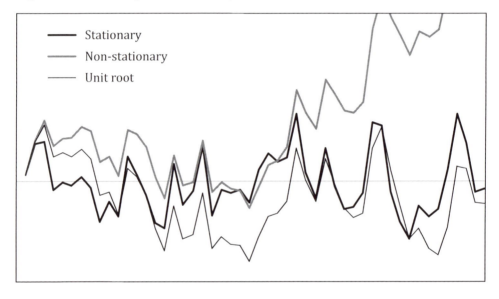

Example 1.2 Figure 1.1 shows examples of stationary, non-stationary, and unit root time series. All three series were generated by a simple autoregressive process with one lag, an $AR(1)$ process defined as $y_t = a_1 y_{t-1} + \varepsilon_t$, where ε_t are normal iid with zero mean and variance $\sigma^2 = 9$. With such an $AR(1)$ process, the necessary and sufficient condition for stationarity is $|a_1| < 1$. If $|a_1| \geq 1$, then the time series is non-stationary, with $|a_1| > 1$ it explodes and with $|a_1| = 1$ it contains a unit root. The formal necessary and sufficient conditions for time series stationarity will be described in sections 2.4 and 2.5. The three time series in the figure were generated by the following processes:

stationary: $y_t = 0.6 y_{t-1} + \varepsilon_t$, $a_1 = 0.6 < 1$,
non-stationary: $y_t = 1.1 y_{t-1} + \varepsilon_t$, $a_1 = 1.1 > 1$,
unit root: $y_t = y_{t-1} + \varepsilon_t$, $a_1 = 1$.

We can distinguish clear visual differences between the three time series. The stationary time series tends to return often to its initial value. The non-stationary time series explodes after a while. Finally, the time series containing a unit root can resemble a stationary time series, but it does not return to its initial value as often. These differences can be more or less pronounced on a visual plot. Nevertheless, a visual plot cannot replace the formal stationarity tests described in sections 3.4, 3.5, and 5.

1.4 TRANSFORMATIONS OF TIME SERIES

In most cases some transformations of time series of economic data are necessary before we can proceed with estimation. Usually we apply transformations in order to achieve stationarity. However, sometimes it is natural to apply transformations because the transformed variable corresponds to what we are actually interested in. A typical example is a macroeconomic variable in levels versus the variable's growth rate. An example of this is prices versus inflation. If we are interested in analyzing inflation, then we want to transform prices (in levels) into inflation first. Achieving stationarity through the transformation is an extra benefit.

Depending on the type of transformation that we must apply in order to make a time series stationary, we can make a basic distinction of the time series into *difference stationary*, *trend stationary*, and *broken trend stationary* series. *Difference stationary* time series become stationary after differencing, *trend stationary* series after detrending, and *broken trend stationary* series after detrending with a structural change incorporated (more on broken trend stationary series will be introduced in section 3.5).

If a series must be differenced n times to become stationary, then it is *integrated of the order n*, which we denote as $I(n)$. Thus, a series that is stationary without any differencing can be also denoted as $I(0)$. The definition assumes that n is an integer. Its extension to fractional values of n is covered by the concept of fractional integration; the topic is beyond the scope of the book but Hosking (1981) and Mills and Markellos (2008) can serve as useful references.

Prior to *differencing* and *detrending*, the most common transformation is to *take a natural logarithm* of the data in order to deal with a sort of non-linearity or to reduce an exponential trend into a linear one. For example, if we are interested in growth rates, it is natural to apply *logarithmic differencing*, which means that we first take natural logarithms of the data and then difference them.

1. *Taking a natural logarithm* is applied when the data perform exponential growth, which is a common case in economics. For example, if a GDP of

a country grows each year roughly by 3% when compared to preceding year, then the time series of yearly GDP contains an exponential trend. In such a case, by taking a natural logarithm we receive data that grow linearly.

2. *Differencing* is the most common approach applied in order to achieve stationarity. To difference a time series, we apply the transformation $\Delta y_t = y_t - y_{t-1}$, where Δy_t is the so-called first difference. To obtain second differences denoted as $\Delta^2 y_t$ we apply the identical transformation on first differences $\Delta^2 y_t = \Delta y_t - \Delta y_{t-1}$. In this way we can create differences of even higher orders. Although any time series becomes stationary after a sufficient order of differencing, differencing of a higher than second order is almost never used in econometrics. The reason is that by each differencing we lose one observation and, more important, by each differencing we lose a part of the information contained in the data. In addition, higher order differences have no clear economic interpretation. Second differences are already linear growth rates of the linear growth rates obtained by first differencing.

3. *Detrending* is a procedure that removes linear or even higher order trends from the data. To detrend a time series, we run a regression of the series on a constant, time t, and eventually its higher powers as well. Residuals from such a regression represent the detrended time series. The degree of the time polynomial included in the regression can be formally tested by an *F*-test prior to detrending. Trending time series are never stationary, because their mean is not constant. Therefore, detrending also helps to make such time series stationary. More details about trends in time series will be given in the next section and in section 3.2.

Example 1.3 We can illustrate the above approaches in the following way. Usually economic data grow exponentially. This means that for a variable X we have the growth equation $X_t = (1 + g_t) X_{t-1}$ in the discrete case, or $X_t = X_{t-1} e^{g_t}$ in the continuous case, where g_t is a growth rate in between two successive periods or the rate of return depending on the nature of X. By logarithmic differencing we obtain $\ln X_t - \ln X_{t-1} = \ln(1 + g_t) \approx g_t$ in the discrete case or $\ln X_t - \ln X_{t-1} = g_t$ in the continuous case. Specifically, let us consider a time series of price levels $\{P_t\}_{t=1}^{T}$. By logarithmic differencing we receive the series of inflation rates $\pi_t = \ln P_t - \ln P_{t-1}$.

The above mentioned differences were always just differences between two successive periods. If the data exhibit a seasonal pattern, it is more fruitful to apply differences between the seasonal periods. For example, with quarterly data we can apply fourth seasonal logarithmic differencing to obtain $\ln X_t - \ln X_{t-4}$. Such a procedure removes the seasonal pattern from the data and also decreases the variance of the series (of course if the seasonal pattern really has a period of four quarters). We will deal more with seasonal patterns in the next section and in section 3.3.

1.5 TREND, SEASONAL, AND IRREGULAR PATTERNS

With some simplifying, a general time series can consist of three basic components, *the deterministic trend, the seasonal pattern,* and *the irregular pattern.* Our task by estimation and forecasting is to decompose the series into these three components. A series can be written as:

$$y_t = T_t + S_t + I_t , \tag{1.1}$$

where the three components can be described in more detail as follows.

1. The *deterministic trend* T_t can be generally described as a trend polynomial $T_t = \sum_{i=0}^{n} a_i t^i$. Usually we will deal only with linear or quadratic trends ($n = 1$ or 2). If the series grows exponentially, it is a good idea to take a natural logarithm in order to transform exponential growth into linear growth. How to estimate and remove the trend from a time series is described in section 3.2. Other than deterministic trends, section 3.2 deals also with so-called *stochastic trends.* However, stochastic trends can be viewed rather as a part of the irregular pattern.

2. The *seasonal pattern* S_t can be described as $S_t = c \sin(t2\pi/d)$, where d is the period of the seasonal pattern. For example if we look at the monthly number of visitors to a sea resort, then the period of the seasonal pattern of such series would be very likely 12 months. Another way to describe seasonal patterns is to incorporate them into the irregular pattern. The issue of seasonality will be treated again in section 3.3.

3. The *irregular pattern* I_t can be expressed by a general *ARMA* model, as described in the following section. In fact, most of the following sections as well as most of univariate time series econometrics deals particularly with the estimation of irregular patterns.

Example 1.4 As an example of the above components we show the decomposition of a time series into trend, seasonal and irregular patterns on a hypothetical time series in figure 1.2. The time series in the picture consists of the trend $T_t = 2 + 0.3t$, the seasonal pattern $S_t = 4\sin(t2\pi/6)$, and the irregular pattern $I_t = 0.7I_{t-1} + \varepsilon_t$, where ε_t are normal i.i.d. with 0 mean and variance $\sigma^2 = 9$.

Figure 1.2: Decomposition of a time series into deterministic trend, seasonal and irregular patterns.

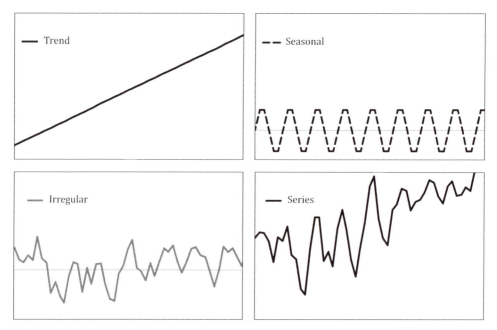

1.6 *ARMA* MODELS OF TIME SERIES

ARMA models are the most common processes used to estimate stationary irregular or eventually also seasonal patterns in time series. The abbreviation *ARMA* stands for *autoregressive moving average*, which is a combination of *autoregressive* and *moving average* models. The individual models and their combination are described in the following list.

1. *Autoregressive process of the order p, AR(p)*, is described as

$$y_t = a_0 + \sum_{i=1}^{p} a_i y_{t-i} + \varepsilon_t. \tag{1.2}$$

2. *Moving average process of the order q, MA(q)*, is described as

$$y_t = \sum_{i=0}^{q} \beta_i \varepsilon_{t-i}. \tag{1.3}$$

3. *Autoregressive moving average process of the orders p and q, ARMA(p,q), is described as*

$$y_t = a_0 + \sum_{i=1}^{p} a_i y_{t-i} + \sum_{i=0}^{q} \beta_i \varepsilon_{t-i}. \tag{1.4}$$

The coefficient β_0 in equations (1.3) and (1.4) is typically normalized to 1. Note that there is no trend in the equations above. This is so because we estimate the irregular pattern only. Therefore, we work already with *detrended, differenced,* or *logarithmic differenced* time series.

   The estimation of a time series with an *ARMA* model makes sense only if the series is stationary. Intuitively a time series should be stationary in order to employ it for meaningful analysis. Non-stationary time series are unpredictable, because they tend to "explode". However, we can specify an *ARMA* process that generates non-stationary time series, as we did in example 1.2. In that example non-stationary and unit root containing time series were generated by $AR(1)$ processes with a_1 = 1.1 and a_1 = 1.0, respectively. In general, there are necessary and sufficient conditions on the coefficients a_i and β_i ensuring that the generated series is stationary. These conditions will be described in section 2, which deals with difference equations. These conditions are also crucial for the construction of stationarity tests, which are described in sections 3.4 and 3.5.

   In terms of notation the *ARMA* models are frequently denoted as *ARIMA* models. If a series was differenced n times, in order to make it stationary, and then estimated by an *ARMA(p,q)* model, then we can say that it was estimated by an *ARIMA(p,n,q) model*. The *I* inserted in the abbreviation *ARMA* and the n in the parentheses stand for *integrated of the order n*, as described earlier.

1.7 STYLIZED FACTS ABOUT TIME SERIES

We mentioned already that time series of economic variables usually have some properties that are endemic to economic data. In the following list we discuss these properties systematically and make references to the chapters where the related topics are presented in more detail.

1. *The trend*
Economic time series very often contain a trend. Their growth is usually not only linear but may be exponential, as mentioned in example 1.3. Therefore, even after we take a natural logarithm of the data, a linear trend still persists. Such behavior is typical for variables that naturally grow over time in a long run. Typical examples are GDP, price indices, prices of stocks, etc. When we estimate such a series, we usually apply logarithmic differencing, which yields

a growth rate in between two desired periods, or the rate of return. First logarithmic differencing may yield for example a yearly growth rate of aggregate
output or daily rate of return on a financial instrument or product. If such
growth rates or rates of return are stationary, then we can estimate them with
an *ARMA* model. If they are not stationary, then we can make them stationary
by further differencing and only after that estimate them by an *ARMA* model.
The most common transformations applied in order to remove the trend and
to achieve stationarity were described in section 1.4. The trend component of
time series was mentioned in section 1.5. More about trends will be presented
in section 3.2.

2. *Trend breaks and structural changes*
To make things more complicated, the trend mentioned in the previous point is
usually not constant over time. For example GDP can grow by 4% for 10 years
and 2% for the following 10 years. Similar cases can happen with inflation or
stock prices. We say that such time series experience a structural change or contain a structural break. Moreover, structural change can involve not only change
in the trend coefficient (in the growth rate) but also in the intercept. Structural
changes in time series are usually caused by some real historical or economic
events. For example the oil shocks in the 1970s were followed by a significant
slowdown of economic growth in most industrialized countries. The issue of
trend breaks and structural changes will be studied in sections 3.5 and 3.6.

3. *The mean running up and down*
Some time series, for example freely floating exchange rates, do not show any
persistent tendency to increase or decrease. On the other hand, they do not
return to their initial value very often either. Rather they alternate between
relatively long periods of increases and decreases. As was already suggested
in example 1.2, such behavior is typical for series that contain a unit root. The
simplest process containing a unit root is the so-called *random walk*. This is
defined by the equation $y_t = y_{t-1} + \varepsilon_t$, where ε_t is white noise. Our feeling that exchange rates or stock prices behave as a random walk has a noble counterpart
in economic theory, namely in the *information efficiency hypothesis*. This hypothesis is described in example 1.5 that is introduced at the end of the section.
More about unit roots and random walks will be given in sections 3.2 and 3.4.

4. *High persistence of shocks*
This observation is based on the fact that any shock that occurs at time t has
typically a long persistence in economic time series. Again it is related to the
fact that the underlying data generating processes are either non-stationary
or close to unit root processes. In such a case the coefficients a_i and β_i in *ARMA*
models have relatively high values. Therefore, any past shock is transferred to

future dates in large magnitude. Also, this point is closely related to point 2 on trend breaks and structural changes. If the shock has high persistence, it can appear as a structural change in the data.

5. *Volatility is not constant*

Along with time series that have constant variance (*homoskedastic* series) many economic time series do not have constant variance (*heteroskedastic* series). For example, in the case of data generated on financial markets (e.g. stock prices, exchange rates, etc.), we can observe periods of high and low volatility, which is an indisputable sign of changing variance. Time series with changing variance are called *conditionally heteroskedastic* and are usually estimated with the *ARCH* (autoregressive conditional heteroskedasticity) class of models; these models will be described in section 3.7.

6. *Non-stationarity*

All of the previous five points have one common consequence. Time series of economic data are in most cases non-stationary. Therefore, some transformations are usually needed in order to make them stationary. These transformations were described in section 1.4. Formal tests of stationarity will be introduced in sections 3.4, 3.5, and 5.

7. *Comovements in multiple time series*

Some time series can share comovements with other time series. This occurs for example, when shocks to one series are correlated with shocks to other series. In today's open world, where national economies are closely linked by many channels (e.g. international trade, international investment, and foreign exchange markets), such behavior is not surprising. If comovement is a result of some long term equilibrium towards which the two series tend to return after each shock, then such series are called to be *cointegrated*. More on cointegration and multiple time series comovements will be presented in section 4.

Example 1.5 *Hypothesis of the information efficiency of foreign exchange markets*
The information efficiency hypothesis assumes that prices on the markets reflect all available information. To prevent any arbitrage opportunities under such conditions it must hold that today's expectation of tomorrow's exchange rate equals today's exchange rate. Such a statement can be written as $E_t(y_{t+1}|\Omega_t) = y_t$, where Ω_t stands for the information available at time t and y_t for an exchange rate at time t. The reader can easily verify that the random walk fits this condition. However, more complicated processes exist, like the *ARCH*-type processes that can also suit this hypothesis. In general, such processes are called *martingales*.

2.

DIFFERENCE EQUATIONS

The equations used to describe time series data generating processes outlined in the previous section are in mathematical terminology called *difference equations*. The theory of difference equations constitutes the basic mathematical background for time series econometrics. In this section we will briefly introduce the major components of this theory. We will focus on those components that are important for econometric time series analysis. From this point of view mainly the *stability conditions* and the relation between the *stability of a difference equation* and the *stationarity of a time series* are crucial (see sections 2.4 and 2.5). For a full scale treatment of the difference equations and more details on the topic see for example Goldberg (1986) and Agarwal (2000).

2.1 LINEAR DIFFERENCE EQUATIONS

It was noted above that equations used to model time series data generating processes introduced in the previous section are so-called *difference equations*. To be more precise, we should say that they all belong to a subset of difference equations called *linear difference equations*. This is for example the case with equations (1.2), (1.3), and (1.4) modeling the *AR*, *MA*, and *ARMA* processes, respectively. They are *difference equations*, because they contain the current and lagged values of variables. They are *linear difference equations*, because these variables are raised only to the first power, which means that only a linear combination of present and lagged values appears in the equation. Moreover, they are *linear stochastic difference equations*, because they contain some stochastic component, that is, some random variables.

Formally a *p-th order linear difference equation* can be written as

$$y_t = a_o + \sum_{i=1}^{p} a_i y_{t-i} + x_t,$$ (2.1)

where x_t is the so-called *forcing process* that can be any function of time t, current and lagged values of variables other than y, and for the linear difference equation to deserve the attribute "stochastic", it should be also a function of stochastic variables (e.g. stochastic disturbances).

2.2 LAG OPERATOR

The lag operator is a useful tool that helps to write and adjust difference equations and to express their solutions in a simple and compact way. The *lag operator L* is a linear operator, which when applied to a variable y_t yields its lagged value y_{t-1}. It can be defined as:

$$Ly_t = y_{t-1}, \text{ or for higher lags } L^i y_t = y_{t-i}.$$

Equation (1.4), describing an *ARMA(p,q)* process, can be written with the use of lag operators as

$$A(L)y_t = a_0 + B(L)\varepsilon_t,$$ (2.2)

where $A(L)$ and $B(L)$ are the following polynomials of L:

$$A(L) = 1 - a_1 L - a_2 L^2 - \cdots - a_p L^p \text{ and } B(L) = \beta_0 + \beta_1 L + \beta_2 L^2 + \cdots + \beta_q L^q.$$

Although L is an operator, most of its algebraic properties are analogous to those of a simple variable. The major properties of the lag operator L are listed below:
1. L applied to a constant yields a constant: $Lc = c$.
2. The distributive law holds: $(L^i + L^j)y_t = L^i y_t + L^j y_t = y_{t-i} + y_{t-i}$.
3. The associative law for multiplication holds: $L^i L^j y_t = L^{i+j} y_t = y_{t-i-j}$.
4. L raised to a negative power is a *lead operator*: $L^{-i} y_t = y_{t+i}$.
5. From 2 and 3 above follows that for $|a| < 1$, $(1 + aL + a^2 L^2 + a^3 L^3 + \cdots) y_t = $ $= y_t/(1-aL)$.

2.3 THE SOLUTION OF DIFFERENCE EQUATIONS

Solving a general linear difference equation (2.1) involves expressing the value of y_t as a function of the elements of the forcing process sequence $\{x_t\}$, time t, and potentially also of the elements of the sequence $\{y_t\}$ called *initial conditions*. The solution process is quite similar to the process of solving linear differential equations. In the general case, finding the solution involves the following steps:

1. All the so-called *homogeneous solutions* of the *homogeneous part* of a linear difference equation must be found. The homogeneous part of equation (2.1) is defined as

$$y_t = \sum_{i=1}^{p} a_i y_{t-i} \text{ or, rewritten, } y_t - \sum_{i=1}^{p} a_i y_{t-i} = 0, \tag{2.3}$$

which means that the constant a_0 and the forcing process x_t from the original equation are left out. Such a homogeneous equation has p linearly independent solutions that we will denote as $H_i(t)$. Homogeneous solutions are functions of time t only. Any linear combination of the homogeneous solutions $H_i(t)$ is also a solution to equation (2.3).

2. One solution of the whole linear difference equation (2.1) must be found. Such a solution is called a *particular solution*, denoted as $P(\{x_t\},t)$. A particular solution can be a function of time t and the elements of the forcing process $\{x_t\}$.

3. The *general solution* of a linear difference equation is any linear combination of the p homogeneous solutions $H_i(t)$ plus the particular solution $P(\{x_t\},t)$. Let us denote the general solution as $G(\{x_t\},t)$. It can be written in the following way:

$$G(\{x_t\},t) = \sum_{i=1}^{p} C_i H_i(t) + P(\{x_t\},t), \tag{2.4}$$

where C_i are arbitrary constants. Clearly there are infinitely many general solutions as there is an infinity of such constants.

4. If the *initial conditions* for the values of y at the initial periods are specified, then the arbitrary constants can be eliminated by imposing these conditions on the general solution. Ideally, if the initial values are known for p initial time periods ($y_0, y_1, ..., y_{p-1}$), then all the arbitrary constants can be eliminated and we obtain one *unique solution*.

Before we describe the general process of finding homogeneous, particular, and unique solutions, we will introduce some more intuitive simple methods

of *expressing particular solutions in terms of lag operators* and of *finding par-*
ticular and unique solutions by iteration.

2.3.1 PARTICULAR SOLUTION AND LAG OPERATORS

It was already mentioned that the *lag operator* with its simple algebraic
properties can be used to express particular solutions of difference equations in a simple way. We have just shown that a general *ARMA(p,q)* model
$y_t = a_0 + \sum_{i=1}^{p} a_i y_{t-i} + \sum_{i=0}^{q} \beta_i \varepsilon_{t-i}$ can be rewritten as equation (2.2),
$A(L)y_t = a_0 + B(L)\varepsilon_t$, where

$$A(L) = 1 - a_1 L - a_2 L^2 - \cdots - a_p L^p \text{ and } B(L) = \beta_0 + \beta_1 L + \beta_2 L^2 + \cdots + \beta_q L^q.$$

The particular solution to this equation can be simply expressed as

$$y_t = \frac{a_0}{A(L)} + \frac{B(L)}{A(L)} \varepsilon_t. \tag{2.5}$$

Unfortunately, such a solution does not tell us anything about the specific coefficients associated with the parameters and the sequence of shocks $\{\varepsilon_t\}$ because
$1/A(L)$ and $B(L)/A(L)$ are not numbers but operators. To obtain the coefficients
of the particular solution we must solve the polynomials $A(L)$ and $B(L)$ with
respect to L, which means finding their characteristic roots. Such a procedure
is shown for the simplest case of an $AR(1)$ process in example 2.1 below. Equation (2.5) is only a particular solution of the *ARMA(p,q)* equation, which is not
unique. *Lag operators cannot be used to express homogeneous solutions and so*
they cannot be used to express general solutions.

Example 2.1 The $AR(1)$ process $y_t = a_0 + a_1 y_{t-1} + \varepsilon_t$ can be written as $A(L)$
$y_t = a_0 + \varepsilon_t$, where $A(L) = (1 - a_1 L)$. The polynomial $A(L)$ is of the first order only
and so it has just one characteristic root, which is equal to $1/a_1$. The solution is

$$y_t = a_0/(1 - a_1 L) + \varepsilon_t/(1 - a_1 L).$$

Now consider only the case of $|a_1| < 1$. Using the properties of the lag operator,
the solution can be written as $y_t = (1 + a_1 L + a_1^2 L^2 + \cdots)a_0 + (1 + a_1 L + a_1^2 L^2 + \cdots)\varepsilon_t$.
Finally, application of the lag operator yields $y_t = (a_0 + a_1 a_0 + a_1^2 a_0 + \cdots) +$
$+(\varepsilon_t + a_1 \varepsilon_{t-1} + a_1^2 \varepsilon_{t-2} + \cdots)$, which can be simplified as

$$y_t = a_0 / (1 - a_1) + \sum_{i=0}^{\infty} a_1^i \varepsilon_{t-i}. \tag{2.6}$$

2.3.2 SOLUTION BY ITERATION

Simple difference equations can be solved by *iteration. This methodology again enables finding only particular solutions.* However, if we know the *initial conditions* (initial values of y_t), then we can iterate from these to obtain a *unique solution.*

Again we will demonstrate the solution procedure on the simple case of an $AR(1)$ process $y_t = a_0 + a_1 y_{t-1} + \varepsilon_t$. The equation must hold also for y_{t-1}, y_{t-2}, etc. Therefore, we can substitute into the above $AR(1)$ process the expression for y_{t-1}, which takes the form of $y_{t-1} = a_0 + a_1 y_{t-2} + \varepsilon_{t-1}$. In a similar manner we can susbstitute y_{t-2} with the expression $y_{t-2} = a_0 + a_1 y_{t-3} + \varepsilon_{t-2}$, and continue infinitely to obtain the expression

$$y_t = a_0 + a_1 (a_0 + a_1 (a_0 + a_1 (\ldots) + \varepsilon_{t-2}) + \varepsilon_{t-1}) + \varepsilon_t =$$

$$= (a_0 + a_0 a_1 + a_0 a_1^2 + \cdots) + (\varepsilon_t + a_1 \varepsilon_{t-1} + a_1^2 \varepsilon_{t-2} + \cdots)$$

that can be written in a more compact way as

$$y_t = \sum_{i=0}^{\infty} a_0 a_1^i + \sum_{i=0}^{\infty} a_1^i \varepsilon_{t-i}.$$

If $|a_1| \geq 1$, then the solution is not convergent. If $|a_1| < 1$, then we can compute the first sum and obtain the result expressed by equation (2.6). Thus, we obtain the same result as when using lag operators in example 2.1.

As in example 2.1 we obtained only a particular solution. The iteration methodology does not produce *homogeneous solutions* of the homogeneous part of an $AR(1)$ equation $y_t = a_0 + a_1 y_{t-1} + \varepsilon_t$. For the moment, it can be verified that the homogeneous solution is $y_t = Ca_1^t$, where C is an arbitrary constant. If we combine this homogeneous solution with the particular solution described by equation (2.6), then we obtain the *general solution* of the $AR(1)$ equation for $|a_1| < 1$, which is

$$y_t = Ca_1^t + a_0 / (1 - a_1) + \sum_{i=0}^{\infty} a_1^i \varepsilon_{t-i}. \qquad (2.7)$$

Knowing the initial condition y_0 we can substitute it into the solution and eliminate the arbitrary constant C:

$y_0 = C + a_0 / (1 - a_1) + \sum_{i=0}^{\infty} a_1^i \varepsilon_{0-i}$, thus $C = y_0 - a_0 / (1 - a_1) - \sum_{i=0}^{\infty} a_1^i \varepsilon_{0-i}$. Now we can

substitute the constant C into the general solution and obtain the *unique solution:*

$$y_t = (y_0 - a_0/(1-a_1) - \sum_{i=0}^{\infty} a_1^i \varepsilon_{0-i}) a_1^t + a_0/(1-a_1) + \sum_{i=0}^{\infty} a_1^i \varepsilon_{t-i} , \text{ which can be further}$$

simplified as

$$y_t = (y_0 - a_0/(1-a_1)) a_1^t + a_0/(1-a_1) + \sum_{i=0}^{t-1} a_1^i \varepsilon_{t-i} . \qquad (2.8)$$

This procedure, that led us from a particular solution obtained by iteration to the general and unique solutions, could obviously be used also in the case when the particular solution was obtained by the application of lag operators. Nevertheless, the iteration methodology is a bit more powerful in the sense that *we can obtain the unique solution directly by iteration from the initial condition y_0.* If we have an $AR(1)$ process $y_t = a_0 + a_1 y_{t-1} + \varepsilon_t$, it must hold that

$$y_1 = a_0 + a_1 y_0 + \varepsilon_1 ,$$

$$y_2 = a_0 + a_1 y_1 + \varepsilon_2 = a_0 + a_1(a_0 + a_1 y_0 + \varepsilon_1) + \varepsilon_2 ,$$

$$y_3 = a_0 + a_1 y_2 + \varepsilon_3 = a_0 + a_1(a_0 + a_1(a_0 + a_1 y_0 + \varepsilon_1) + \varepsilon_2) + \varepsilon_3 , \text{ etc.}$$

until we obtain

$$y_t = \sum_{i=0}^{t-1} a_0 a_1^i + a_1^t y_0 + \sum_{i=0}^{t-1} a_1^i \varepsilon_{t-i} .$$

In the case of $|a_1| < 1$ we can compute the first sum and obtain

$$y_t = a_0/(1-a_1) - a_1^t a_0/(1-a_1) + a_1^t y_0 + \sum_{i=0}^{t-1} a_1^i \varepsilon_{t-i} ,$$

which is identical to the solution expressed by equation (2.8).

Note that in the case of the particular solution obtained by iteration, we *iterated backward*. In this way we obtain the so-called *backward looking solution.* An alternative way is to *iterate forward* and to obtain a *forward looking solution.* Forward looking solutions are functions of future realizations of shocks ε_t, which is not very useful in time series econometrics. The fact is understandable due to the lack of available data from the future. However, such solutions are often used in rational expectations models.

We have shown how to solve difference equations using the iteration method and the method of lag operators. These methods enable obtaining only the particular solution, but in the case of the iteration method combined with the initial condition, the unique solution can also be obtained. Further, it is straightforward to see that these methods can be applied only with the simplest difference equations. In more complicated cases, such as a general $ARMA(p,q)$ specification, a general solution methodology must be applied. In addition, the two methods do not lead to homogeneous solutions. If we want to obtain homogeneous solutions and hence also the general solution, we must follow the general procedure described in the following two sections.

2.3.3 HOMOGENOUS SOLUTION

Here we will describe the procedure to find *homogeneous solutions of a general p-th order linear homogeneous difference equation* (2.3):

$$y_t = \sum_{i=1}^{p} a_i y_{t-i} \text{ or rewritten as } y_t - \sum_{i=1}^{p} a_i y_{t-i} = 0,$$

which can be also written in terms of lag operators as

$$A(L)y_t = 0, \text{ where } A(L) = 1 - a_1 L - a_2 L^2 - \cdots - a_p L^p = 1 - \sum_{i=1}^{p} a_i L^i. \qquad (2.9)$$

Notice that this homogeneous equation is a homogeneous part of an $AR(p)$ equation but also of an $ARMA(p,q)$ equation, and in general of any p-th order linear difference equation.

   In the previous section we saw that the homogeneous solution to the homogeneous part of an $AR(1)$ equation takes the form of a_1^t. Knowing this, we will try to find solutions to the general homogeneous equation (2.3) in the form of α^t. Notice that there will be p independent homogeneous solutions.

   By substituting α^t to the homogeneous equation (2.3) and dividing the whole equation by α^{t-p} we obtain

$$\alpha^p - a_1 \alpha^{p-1} - a_2 \alpha^{p-2} - \cdots - a_p = \alpha^p - \sum_{i=1}^{p} a_i \alpha^{p-i} = 0, \qquad (2.10)$$

which is the so-called *characteristic equation*. Notice that if we divide the characteristic equation by α^p and substitute L for $1/\alpha$, we will obtain

$$1 - a_1 L - a_2 L^2 - \cdots - a_p L^p = A(L) = 0, \qquad (2.11)$$

where $A(L)$ is the polynomial of the lag operator from equation (2.9). Equation (2.11) is called the *inverse characteristic equation* and the L's that solve it are inverse values of the α's that solve the characteristic equation (2.10).

   Now, we search for α's that solve the characteristic equation (2.10). It is a polynomial equation that will have p *characteristic roots* $\{\alpha_i\}_{i=1}^{p}$. In general some of the roots can be multiple and some can be complex. We will distinguish these cases in the following list and assign one homogeneous solution to each of the roots, so that we obtain p linearly independent homogeneous solutions $\{H_i(t)\}_{i=1}^{p}$.

1. *The root α_j is real and unique.*
In this simplest case the corresponding homogeneous solution is indeed
$H_j(t) = \alpha_j^t$.

2. *The root α_j is real and multiple.*
We have k identical roots α_j, where k is the root's multiplicity. In this case the corresponding k linearly independent homogeneous solutions are $H_j(t) = \alpha_j^t$, $H_{j+1}(t) = t\alpha_j^t$, $H_{j+2}(t) = t^2\alpha_j^t$, ..., $H_{j+k-1}(t) = t^{k-1}\alpha_j^t$.

3. *The root α_j is complex.*
Such a root will necessarily come in a conjugate complex pair which can be written as $\gamma_j \pm i\theta_j$. The two corresponding homogeneous solutions will also be complex and will take the form of $H_j(t) = (\gamma_j + i\theta_j)^t$ and $H_{j+1}(t) = (\gamma_j - i\theta_j)^t$.

So for each of the p roots α_i that solve the characteristic equation (2.10) we obtained a homogeneous solution $H_i(t)$ that solves the linear homogeneous difference equation (2.3). Moreover, these solutions are linearly independent and their linear combinations are also solutions to the homogeneous difference equation (2.3).

2.3.4 PARTICULAR SOLUTION

We have already shown how to find *particular solutions* by the iteration method and how to express such solutions easily by means of lag operators. Unfortunately, there is no easy-to-follow technique leading to a particular solution. The choice of the right way is often led by intuition and depends on the nature of the forcing process $\{x_t\}$.

For example, if all the elements of $\{x_t\}$ are equal to 0, then the p-th order linear difference equation (2.1) reduces to

$$y_t = a_o + \sum_{i=1}^{p} a_i y_{t-i},$$

and it seems reasonable to try to find a particular solution in the form of a constant $y_t = c$. Indeed, substituting this in the above equation leads to $c = a_o + \sum_{i=1}^{p} a_i c$, which can be solved as $c = a_o / (1 - \sum_{i=1}^{p} a_i)$. This is possible only if $1 - \sum_{i=1}^{p} a_i \neq 0$. If $1 - \sum_{i=1}^{p} a_i = 0$, then the particular solution takes the form $y_t = ct$. Analogically it can be shown that in this case $c = a_o / (\sum_{i=1}^{p} i a_i)$.

The method, that is probably closest to an instructive style, is called the *method of undetermined coefficients*. Using this method we benefit from the fact that a particular solution of a linear difference equation must be also linear. Then, the particular solution is assumed to be a linear combination of a constant c, time t, and the elements of the forcing process $\{x_t\}$, because we know that there is hardly anything else it could depend on. We substitute this so-called *challenge solution* into the difference equation and solve for the constants of the linear combination. Even though it sounds simple, the practical application may be cumbersome.

2.4 STABILITY CONDITIONS

The *stability of homogeneous linear difference equations* is closely linked to the concept of the *stationarity of time series*. In this sense, *stability conditions* represent a result of the theory of difference equations that has the greatest importance for econometric analysis of time series. If a linear homogeneous difference equation is *stable*, then its solution converges to zero as $t \to \infty$. If it is *unstable*, then its solution diverges.

The stability of the homogeneous part of a linear difference equation that describes the time series generating process is the *necessary condition* for the time series stationarity. In section 2.3.3 we have already mentioned that a *general p-th order linear homogeneous difference equation* (2.3) forms the homogeneous part of a difference equation describing any general *ARMA(p,q)* process. That is why stability conditions represent necessary conditions for the stationarity of a wide range of time series, namely of any time series that were generated by a general *ARMA(p,q)* process.

In section 2.3.2 we saw that the homogeneous solution of the homogeneous part of an *AR(1)* equation $y_t = a_1 y_{t-1}$ takes the form of $y_t = C a_1^t$, because a_1 is the only characteristic root of the corresponding characteristic equation.[3] Obviously such solution is *stable* and converges to zero if $|a_1| < 1$ and is *unstable* and diverges if $|a_1| > 1$. If $a_1 = 1$, then the solution remains $y_t = C$ forever and we say similarly as in the time series context that the equation contains a *unit root*.

For a first order homogeneous linear difference equation $y_t = a_1 y_{t-1}$ we can summarize that:

1. If $|a_1| < 1$, then the equation and its solution are *stable*.
2. If $|a_1| > 1$, then the equation and its solution are *unstable*.
3. If $|a_1| = 1$, then the equation is unstable and contains a *unit root*.

---

3   Note that the homogeneous solution of the homogeneous part of an AR(1) equation is also the homogeneous part of any *ARMA(1,q)* process.

Similarly we can describe stability conditions for a *general p-th order linear homogeneous difference equation* (2.3):

$$y_t = \sum_{i=1}^{p} a_i y_{t-i},$$

whose corresponding *characteristic equation* is equation (2.10):

$$\alpha^p - a_1 \alpha^{p-1} - a_2 \alpha^{p-2} - \cdots - a_p = 0.$$

Here we conclude that

1. If all *characteristic roots* $\{\alpha_i\}_{i=1}^{p}$ lie within the unit circle, that is $|\alpha_i| < 1$ for all *i*, then the equation and its solution are *stable*.
2. If at least one *characteristic root* α_i lies outside the unit circle, that is $|\alpha_i| > 1$, then the equation and its solution are *unstable*.
3. If at least one *characteristic root* α_i lies on the unit circle, that is $|\alpha_i| = 1$, then the equation is unstable and contains a *unit root*.

Sometimes stability conditions are described in terms of the roots of the *inverse characteristic equation* (2.11). The roots of the inverse characteristic equation are the inverse values of the roots of the characteristic equation. Therefore, the stability conditions require the opposite, that all the inverse characteristic roots lie outside the unit circle.

It is often difficult to compute all the characteristic roots. Fortunately there are some necessary and sufficient conditions for stability. These conditions are expressed directly in terms of the coefficients a_i as:

1. $\sum_{i=1}^{p} a_i < 1$ is a *necessary condition for stability*.

2. $\sum_{i=1}^{p} |a_i| < 1$ is a *sufficient condition for stability*.

3. If $\sum_{i=1}^{p} a_i = 1$, then the difference equation contains a *unit root*, which means that at least one of the characteristic roots equals unity. This condition is used when testing for unit roots in time series. Such tests are described in sections 3.4 and 3.5.

2.5 STABILITY AND STATIONARITY

In the previous section we have stated that the *necessary condition for stationarity* of a time series generated by a general *ARMA(p,q)* process is the stability of the corresponding *p*-th order linear homogeneous difference equation (2.3).

However, it is only a necessary condition. Except for its homogeneous part, a general $ARMA(p,q)$ specification contains also the forcing process x_t, which is described as

1. $x_t = a_0 + \varepsilon_t$ in the case of an $AR(p)$ process,

2. $x_t = \sum_{i=0}^{q} \beta_i \varepsilon_{t-i}$ in the case of a $MA(q)$ process (here the forcing process is the whole right side of the $MA(q)$ equation),

3. $x_t = a_0 + \sum_{i=0}^{q} \beta_i \varepsilon_{t-i}$ in the case of a general $ARMA(p,q)$ process.

The particular solution associated with this forcing process can cause the time series to be non-stationary, even if the homogeneous solution is stable. This is not the case with any AR process and with any finite MA process, where the stability of the corresponding homogeneous equation is not only a necessary but also a sufficient condition for stationarity. However, this can be the case with an infinite MA process. Therefore, for infinite MA processes some additional conditions for stationarity are needed. We summarize the important points on the stationarity issue below.

1. $AR(p)$ *process* $y_t = a_0 + \sum_{i=1}^{p} a_i y_{t-i} + \varepsilon_t$
The stability of the corresponding p-th order linear homogeneous difference equation is the necessary and sufficient condition for the stationarity of the generated time series.

2. $MA(q)$ *process* $y_t = \sum_{i=0}^{q} \beta_i \varepsilon_{t-i}$
Here the corresponding homogeneous difference equation is $y_t = 0$, which is obviously stable. However, the forcing process and the particular solution associated with it can cause the generated time series to be non-stationary.
(a) If q is finite, then the generated time series will be stationary.
(b) If q is infinite, then the necessary and sufficient condition for the stationarity of the generated time series is that the sums $(\beta_s + \beta_1\beta_{s+1} + \beta_2\beta_{s+2} + \cdots)$ are finite for all s. Note that in the case of a finite MA process these sums are obviously finite, because they contain a finite number of summands.

3. $ARMA(p,q)$ *process* $y_t = a_0 + \sum_{i=1}^{n} a_i y_{t-i} + \sum_{i=0}^{q} \beta_i \varepsilon_{t-i}$
Here we can combine the two previous cases and obtain the following necessary and sufficient condition for the stationarity of the generated time series:
(a) The corresponding p-th order linear homogeneous difference equation must be stable.
(b) The sums $(\beta_s + \beta_1\beta_{s+1} + \beta_2\beta_{s+2} + \cdots)$ must be finite for all s.

Using the above conditions we have related the econometric concept of time series stationarity with the mathematical concept of the stability of linear homogeneous difference equations. Nevertheless, one more condition for the stationarity of time series is needed. As stated in section 1.3, the stationarity of a time series requires that its mean, variance, and covariances are constant. Even if the homogeneous part of the difference equation generating the time series is stable, its homogeneous solution is not constant, it only converges to zero. This means that the homogeneous solution will be constant (equal to zero) only after a sufficiently long time t. Therefore, the above listed necessary and sufficient conditions hold only for sufficiently large time periods, that is for time periods that are sufficiently distant from the initial period $t = 0$. As one might expect in time series econometrics, time does matter.

3.
UNIVARIATE TIME SERIES

In this chapter we introduce the essential concepts and tools for analyzing a single time series. First, following the exposition in chapters 1 and 2, we discuss the estimation of ARMA models. Then we introduce trend and seasonality in time series. Testing for unit roots is discussed as an individual topic as well as in conjunction with the concept of broken trend stationarity. We also contrast methods that treat structural change in time series exogenously with those that take an endogenous approach. Changing variance and non-linear structure are discussed at the end of the chapter.

3.1 ESTIMATION OF AN *ARMA* MODEL

As mentioned earlier, an *ARMA* model is a standard building block of time series econometrics. In this section we will describe how to estimate the time series (true) data generating process with an *ARMA* model. We will follow the so-called *Box-Jenkins methodology* (see Box and Jenkins, 1976). The aim of the methodology is to find the most *parsimonious* model of the data generating process. By the most parsimonious we mean a model that fits the data well and at the same time uses the minimum number of parameters; thus it leaves a high number of degrees of freedom. The search for parsimony is common for all branches of econometrics, not only for time series analysis. In fact it is the general principal of estimation. In estimation, our aim is not to achieve a perfect fit, but to achieve a reasonable fit with few parameters. A perfect fit can be always achieved trivially, if we use as many parameters as data points. However, such an extremely overparametrized model does not tell us much about the nature of the events and decisions that generated the data.

The Box-Jenkins methodology can be divided into three main stages. The first is to *identify* the data generating process, the second is to *estimate* the parameters of this process, and the third is to *diagnose* the residuals from the estimated model. If the process was identified and estimated correctly, then such residuals should be diagnosed as white noise.

Most of the tools and procedures of the Box-Jenkins methodology require that the time series is *stationary* and the estimated process *invertible*. The concept of stationarity was explained in section 1.3. The concept of invertibility will be explained below, in subsection 3.1.2. In short it means that the process can be represented by a finite-order or convergent autoregressive process.

In the following subsections we will first describe the tools needed for the application of the Box-Jenkins methodology and after that we will clarify the sequence and logic in which they should be applied.

3.1.1 AUTOCORRELATION FUNCTION – ACF

The basic tools of the Box-Jenkins methodology are the *autocorrelation function* and the *partial autocorrelation function* (*ACF* and *PACF*). These functions help to identify the parameters p and q of the *ARMA(p,q)* data generating process. That is, the number of *AR* and *MA* lags that should be included in the model. We will start with a description of the *ACF*.

Let us denote the *ACF* of a time series $\{y_t\}$ as ρ_s, where s represents a specific number of lags. The *ACF* is defined as

$$\rho_s = \frac{cov(y_t, y_{t-s})}{var(y_t)}. \tag{3.1}$$

Because we consider stationary time series, the *ACF* expressed by equation (3.1) is only a function of the time difference of the length s and not of the time t itself. Remember that one of the stationarity conditions is the independence of $var(y_t)$ and $cov(y_t, y_{t-s})$ from time t. The independence of the *ACF* from time then follows from its construction. The stationarity of $\{y_t\}$ also ensures that the *ACF* is equal to the correlation between y_t and y_{t-s}, $corr(y_t, y_{t-s})$. Because $var(y_t) = var(y_{t-s})$, we can write

$$corr(y_t, y_{t-s}) = cov(y_t, y_{t-s}) / \sqrt{var(y_t)var(y_{t-s})} = cov(y_t, y_{t-s}) / var(y_t) = \rho_s.$$

In order to obtain specific results, first consider an $AR(1)$ process $y_t = a_0 + a_1 y_{t-1} + \varepsilon_t$. To compute the ACF we need to obtain $var(y_t)$ and $cov(y_t y_{t-s})$. Let us denote $var(\varepsilon_t)$ by σ^2, then because y_{t-1} and ε_t are uncorrelated, we can write

$$var(y_t) = var(a_0 + a_1 y_{t-1} + \varepsilon_t) = a_1^2 var(y_{t-1}) + \sigma^2.$$

We assume the time series $\{y_t\}$ is stationary, thus $var(y_t) = var(y_{t-1})$. Substitution of this identity yields the equation $var(y_t) = a_1^2 var(y_t) + \sigma^2$. Solving this equation for variance we obtain

$$var(y_t) = \frac{\sigma^2}{1 - a_1^2}.$$

For covariances we can write similarly

$$cov(y_t, y_{t-1}) = cov(a_0 + a_1 y_{t-1} + \varepsilon_t, y_{t-1}) = a_1 var(y_{t-1}) = a_1 var(y_t),$$

$$cov(y_t, y_{t-2}) = cov(a_0 + a_1 y_{t-1} + \varepsilon_t, y_{t-2}) = a_1 cov(y_{t-1}, y_{t-2})$$

$$= a_1 cov(y_t, y_{t-1}) = a_1^2 var(y_t)$$

and for the general case of $cov(y_t y_{t-s})$ we obtain through iteration

$$cov(y_t, y_{t-s}) = cov(a_0 + a_1 y_{t-1} + \varepsilon_t, y_{t-s}) = a_1 cov(y_{t-1}, y_{t-s})$$

$$= a_1^2 cov(y_{t-2}, y_{t-s}) = \ldots = a_1^{s-1} cov(y_{t-s+1}, y_{t-s})$$

$$= a_1^{s-1} cov(y_t, y_{t-1}) = a_1^s var(y_t).$$

Now we can compute the ACF for an $AR(1)$ process. By substituting the expression for $cov(y_t y_{t-s})$ into equation (3.1) we obtain

$$\rho_s = \frac{cov(y_t, y_{t-s})}{var(y_t)} = \frac{a_1^s var(y_t)}{var(y_t)} = a_1^s.$$

Second, consider an $MA(1)$ process $y_t = \varepsilon_t + \beta_1 \varepsilon_{t-1}$. In similar manner as in case of the $AR(1)$ process we compute variance and covariances so that we have

$$var(y_t) = var(\varepsilon_t + \beta_1 \varepsilon_{t-1}) = (1 + \beta_1^2) \sigma^2,$$

$$cov(y_t, y_{t-1}) = cov(\varepsilon_t + \beta_1 \varepsilon_{t-1}, \varepsilon_{t-1} + \beta_1 \varepsilon_{t-2}) = \beta_1 \sigma^2,$$

$$cov(y_t, y_{t-2}) = cov(\varepsilon_t + \beta_1 \varepsilon_{t-1}, \varepsilon_{t-2} + \beta_1 \varepsilon_{t-3}) = 0,$$

$$cov(y_t, y_{t-3}) = cov(\varepsilon_t + \beta_1\varepsilon_{t-1}, \varepsilon_{t-3} + \beta_1\varepsilon_{t-4}) = 0 \text{ , etc.}$$

After proper substitution we obtain the *ACF* for the *MA*(1) process that is for different lags defined as

$$\rho_0 = 1,$$

$$\rho_1 = \beta_1 / (1 + \beta_1^2),$$

$$\rho_s = 0 \quad \text{for any } s > 1.$$

After computing the theoretical *ACF* of the *AR*(1) and *MA*(1) processes we can summarize the following results:

1. For the *AR*(1) process $y_t = a_0 + a_1 y_{t-1} + \varepsilon_t$, where $|a_1| < 1$ (a sufficient and necessary condition for the stationarity of such a process) the *ACF* is defined as

$$\rho_s = a_1^s.$$

The *ACF* performs a direct exponential or oscillating decay, because $|a_1| < 1$. The decay is direct if $1 > a_1 > 0$ and oscillating if $-1 < a_1 < 0$. It can be shown that the same behavior holds for any stationary *AR*(*p*) process. The *ACF* decays, and the decay might be direct or oscillating.

2. For the *MA*(1) process $y_t = \varepsilon_t + \beta_1\varepsilon_{t-1}$ (such a process is always stationary) the *ACF* is defined as

$$\rho_0 = 1,$$

$$\rho_1 = \beta_1 / (1 + \beta_1^2),$$

$$\rho_s = 0 \quad \text{for any } s > 1.$$

The *ACF* is different from zero for $s \leq 1$ and is zero for $s > 1$. It can be shown that for any *MA*(*q*) process the autocorrelation function is different from zero for $s \leq q$ and is zero for $s > q$.
    The above-mentioned autocorrelation functions are theoretical functions. They are computed based on true data generating processes. However, in estimation we do not know the true data generating process. In fact, our task is almost the opposite. We have the data, that is, the time series, and we want to estimate the data generating process with an *ARMA*(*p,q*) model. Fortunately, we can use the *sample counterparts* of the theoretical autocorrelation functions mentioned above. The *sample autocorrelation function* (the sample *ACF*) is defined as

$$\hat{\rho}_s = \frac{\sum_{t=s+1}^{T}(y_t - \bar{y})(y_{t-s} - \bar{y})}{\sum_{t=1}^{T}(y_t - \bar{y})^2}, \tag{3.2}$$

where $\bar{y} = \dfrac{1}{T}\sum_{t=1}^{T}y_t$ is the sample mean.

Having observations $\{y_t\}_{t=1}^{T}$, equation (3.2) enables computing the sample ACF and comparing it with the theoretical autocorrelation functions computed for different ARMA(p,q) processes according to equation (3.1). If the sample ACF resembles an oscillatory or direct decay, we can assume that the data were generated by a AR(p) process. If the sample ACF is different from zero until the lag s = q and goes almost to zero for lags s > q, then we can assume that the true data generating process was MA(q). A more general algorithm that enables assigning an appropriate ARMA(p,q) process to a certain behavior of the sample ACF (and also sample PACF) is offered in Table 1 in subsection 3.1.6.

3.1.2 PARTIAL AUTOCORRELATION FUNCTION – PACF

Another tool helping to identify the correct number of lags p, q of the true ARMA(p,q) data generating process is the *partial autocorrelation function* (PACF). The PACF gives correlations similar to the ACF correlations between the elements of the time series $\{y_t\}_{t=1}^{T}$. However, in this case the correlation between y_t and y_{t-s} is netted out of the effects of $y_{t-1}, y_{t-2}, ..., y_{t-s+1}$. Notice that in the case of an AR(1) process $y_t = a_0 + a_1 y_{t-1} + \varepsilon_t$ we have a correlation between y_t and y_{t-2}, even though y_{t-2} does not directly appear in the AR(1) equation. This correlation is intermediated through y_{t-1}. Because y_t is correlated with y_{t-1} and y_{t-1} is correlated with y_{t-2}, we obtain the correlation between y_t and y_{t-2}:

$$\rho_2 = corr(y_t, y_{t-2}) = corr(y_t, y_{t-1})corr(y_{t-1}, y_{t-2}) = \rho_1^2.$$

The aim of the PACF is to eliminate such intermediated correlations in the AR(p) processes. To derive the theoretical PACF we assume that we have the autocorrelation function ρ_s for our time series $\{y_t\}$. If we want to obtain the PACF for the first lag, we suppose for the moment that the time series was generated by an AR(1) process, that is,

$$y_t = a_0 + \phi_{11} y_{t-1} + \varepsilon_t,$$

where the coefficient at the first lag ϕ_{11} equals the desired PACF. Knowing the ACF for the first lag ρ_1, it must hold that

$$\rho_1 = corr(y_t, y_{t-1}) = corr(a_0 + \phi_{11}y_{t-1} + \varepsilon_t, y_{t-1}) = \phi_{11}.$$

Then as a result

$$\phi_{11} = \rho_1,$$

which is not surprising, because for the first lag there are no intervening lags in between, so that the *PACF* for the first lag ϕ_{11} equals the *ACF* for the first lag ρ_1. To compute the *PACF* for the second lag ϕ_{22}, we assume that the time series was generated by an *AR*(2) process described as:

$$y_t = a_0 + \phi_{21}y_{t-1} + \phi_{22}y_{t-2} + \varepsilon_t,$$

where the coefficient at the second lag ϕ_{22} equals the desired *PACF*. Knowing the *ACF* for the first and second lags, ρ_1 and ρ_2, it must hold that

$$\rho_1 = corr(y_t, y_{t-1}) = corr(a_0 + \phi_{21}y_{t-1} + \phi_{22}y_{t-2} + \varepsilon_t, y_{t-1}) = \phi_{21} + \phi_{22}\rho_1,$$

$$\rho_2 = corr(y_t, y_{t-2}) = corr(a_0 + \phi_{21}y_{t-1} + \phi_{22}y_{t-2} + \varepsilon_t, y_{t-2}) = \phi_{21}\rho_1 + \phi_{22}.$$

These two equations can be solved for ϕ_{22} so that we have

$$\phi_{22} = (\rho_2 - \rho_1^2)/(1 - \rho_1^2).$$

We can continue the procedure until we obtain the *PACF* for any general lag s, denoted as ϕ_{ss}. In such a case we must suppose that the time series was generated by an *AR*(s) process and that we know the *ACF* for all lags until s. In this manner we obtain the following expression for the *PACF* of any general lag s greater than 2 defined as

$$\phi_{ss} = \frac{\rho_s - \sum_{j=1}^{s-1} \phi_{s-1,j}\rho_{s-j}}{1 - \sum_{j=1}^{s-1} \phi_{s-1,j}\rho_j} \quad \text{for } s > 2, \tag{3.3}$$

where $\phi_{sj} = \phi_{s-1,j} - \phi_{ss}\phi_{s-1,s-j}$.

The theoretical *PACF* derived above will have a specific behavior for time series generated by different *ARMA*(p,q) processes. As in the previous section, for simplicity we will first consider *AR*(1) and *MA*(1) processes.

1. The *AR*(1) process $y_t = a_0 + a_1 y_{t-1} + \varepsilon_t$, where $|a_1| < 1$ (a sufficient and necessary condition for the stationarity of such a process).

The *PACF* is different from zero until lag $s = 1$ and equals zero for all lags $s > 1$. Similarly, if the data were generated by an *AR(p)* process, then there is no direct correlation between y_t and y_{t-s} for $s > p$. The *PACF* is thus different from zero up to the lag $s = p$ and equals zero for any lag $s > p$.

2. The *MA(1)* process $y_t = \varepsilon_t + \beta_1 \varepsilon_{t-1}$ (such a process is always stationary).
    If $\beta_1 \neq -1$, using the lag operator we can rewrite the *MA(1)* equation as $y_t/(1 + \beta_1 L) = \varepsilon_t$. We suppose the *MA(1)* process to be not only stationary but also *invertible*, thus having a convergent infinite order *AR* representation as $y_t = \beta_1 y_{t-1} - \beta_1^2 y_{t-2} + \beta_1^3 y_{t-3} - \cdots + \varepsilon_t$. Note that the necessary and sufficient condition for the convergence of this infinite order *AR* equation and therefore also for the invertibility of the *MA(1)* equation is that $|\beta_1| < 1$. Because the *MA(1)* process has a convergent infinite order *AR* representation, the *PACF* will never go directly to zero. Rather it will decay exponentially to zero, while the decay will be direct if $\beta_1 < 0$ and oscillatory if $\beta_1 > 0$. It can be shown that for any invertible *MA(q)* process the *PACF* will decay to zero either in a direct or oscillatory way.

We have just shown that the *MA(1)* process must be *invertible*, if we want to obtain a meaningful *PACF*. As it was already mentioned in the beginning of section 3.1, the invertibility of any *ARMA(p,q)* process means that it can be represented by a finite-order or convergent infinite autoregressive process. In general we need any *ARMA(p,q)* process to be invertible for its *PACF* to make sense. In a more exact way an *ARMA(p,q)* process

$$y_t = a_0 + \sum_{i=1}^{p} a_i y_{t-i} + \sum_{i=0}^{q} \beta_i \varepsilon_{t-i}$$

is invertible if all the roots L_i of the polynomial $\sum_{i=0}^{q} \beta_i L^i$ lie outside the unit circle ($|L_i| > 1$). In this case the polynomial can be rewritten as

$$\prod_{i=0}^{q}(L - L_i) = -\prod_{i=0}^{q} L_i(1 - r_i L),$$

where r_i stands for $1/L_i$, thus $|r_i| < 1$. The *ARMA(p,q)* process can be then rewritten as

$$\frac{-y_t}{\prod_{i=0}^{q} L_i(1 - r_i L)} = \frac{-a_0}{\prod_{i=0}^{q} L_i(1 - r_i L)} + \frac{-\sum_{i=1}^{p} a_i y_{t-i}}{\prod_{i=0}^{q} L_i(1 - r_i L)} + \varepsilon_t.$$

Because all $|r_i| < 1$, all elements in the equation above can be extended step by step into convergent sums, which yields a convergent infinite *AR* representation of the original *ARMA(p,q)* process.

The *PACF* given by equation (3.3) is a theoretical function computed from the theoretical *ACF* (ρ_s). In practice, when we estimate a time series, we know neither the theoretical *ACF* nor the theoretical *PACF*. Similarly as in the case of *ACF* we use the *sample partial autocorrelation function* (sample *PACF*) instead of the theoretical one. We obtain the sample *PACF* simply by replacing the theoretical *ACF* (ρ_s) by its sample counterpart $\hat{\rho}_s$ in equation (3.3). One other way to obtain the sample *PACF* is to apply the *OLS* method to estimate the equation $y_t = a_0 + \phi_{i1} y_{t-1} + \phi_{i2} y_{t-2} + \cdots + \phi_{ii} y_{t-i} + \varepsilon_t$. The coefficient estimates will then equal the appropriate elements of the sample *PACF*.

To summarize, having the observations $\{y_t\}_{t=1}^{T}$, we can compute the sample *PACF* and compare it with theoretical partial autocorrelation functions computed for different *ARMA(p,q)* processes. If the sample *PACF* resembles an oscillating or direct decay, we can assume that the data were generated by some *MA(q)* process. If the sample *PACF* is different from zero until the lag $s = p$ and goes almost to zero for lags $s > p$, then we can assume that the true data generating process was an *AR(p)*. A general algorithm that enables assigning the appropriate *ARMA(p,q)* process to a certain behavior of the sample *PACF* (and also sample *ACF*) is provided in Table 1 in subsection 3.1.6.[4]

3.1.3 Q-TESTS

In the previous section, we described the autocorrelation and partial autocorrelation functions as useful tools that help us to determine the number of lags p and q of the true *ARMA(p,q)* data generating process. The application of these functions is rather intuitive. The sample counterparts of these functions are compared to the theoretical functions for different *ARMA* models. If the pattern of the sample *ACF* and *PACF* resembles the theoretical *ACF* and *PACF* of an *ARMA(p,q)* process, then p and q very likely represent the true number of lags. However, in practice this procedure is rarely so straightforward and easy. The sample *ACF* and *PACF* can often appear to be ambiguous. Then it becomes very difficult to discover a clear pattern. Indeed, the sample *ACF* and *PACF* are random variables and as such can deviate from the expected pattern by pure chance. As a result, the assessment of the correct number of lags based on the sample *ACF* and *PACF* is to an extent a matter of experience.

To increase the chance that the chosen number of lags is correct, we can use another tool – the *Q-tests*. The *Q-tests* based on *Q*-statistics offer a statisti-

---

4   The *ARMA* model is one of the key building blocks of empirical econometrics for capturing an underlying process in data. An interesting application of the *ARMA* specification as an alternative to the random walk to model stock returns can be found in Vošvrda and Žikeš (2004). The *ARMA* model is used by Derviz (2002) in conjunction with uncovered interest rate parity.

cally more formal way to assess the correct number of lags. They test whether a group of autocorrelations ρ_s (elements of the *ACF*) is statistically different from zero. Theoretically the sample variance for the sample *ACF* and *PACF* can be computed as well as *t*-tests of these functions formulated for each lag *s* separately. However, such tests have low power, because they are always based on only one value of the sample *ACF* and *PACF*, for one particular *s*. The *Q*-statistics are based on a group of sample autocorrelations $\hat{\rho}_s$, and therefore their power is higher.

In practical application two well known types of *Q*-tests are used: the *Box-Pierce Q-test* (Box and Pierce, 1970) and the *Ljung-Box Q-test* (Ljung and Box, 1978). The former test performs well only in very large samples, while the latter test uses a *Q*-statistics that is adjusted in order to perform better in small samples. That is why the Ljung-Box *Q*-test is usually the preferred one, but for the sake of completeness both are introduced here.

1. *Box-Pierce Q-test*
The Box-Pierce *Q*-test is based on the *Box-Pierce Q-statistics* defined as

$$Q = T \sum_{i=1}^{k} \hat{\rho}_i^2, \tag{3.4}$$

where $\hat{\rho}_i$ are the elements of the sample *ACF* defined by equation (3.2). Under the null hypothesis that all autocorrelations up to the lag *k* are zero, the *Q*-statistics is asymptotically χ^2 distributed with *k* degrees of freedom; this holds only in the case that the time series was generated by a stationary *ARMA* process.

2. *Ljung-Box Q-test*
The Ljung-Box *Q*-test is based on the *Ljung-Box Q-statistics* defined as

$$Q = T(T+2) \sum_{i=1}^{k} \frac{\hat{\rho}_i^2}{T-i}, \tag{3.5}$$

where $\hat{\rho}_i$ are as in the previous case the elements of the sample *ACF* defined by equation (3.2). Under the null hypothesis that all autocorrelations up to the lag *k* are zero, the *Q*-statistics is χ^2 distributed with *k* degrees of freedom; this holds only in the case that the time series was generated by a stationary *ARMA* process.[5]

When we search for the appropriate number of lags of an *ARMA(p,q)* model, we should compute the *Q*-statistics for *k* starting at 1 and continue until a reasonably high *k*. A reasonable upper bound of *k* verified by practice should not

---

5   Some applications of the Ljung-Box *Q*-test on data from the Central and Eastern European region can be found in Gurgul, Majdosz, and Mestel (2006), Vošvrda and Žikeš (2004) or Žikeš and Bubák (2006b).

be higher then a quarter of the sample size $(T/4)$. In any event, the choice of the upper k is a matter of experience and also of the nature of the data whose generating process we want to model. The testing procedure is standard. If the critical value of χ_k^2 is exceeded by the appropriate Q-statistics, we can say that at least one autocorrelation from the set $\{\rho_i\}_{i=1}^{k}$ is significantly different from zero.

Unlike the analysis of the *ACF* and the *PACF* there is no straightforward algorithm that assigns the most appropriate *ARMA(p,q)* model to various patterns of the Q-tests' results. Both methodologies should be applied together and their results should not contradict each other. In practice, Q-tests are more useful to diagnose the residuals from the estimated model rather than searching for the correct number of lags p and q. The diagnostics of residuals is described in the next section.

3.1.4 DIAGNOSTICS OF RESIDUALS

Residuals from a correctly specified model that captures the data generating process well should be *white noise*. This means that they should contain no further information that could help with estimation. White noise has all autocorrelations equal to zero. That is why Q-tests represent a suitable, but limited, tool to test whether a time series is white noise.

After we choose the lags p and q and estimate the *ARMA(p,q)* model, we should test the residuals of that model for being white noise. For this purpose we use the Q-tests described in the previous chapter. The testing procedure is almost the same. The only difference is that the Q-statistics defined by equations (3.4) and (3.5) have χ^2 distributions with less degrees of freedom. The degrees of freedom are decreased by the number of parameters included in the estimated *ARMA(p,q)*. This means that the χ^2 distribution has $(k - p - q - 1)$ degrees of freedom if a constant is included in the model, or $(k - p - q)$ degrees of freedom if the model is estimated without a constant. Therefore, we can compute the Q-statistics and perform the Q-tests starting only with k higher than $(p + q + 2)$ or $(p + q + 1)$ and continue maximally until a reasonable value of $k = T/4$. If the residuals are white noise, then all autocorrelations should be zero; therefore, we should not be able to reject the null hypothesis for each k. This means that the Q-statistics should not exceed the appropriate χ^2 critical values for any k in case of the residuals being white noise.

3.1.5 INFORMATION CRITERIA

It can happen that several different *ARMA(p,q)* models seem to be appropriate for our data. This occurs if the pattern of the sample *ACF* and *PACF* can be interpreted in several different ways and if the residuals from several different models are diagnosed to be white noise. In such a case we can use *information criteria* to select the model that is the best. By the best we mean the most *parsimonious* model that satisfactorily captures the dynamics of the data.

The most common measure of goodness of fit is the R^2. The problem with the R^2 is that it enables only a comparison of models of the same form and, moreover, models with the same number of explanatory variables. The R^2 would never decrease if we added one more variable in the model and in most cases it would increase. For example we can use the R^2 only to compare linear models that use the same number of explanatory variables, whereas these explanatory variables can differ across the models. This is not exactly what we need in univariate time series econometrics. Here the explanatory variables are given and so cannot differ to such an extent as in cross sectional econometrics. They are the lags of y_t in *AR* models and the lags of ε_t in *MA* models. In time series econometrics we usually want to compare different *ARMA(p,q)* models, where the difference resides in the number of lags p and q, thus in the number of explanatory variables. For this comparison we must use information criteria instead of the R^2.

Most frequently, the following information criteria are used:

the *Akaike information criterion (AIC)* (see Akaike, 1978) defined as

$$AIC = T \ln SSR + 2n,$$ (3.6)

the *Schwarz Bayes information criterion (SBIC)* (see Schwarz, 1978) defined as

$$SBIC = T \ln SSR + n \ln T,$$ (3.7)

and the *Hannan-Quinn information criterion (HQIC)* (see Hannan and Quinn, 1979) defined as

$$HQIC = T \ln SSR + 2n(\ln(\ln T)),$$ (3.8)

where *SSR* is the sum of the residuals' squares; n is the number of explanatory variables ($n = p + q + 1$ if a constant term is included); and T is the number of usable observations. The number of usable observations T should be the same for all the compared models. If we add lagged variables in the model we lose some observations. This happens also by differencing. As a result if we compare several models, we should use for the estimation of all these models only those observations that are usable in the model with the highest number of lagged variables. For example if we compare *AR(1)*, *AR(2)*, and *AR(3)* models with 100 data points, then we should use only 97 observations for the purpose of the comparison.

To select the best model the value of the *information criteria is to be mini-mized*. The problem is that the information criteria will usually suggest choosing a model with more parameters (more explanatory variables) than the true data generating process has. This is a more serious problem in the case of the *AIC* that is biased towards choosing an overparametrized model. The *SBC* is at least asymptotically consistent. This means that if the number of observations goes to infinity the *SBC* will enable us to select the right model. In plain terms the *SBC* imposes a heavier penalty on overparametrized models. The Hannan-Quinn information criterion aims to combine the approach of the *AIC* and *SBIC* in allowing less parsimonious specification with a heavy penalty for excessive parameters.

3.1.6 BOX-JENKINS METHODOLOGY

In the previous subsections we introduced the tools necessary for the application of the Box-Jenkins methodology. Now we will describe the sequence and logic in which they should be applied – *the algorithm of the Box-Jenkins method-ology.* In essence the Box-Jenkins methodology consists of the following three steps:

1. *Identification*
2. *Estimation*
3. *Diagnostic checking.*

Of course, such an algorithm represents a simplification as any generalization does. In reality we must rely also on intuition and experience. Our starting point is the data. We have a time series $\{y_t\}_{t=1}^T$ and we want to estimate its data generating process by an *ARMA(p,q)* model. In order to achieve this goal we should proceed in the following steps:

1. Plot the sample *ACF* and *PACF* for lags from $s = 1$ to $s = T/4$ and compare the pattern of these functions to the patterns of the theoretical *ACF* and *PACF* of *ARMA(p,q)* models with a different number of lags p and q. These theoretical patterns are summarized in the table below. Based on this comparison we choose the most appropriate number of lags p and q for our *ARMA* model.
2. Estimate the *ARMA(p,q)* model with the lags p and q chosen in the previous step and save the residuals. To estimate *AR* models without any *MA* terms a simple OLS can be used in order to obtain consistent and asymptotical-ly normal coefficient estimates. Such models are simple linear regression models with stochastic regressors. However, *ARMA* models are non-linear

Table 1: The ACF and PACF of different ARMA models.

ARMA process	*ACF* pattern
White noise	$\rho_s = 0$ for all s
$AR(1)$	Direct or oscillating decay, $\rho_s = a_1^s$
$AR(p)$	Direct or oscillating decay
$MA(1)$	$\rho_1 \neq 0; \rho_s = 0$ for $s > 1$
$MA(q)$	$\rho_s \neq 0$ for $s \leq q; \rho_s = 0$ for $s > q$
$ARMA(p, q)$	Direct or oscillating decay beginning at lag q
ARMA process	*PACF* pattern
White noise	$\Phi_{ss} = 0$ for all s
$AR(1)$	$\Phi_{11} = \rho_1; \Phi_{ss} = 0$ for $s > 1$
$AR(p)$	$\Phi_{ss} \neq 0$ for $s \leq p; \Phi_{ss} = 0$ for $s > p$
$MA(1)$	Direct or oscillating decay
$MA(q)$	Direct or oscillating decay
$ARMA(p, q)$	Direct or oscillating decay beginning at lag p

due to the *MA* terms and must be estimated using non-linear least squares. Non-linear least squares method provides consistent and asymptotically normal coefficient estimates. Additionally, if the error terms are normally distributed, then non-linear least squares estimates, being identical to maximum likelihood coefficient estimates, are also efficient. More details on the technical issue of the estimation of *ARMA* models can be found for example in Greene (2008). Procedures enabling the routine estimation of *ARMA* models form an integral part of most statistical packages.

3. Plot the sample *ACF* and *PACF* for the series of residuals, compute the Q-statistics and perform the Q-tests. The sample *ACF* and *PACF* can be computed as with the original time series for lags from $s = 1$ to $T/4$. The Q-tests can be computed for k starting at $(p + q + 2)$ if we use a constant term in our model, or at $(p + q + 1)$ if our model is without a constant term and k ends maximally at $T/4$. If all the sample autocorrelations and partial autocorrelations are close to zero and if all the Q-tests do not reject the null hypothesis of no autocorrelation, then the estimated model might be the correct one. If this is not the case, then we have to go back to step 1 and change the number of lags p and q.

4. If we got to this point with several possibly correct *ARMA(p,q)* models, then we can choose the one that minimizes the *information criteria*. Such a model has a good chance to be the best approximation of the true data generating process.

Throughout this section we required the time series to be stationary and invertible. So if the *Box-Jenkins methodology* leads us to a choice of a model that is close to being non-stationary or non-invertible, we should be suspicious. For example, if we estimated the data generating process as an *AR*(2) process, $y_t = a_0 + a_1 y_{t-1} + a_2 y_{t-2} + \varepsilon_t$, and got the coefficients a_1 and a_2 such that $a_1 + a_2$ is close to one, then we should review the whole estimation procedure and possibly test the time series for the presence of a unit root (as presented in section 3.4).

3.2 TREND IN TIME SERIES

In the previous sections we described how to estimate the irregular pattern of a time series with an *ARMA* model. However, it was pointed out that many time series of economic data contain a time trend. Other time series can even grow exponentially. Exponentially growing time series are typically transformed by taking a natural logarithm, which generates a time series containing a linear time trend. Any trending time series is not stationary. Therefore, we must first remove the trend from the analyzed data before we can proceed with estimating the irregular pattern. Explaining the trend is another matter. However, in time series econometrics the explanation of the trend is not a priority. Understandably, a more fundamental as well as theoretical background should be used as a tool to explain the source of a specific trend in the data. Nevertheless, time series econometrics is capable of dealing with trends and Mills (2003) serves as a qualified reference covering this topic.

    In the following subsections we will introduce some basic types of trends that can be present in the data. Also we will suggest the appropriate transformations that should be applied in order to remove each of these trends and to make the time series stationary.

3.2.1 DETERMINISTIC TREND

The simplest model that will generate a stochastic time series containing a deterministic trend is the following:

$$y_t = a_0 + a_1 t + \varepsilon_t. \tag{3.9}$$

This equation can be further extended with *AR* and *MA* terms. Moreover, the time trend does not have to be linear, it can also be polynomial. In such a general case the model will be written as:

$$A(L)y_t = a_0 + a_1 t + a_2 t^2 + \cdots + a_n t^n + I_t,$$

$$\text{where } A(L)I_t = B(L)\varepsilon_t.$$

The presence of the deterministic trend implies that the value of y_t increases in each period by a deterministic amount. In the pure linear time trend model described by equation (3.9) this deterministic increase equals a_1.

When attempting to remove the deterministic trend, the appropriate transformation is *detrending*. To detrend a time series $\{y_t\}_{t=1}^{T}$ we run a simple *OLS* regression of y_t on time t or a polynomial of time t. The correct order of the trend polynomial can be assessed with standard t-tests and F-tests. It is also useful to consult the Akaike and Schwarz Bayes information criteria when deciding what order of the polynomial to use in the regression. We receive a detrended time series when we subtract the fitted values of the regression from the original time series, that is, the detrended time series equals the regression residuals.

Differencing is another standard transformation that helps to achieve time series stationarity. However, *differencing* would not be a correct step when our priors suggest that the time series contains a deterministic time trend. Imagine that we difference a time series with a linear deterministic time trend generated by equation (3.9). In that case we would obtain a time series generated by the process $\Delta y_t = a_1 + \varepsilon_t - \varepsilon_{t-1}$. Such a time series is not invertible and cannot be estimated using the Box-Jenkins methodology. The trouble results from the *MA* component. Its polynomial $B(L) = 1 - L$ clearly contains a unit root and therefore does not enable any finite or convergent *AR* representation. On the other hand, differencing is the ideal transformation to be applied on time series that contain a *stochastic trend*.

3.2.2 STOCHASTIC TREND

In the simplest case, a time series that contains a stochastic trend can be generated by the following model:

$$y_t = y_{t-1} + \varepsilon_t \text{ or } \Delta y_t = \varepsilon_t. \qquad (3.10)$$

Such a process is called a *random walk*. Using the name "stochastic trend" is a matter of terminology. Indeed, a random walk model is not what we would intuitively imagine under the term trend. However, there is some logic to this terminology. Similarly as in the case of a deterministic trend, a time series generated by the random walk model will increase in each period by a given amount. Unlike the deterministic case this increase is stochastic and is given by the concrete realization of the random disturbance ε_t. The solution of equation (3.10) yields

$$y_t = y_0 + \sum_{i=1}^{t} \varepsilon_i .$$

Equation (3.10) can be augmented with *MA* coefficients, which yields a more complicated process containing a stochastic trend. Such a process can be generally described by the equation

$$y_t = y_{t-1} + B(L)\varepsilon_t . \tag{3.11}$$

A time series generated by the random walk model will be obviously non-stationary, because it contains a unit root. Therefore, it cannot be estimated with the tools of the Box-Jenkins methodology. Again we must first remove the stochastic trend before we can proceed to further estimation.

The appropriate transformation that removes the stochastic trend is *differencing*. After differencing equation (3.11), we receive $\Delta y_t = B(L)\ \varepsilon_t$, which is a stationary time series.

3.2.3 STOCHASTIC PLUS DETERMINISTIC TREND

Deterministic and stochastic trends can be combined in one process. The simplest version of such a process can be described by the equation

$$y_t = a_0 + y_{t-1} + \varepsilon_t \text{ or } \Delta y_t = a_0 + \varepsilon_t . \tag{3.12}$$

Such a process is called a *random walk with drift*. The value of y_t increases in each period by $a_0 + \varepsilon_t$. This means that the increase is given by the deterministic amount a_0 plus the concrete realization of the random disturbance ε_t. This property makes the random walk with drift a combination of a deterministic and stochastic trend. It becomes even clearer when we solve equation (3.12). The solution can be written as

$$y_t = y_0 + a_0 t + \sum_{i=1}^{t} \varepsilon_i .$$

Similarly as with pure stochastic trends, equation (3.12) can be augmented with *MA* coefficients, which yields a more complicated process described by the equation

$$y_t = a_0 + y_{t-1} + B(L)\varepsilon_t . \tag{3.13}$$

A time series generated by the random walk with drift model is non-stationary, because it contains a combination of a unit root and a deterministic trend. The appropriate transformation that removes the combination of stochastic and deterministic trends is *differencing*. It yields a time series generated by the process $\Delta y_t = a_0 + B(L)\ \varepsilon_t$, which is already stationary.

3.2.4 ADDITIONAL NOTES ON TRENDS IN TIME SERIES

We have just seen that time series can contain a deterministic trend, a stochastic trend, or a combination of both. Trending time series are not stationary and must be made stationary by the appropriate transformations. Different transformations are needed for different types of trend. When removing the trend we must be very careful in our choice of the transformation. If our priors suggest the presence of a stochastic trend, we should apply differencing. On the other hand, if we suppose the presence of a deterministic trend only, we should choose detrending.

In practice this decision might be tricky, because it is often not clear what type of trend we should expect to be present in the data. Moreover, even if we have good reasons to assume a pure deterministic trend, we can rarely be sure that the trend is constant over time and that there are no trend breaks. With the occurrence of trend breaks, detrending without controlling for such breaks would not be the right transformation. The potential presence of trend breaks is the reason why differencing is often more secure then detrending. In practice, for the correct choice of the transformation we should consult the results of unit root tests and the *ARMA* estimation applied on the transformed time series. If the choice of the transformation was correct, then the transformed time series should be stationary (should not contain a unit root) and should be estimatable with an *ARMA* model. We use the terms *trend stationary time series* and *difference stationary time series* for time series that can be made stationary by detrending and differencing, respectively. Time series that become stationary after *n*-th order of differencing are called *integrated of the order n*, which we denote as $I(n)$.[6]

In practical applications the estimation procedure should proceed by the following steps:

1. *Detect* the trend.
2. *Remove* the trend by the appropriate transformation.
3. *Estimate* the transformed time series.

---

6   When *n* is not an integer but a fraction, then time series is fractionally integrated. The process is weakly stationary for $n < 0.5$. For $n \geq 0.5$, variance is not finite, so the process is non-stationary.

There also exist more complex models of trending time series that require joint estimation of trending and stationary components. Some of these models are introduced very briefly in the following list.

1. *Random walk plus noise model*

$$y_t = z_t + \varepsilon_t, \ z_t = z_{t-1} + \eta_t,$$ (3.14)

where ε_t and η_t are independent white noise processes.

2. *General trend plus irregular model*

$$y_t = z_t + \varepsilon_t, \ z_t = z_{t-1} + a_0 + \eta_t,$$ (3.15)

where ε_t and η_t are independent white noise processes.

3. *Local linear trend model*

$$y_t = z_t + \varepsilon_t, \ z_t = z_{t-1} + a_t + \eta_t, \ a_t = a_{t-1} + \delta_t,$$ (3.16)

where ε_t, η_t, and δ_t are mutually independent white noise processes.

From the exposition above it is obvious that the additive decomposition of any time series into trend, seasonal, and irregular patterns described in section 1.5 with equation (1.1), $y_t = T_t + S_t + I_t$, is in some cases misleading. The trend can be treated as a simple additive component only if it is a pure deterministic trend. If the time series is described by a random walk or a random walk with drift model, then the stochastic trend contained in such a time series cannot be represented as a simple additive component.

3.3 SEASONALITY IN TIME SERIES

In section 1.5 we proposed a decomposition of any time series into trend, seasonal and irregular patterns. Various types of trend and the way to remove them were described in the previous section. In this section we will elaborate in more detail on the issue of seasonal patterns. A *seasonal pattern* is typical for time series that are related to some real seasonal activities (e.g. agriculture or tourism). A seasonal pattern may also appear through policy or accounting practices (e.g. spending or investments). In order to observe a seasonal pattern in a time series, the data must be collected more often than the period of the seasonal pattern. The choice of the terminology itself suggests that the data-collecting period of seasonal patterns is less than or equal to one year. Because seasonal patterns are usually related to some cyclical variation during yearly seasons, most seasonal patterns can be expected to have periods of 3, 6, or 12 months. Therefore, we will rarely observe any seasonal pattern in yearly data. On the other hand, we can almost always expect some seasonal patterns in quarterly, monthly, weekly, or daily data. For example, monthly data of agricultural production in any temperate zone country will most likely contain a seasonal pattern with the period of 12 months. Still, there are some special cases where the period of the seasonal pattern is greater than one year. For example, if we want to detect the business cycle in GDP data, we can expect its period to be greater than one year. However, the particular issue of the business cycle would be more complex, because business cycles are irregular to an extent.

Time series that contain seasonal patterns are not necessarily non-stationary. However, if we disregard the presence of the seasonal pattern when estimating the data generating process, we will not reach the most parsimonious model and our coefficient estimates will have a relatively high variance.

We already mentioned that the additive decomposition of any time series into trend, seasonal and irregular patterns described in section 1.5 with equation (1.1), $y_t = T_t + S_t + I_t$, is slightly misleading. In the previous section we have seen that the trend cannot always be treated as a pure additive component of a time series. Similarly, in many cases the seasonal pattern is not a pure additive component of a time series. Often seasonal patterns cannot be treated separately, but must be estimated jointly with the irregular pattern. When estimating a time series with a seasonal pattern, we should logically proceed by the following steps:

1. *Detect* the seasonal pattern.
2. *Remove* the seasonal pattern (*deseasonalize the data*) or estimate it jointly with the irregular pattern.
3. *Estimate* the deseasonalized data, if the seasonal pattern was not estimated jointly with the irregular pattern.

For reasons of clear exposition the way seasonal patterns can be *detected* and *estimated*, or *removed*, will be described in reverse order in the following subsections.

3.3.1 REMOVING SEASONAL PATTERNS

The simplest transformation that helps to remove a seasonal pattern is *seasonal differencing*. To apply seasonal differencing we take differences not between successive periods but between seasonal periods. For example, if we have a monthly time series $\{y_t\}_{t=1}^{T}$ that contains a seasonal pattern with the period of 12 months, we apply 12th seasonal differencing, which we denote as $\Delta_{12} y_t = y_t - y_{t-12}$. If the period of the seasonal pattern was really 12 months, then out of all possible types of seasonal differencing the 12th seasonal differencing will yield a time series with the lowest variation. In the general case seasonal differencing is denoted by the operator Δ_s and is defined as

$$\Delta_s y_t = (1 - L^s) y_t = y_t - y_{t-s}.\tag{3.17}$$

If we have a trending time series $\{y_t\}_{t=1}^{T}$ that also contains a seasonal pattern, then seasonal differencing can remove both the trend and the seasonal pattern. Moreover, seasonal differencing will yield a time series that will have a lower variance than time series obtained after regular (e.g. first) differencing. Nevertheless, it can happen that even after seasonal differencing, the time series will still be non-stationary. In such a case we can still apply regular differencing. This means that together we will apply the following transformation:

$$\Delta\Delta_s y_t = (1 - L)(1 - L^s) y_t = (1 - L)(y_t - y_{t-s}) = y_t - y_{t-1} + y_{t-s-1} - y_{t-s}.$$

Sometimes even after seasonal differencing some seasonal pattern remains present in the data. Such a persistent seasonal pattern must be either removed by additional seasonal differencing or estimated jointly with the irregular pattern. The way seasonal patterns can be incorporated into *ARMA* models and estimated jointly with the irregular pattern will be described in the following section.

Often time series provided by various national and international agencies are reported to be deseasonalized. The seasonal pattern is removed from such time series with the application of so-called filters. Even though the underlying methodology can be very sophisticated, we should be cautious when working with such deseasonalized data. The filters applied are usually designed for routine application on many time series. Therefore, they are not necessarily the best way to treat the seasonal pattern in an individual case.

3.3.2 ESTIMATING SEASONAL PATTERNS

When estimating a time series we search for the most parsimonious model. Removing the seasonal pattern first and then estimating the irregular pattern does not always lead to the most parsimonious model. It is often more fruitful to incorporate the seasonal pattern into an *ARMA* model and estimate it jointly with the irregular pattern. *ARMA* models of seasonal data can be either *additive* or *multiplicative*.

An example of an additive $AR(1)$ model of seasonal data with a seasonal period 12 can be specified as:

$$(1-a_1L-a_{12}L^{12})y_t = a_0 + \varepsilon_t \text{ or } y_t = a_0 + a_1 y_{t-1} + a_{12}y_{t-12} + \varepsilon_t.$$

A multiplicative $AR(1)$ model of seasonal data with a seasonal period 12 can be written as

$$(1-a_{12}L^{12})(1-a_1L)y_t = a_0 + \varepsilon_t \text{ or } y_t = a_0 + a_1 y_{t-1} + a_{12}y_{t-12} - a_1 a_{12}y_{t-13} + \varepsilon_t.$$

From the two examples above it is clear that the multiplicative model enables more interaction of the seasonal and regular AR components. This is the reason why multiplicative models of seasonal data are often preferred to purely additive models. Seasonal coefficients can of course be incorporated also into MA processes. In a very general case we can describe *additive and multiplicative ARMA models of seasonal data* with a period s by the following equations:

$$(A(L)-a_sL^s)y_t = (B(L)-\beta_sL^s)\varepsilon_t, \tag{3.18}$$

$$(1-a_sL^s)A(L)y_t = (1-\beta_sL^s)B(L)\varepsilon_t. \tag{3.19}$$

Such models can be estimated by most statistical packages in a similar way as simple $ARMA$ models.

In the previous section we mentioned that some persistent seasonal pattern can still remain in seasonally differenced data. Moreover, a time series that was seasonally differenced can still be non-stationary and require further regular differencing. In such a case we first difference the time series seasonally, then we apply normal differencing, and then we estimate the transformed time series with a seasonal $ARMA$ model. It might be useful to show how such a complex model can look in a concrete case. After seasonal and regular differencing we can, for example, estimate the time series with an $ARMA(1,1)$ model with a multiplicative seasonal MA coefficient. That is, we estimate the following model

$$(1-a_1L)(1-L)(1-L^{12})y_t = a_0 + (1-\beta_sL^s)(1-\beta_1L)\varepsilon_t,$$

which can be rewritten as

$$y_t = a_0 + y_{t-12} + y_t - y_{t-13} + a_1 y_{t-1} - a_1 y_{t-2} - a_1 y_{t-13} + a_1 y_{t-14} +$$

$$+ \varepsilon_t - \beta_1 \varepsilon_{t-1} - \beta_s \varepsilon_{t-s} + \beta_s \beta_1 \varepsilon_{t-s-1}.$$

3.3.3 DETECTING SEASONAL PATTERNS

In order to remove or estimate the seasonal pattern of any time series we must first *detect* it. To do so we use a procedure similar to that for assessing the correct number of lags p and q in an $ARMA(p,q)$ model. That is, we investigate the sample ACF and $PACF$ functions. Imagine the following simple AR and MA seasonal processes with the period s:

$$(1-a_s L^s)y_t = \varepsilon_t \text{ rewritten as } y_t = a_s y_{t-s} + \varepsilon_t, \qquad (3.20)$$

$$y_t = (1-\beta_s L^s)\varepsilon_t \text{ rewritten as } y_t = \beta_s \varepsilon_{t-s} + \varepsilon_t. \qquad (3.21)$$

The theoretical ACF of the AR model (3.20) will exhibit exponential decay at lags s, $2s$, $3s$, etc., and will equal zero for all other lags. Its theoretical $PACF$ will have only one spike at the lag s. The theoretical ACF of the MA model (3.21) will show a single spike at the lag s. Its theoretical $PACF$ will decay exponentially at lags s, $2s$, $3s$, etc.

To summarize, in order to detect the seasonal pattern and its period we can investigate the sample ACF and $PACF$. If any of these functions show decaying periodical spikes, it is very likely that the studied time series contains a seasonal pattern with the same period. Moreover, if the periodical spikes appear in the sample ACF, we can assume a seasonal AR model. If such spikes are present in the sample $PACF$, we can expect a seasonal MA model. Unfortunately, in practice the analysis of a sample ACF or $PACF$ is tricky. Typically, the seasonal $ARMA$ coefficients will interact with the regular $ARMA$ coefficient and the resulting sample ACF or $PACF$ will show a very complex pattern. To see this, we show on Figure 3.1 the sample ACF and $PACF$ of a time series generated by a seasonal multiplicative $AR(1)$ model described by the equation $(1 - 0.4L^4)(1 - 0.4L)$ $y_t = \varepsilon_t$, where $\varepsilon_t \sim N(0,1)$. Already in this very simple case the interpretation of the correlogram is not so straightforward. It is one of the numerous cases when science mingles with art.

3.3.4 HODRICK-PRESCOTT FILTER

A different type of approach to detrending the data is a flexible detrending method designed by Hodrick and Prescott (1997) to analyze business cycles. The technique has become known as the Hodrick-Prescott filter (the HP filter) and in general can be used to obtain a smoothed non-linear representation of a time series that would capture its long-term behavior rather than short-term fluctuations.

The HP filter decomposes a time series y_t into a nonstationary trend τ_t and a stationary residual component c_t, e.g. $y_t = \tau_t + c_t$. Both trend and residual com-

Figure 3.1: Sample ACF and PACF of a multiplicative AR(1) seasonal model.

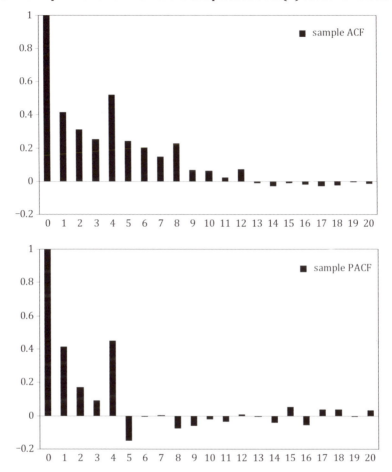

ponents are unobservable. Since c_t is a stationary process, y_t can be considered as a noisy signal for the trend component τ_t. The *HP* filter extracts the trend component τ_t from a series y_t by following this minimization problem:

$$Min_{\{\tau_t\}_{t-1}^T} \left[\sum_{t=1}^{T}(y_t - \tau_t)^2 + \lambda \sum_{t=2}^{T-1}\left[\left(\tau_{t+1} - \tau_t\right) - \left(\tau_t - \tau_{t-1}\right)\right]^2 \right],$$

where λ is a multiplier or a penalty parameter that is used for the adjustment of the sensitivity of the trend to short-term fluctuations.[7] The first term of the

---

7   By taking derivatives of the above loss function with respect to the trend component τ_t, $t = 1, \dots T$, and
     rearranging them, it can be shown that that the solution to the minimization problem can be written in
     the following matrix form: $\mathbf{y}_T = (\lambda\mathbf{F} + \mathbf{I}_T)\boldsymbol{\tau}_T$, where $\mathbf{y}_T$ is a $(T \times 1)$ vector of original series and $\mathbf{F}$ is a $(T \times T)$
     matrix of coefficients (not specified here).

minimization problem puts a penalty on the variance of the stationary component c_t and as such it is a measure of the fit of the time series. The second term is a measure of smoothness as it penalizes the lack of smoothness in the trend component τ_t. There is a conflict between *goodness of fit* and *smoothness*. To keep track of this problem there is a "trade-off" parameter λ. When λ is zero, we assume that there is no noise and the trend component becomes equivalent to the original series (i.e. $y_t = \tau_t$), while as λ diverges to infinity, the trend component approaches a linear trend. Hodrick and Prescott (1997) show that under some conditions the best choice of parameter λ that minimizes the sum of errors is driven by the relative variances of c_t and the second difference of τ_t. Thus, the *HP* filter removes a trend from the data by solving a least squares problem.[8] Hodrick and Prescott (1997) suggest using a value of $\lambda = 1600$ for quarterly data. Similarly, in the literature the following values are suggested for the different frequencies: $\lambda = 100$ for annual data, $\lambda = 14,400$ for monthly data, $\lambda = 260,100$ for weekly data, and $\lambda = 6,250,000$ for daily data; in general it is 100 times the frequency squared.

The *HP* filter is a widely used tool in empirical macroeconomics where it has been used in the study of business cycles. Its use is not limited only to this area, though. Bulíř (2005) analyzed the link between financial market liberalization and exchange rate stability as deviations of exchange rates from the equilibrium level bring forth stabilizing flows of liquidity. The deviations are defined with the *HP* filter: the log of the exchange rate is assumed to consist of the long-term trend level (affected by fundamental factors) and the effects of transitory demand. Using a univariate error-correction framework (see section 4.3 for details on ECMs), it was found that the depth of the market may have implications on how quickly the exchange rate reacts to temporary shocks as more liberalized markets have more stable exchange rates. Further, by using the *HP* filter, Babetskii and Égert (2005) documented periods of overvaluation and undervaluation of the Czech national currency during 1993–2004.

3.4 UNIT ROOTS

Stationarity is the central issue of time series econometrics. Therefore, knowledge of the formal procedures that test for stationarity is essential for any researcher. Such formal tests will be introduced in this section. We will focus on the way stationarity tests are executed in practice, rather than on their theoretical background.

---

8   The *HP* filter can create spurious serial correlation in detrended data (Cogley and Nason, 1995) and also often fails at the beginning and the end of a time series.

Stationarity tests are typically called *unit root tests*, because either null or alternative hypotheses in these tests are formulated in a way that the time series contains a unit root. Theoretically, unit root tests test only for the presence of unit roots. However, because a unit root process lies on the edge between a stationary and non-stationary process, in practice unit root tests distinguish between stationary and non-stationary time series. In this sense, out of all non-stationary processes a unit root process resembles a stationary process the most. Therefore, the unit root tests cover the area where the decision is the most tricky. That is also why in this section we will focus on stationary time series versus those series containing unit root.

The formal *definition of stationarity* was given in section 1.3. According to this definition, a stationary time series $\{y_t\}_{t=1}^{T}$ has the following properties:

1. *a constant and finite long run mean* $\mu = E[y_t]$, to which it tends to revert after any disturbance (*mean reversion*),
2. *a constant and finite variance* $\sigma^2 = var(y_t) = E[(y_t - \mu)^2]$, and
3. *a constant and finite covariance* $\gamma_s = cov(y_t, y_{t-s}) = E[(y_t - \mu)(y_{t-s} - \mu)]$ that can vary only with s but not t.

Other interesting related properties of a stationary time series are:

4. the expected length of times between crossing the long run mean value μ is finite,

and

5. the theoretical autocorrelations ρ_s decrease steadily with s and their sum is finite.

Unlike the "orderly" behavior of stationary time series, the behavior of time series containing a unit root is strikingly troublesome. A time series $\{y_t\}_{t=1}^{T}$ that contains a unit root does not exhibit mean reversion, even if it has a constant long run mean (as for example a random walk). Its variance goes to infinity as t goes to infinity. The expected time between crossing the value of y_0 is infinity. The theoretical autocorrelations ρ_s are not independent of t and converge to 1 for all s as t goes to infinity. Clearly such properties imply that a non-stationary time series cannot be estimated using the Box-Jenkins methodology. In fact, except cointegration analysis (see section 4.3), not much can be investigated with non-stationary time series.

The list of properties of stationary time series versus those containing a unit root would suggest that the stationarity of a time series could be simply decided with a brief look at its correlogram. With a stationary time series, the autocorrelations ρ_s decay steadily with s; this should enable distinguishing one series from others containing a unit root, whose autocorrelations ρ_s should all be close to one. Unfortunately such a property holds only for theoretical auto-correlations of infinite sample time series. With finite samples, even for time series containing a unit root, the autocorrelations will decay. Therefore, we need the formal statistical tests to distinguish between stationary time series and time series that contain a unit root.

In general, the approach to unit root testing implicitly assumes that the in-vestigated time series $\{y_t\}_{t=1}^{T}$ can be written as

$$y_t = TD_t + z_t + \varepsilon_t ,$$

where TD_t is a deterministic component (time trend, seasonal component, etc.), ε_t is a stationary error process, and z_t is a stochastic component. The task is to determine whether this stochastic component contains a unit root (is non-stationary) or is stationary. Even though this is the general idea, each particular unit root test differs in its implementation.

3.4.1 DICKEY-FULLER TEST

Probably the most popular unit root test was introduced by David A. Dickey and Wayne A. Fuller (see Fuller, 1976 and Dickey and Fuller, 1979 and 1981). Here, we will present the simple version of the so-called *Dickey-Fuller test*. In the next section, we will describe an augmented version of the test. In applied research the augmented version is usually used. However, the simple version demonstrates the idea of the test more clearly.

Assume that you have a time series $\{y_t\}_{t=1}^{T}$ generated by a simple $AR(1)$ process

$$y_t = a_1 y_{t-1} + \varepsilon_t , \qquad (3.22)$$

where $\{\varepsilon\}$ are independent normal disturbances with zero mean and variance σ^2. In this simple case the time series $\{y_t\}_{t=1}^{T}$ will be stationary if $|a_1| < 1$ and will contain a unit root if $|a_1| = 1$. In economic time series a_1 will rarely be nega-tive, so that we can limit ourselves to the cases when $a_1 > 0$. One would think that a simple way to test for the presence of the unit root would be to estimate the a_1 coefficient by the OLS (which is equivalent to the MLE in this case) and use a simple one-sided t-test to test the null hypothesis $a_1 = 1$ against the al-ternative $a_1 < 1$. The task is unfortunately not that simple. The problem arises from the null hypothesis of $a_1 = 1$. Under this hypothesis the time series $\{y_t\}_{t=1}^{T}$ is not stationary and it can be shown that the OLS estimate of a_1 is biased to be below one. Moreover, the limiting distribution of the a_1 estimate is not normal. Clearly, the standard t-test cannot help here.

In their classic work (see Fuller, 1976 and Dickey and Fuller, 1979 and 1981) Dickey and Fuller show the properties of the a_1 estimate under the condition that $a_1 = 1$. Moreover, with *Monte Carlo simulations* (see Appendix A), they compute critical values for the t-statistics of the a_1 estimate. This enables testing the hypothesis H_0: $a_1 = 1$ using the standard t-statistics of the a_1 estimate for which the critical values were simulated. It turns out that the simulated critical values are lower than the critical values of the standard t-distribution. This is quite intuitive, because under the H_0 the a_1 estimate is biased downwards. This means that to reject the hypothesis H_0: $a_1 = 1$ the appropriate t-statistics must be lower than would suffice for the rejection, if the estimate of a_1 was not biased downwards. The test is further extended for the cases when the estimated equation contains intercept or intercept plus trend coefficients. Thus the simple Dickey-Fuller test with its three modifications allows testing for *stationarity*, *level stationarity*, and *trend stationarity*. Not surprisingly, the simulated critical values differ for the three cases: they decrease with the number of parameters used.

Note that if we subtract y_{t-1} from both sides of equation (3.22) we obtain

$$\Delta y_t = \gamma y_{t-1} + \varepsilon_t \text{, where } \gamma = a_1 - 1. \tag{3.23}$$

The original null hypothesis H_0: $a_1 = 1$ is now equivalent to the null hypothesis H_0: $\gamma = 0$. Similarly the alternative hypothesis $H_A : a_1 < 1$ transforms into the alternative hypothesis $H_A : \gamma < 0$.

To perform the simple Dickey-Fuller test on a time series $\{y_t\}_{t=1}^{T}$ we estimate one of the test specifications:

Model A: $\Delta y_t = \gamma y_{t-1} + \varepsilon_t$,

Model B: $\Delta y_t = \mu + \gamma y_{t-1} + \varepsilon_t$, or

Model C: $\Delta y_t = \mu + \beta t + \gamma y_{t-1} + \varepsilon_t$.

Depending on whether we want to test for stationarity, level stationarity, or trend stationarity, we choose model A (neither intercept nor trend included), model B (intercept included), or model C (both intercept and trend included), respectively. We compute the t-statistics of the γ estimate defined as

$$t_{DF} = \frac{\hat{\gamma}}{Se(\hat{\gamma})},$$

where $\hat{\gamma}$ and $Se(\hat{\gamma})$ stand for the estimates of γ and its standard error. In order to test the hypothesis

H_0: $\gamma = 0$ of a unit root time series

against the alternative

H_A: $\gamma < 0$ of a stationary time series,

the t-statistics is compared to the Dickey-Fuller critical values that are tabulated in Table 2 in Appendix B for the three models A, B, and C and for different time spans T. If t_{DF} is lower than the appropriate critical value, then we reject the H_0 of the presence of a unit root in favor of the H_A of a stationary time series. If t_{DF} is greater than the appropriate critical value, then we cannot reject the H_0 of the presence of a unit root.

Dickey and Fuller (1981) also designed F-tests for various joint hypotheses on the coefficients μ, β, and γ. Such tests can help make the correct choice among models A, B, and C. We will not present these tests here. The interested reader can find them in Dickey and Fuller (1981). In practice, we usually choose among models A, B, and C based on a visual inspection of the data or economic intuition. If the time series steadily increases, then we will employ model C and test for trend stationarity. Otherwise we will typically use model B and test for level stationarity. Only if the time series clearly seems to oscillate around 0, then we can try to test with the simplest model, model A.[9]

To choose the right model, we can also employ simple t-tests on the significance of the intercept and trend coefficients μ and β. Imagine that we started with model C and rejected H_0; that is, we found that our time series is trend stationary. If the time series is trend stationary, then the estimate of β is unbiased and therefore should be significantly different from zero. If this is not the case, then we should have probably tested for level rather than trend stationarity. Similarly, if we rejected H_0 with model B, then the estimate of μ should be unbiased and thus significantly different from zero. Otherwise we should have used model A to test for stationarity.

3.4.2 AUGMENTED DICKEY-FULLER TEST

The simple Dickey-Fuller test uses models that estimate the tested time series with a simple $AR(1)$ process only. If the time series was generated with a higher order autoregressive process $AR(p)$ or even with an $ARMA(p,q)$ process, then

---

9   In terms of an economic example with real economic data, if we test for the stationarity of yearly GDP, we will most likely choose model C and test for trend stationarity of the (log of) GDP, because our economic intuition tells us that GDP typically grows over time. On the other hand with a time series of interest rates we would probably prefer model B and test for level stationarity.

the residuals from the estimated equations A, B, or C would not be white noise and autocorrelation would be present among them. The *augmented Dickey-Fuller test* (*ADF test*) enables controlling for such autocorrelation in residuals. In other words, it enables testing for the presence of a unit root even in time series that were generated with a higher order than simple $AR(1)$ processes. It is quite unrealistic to assume *ad hoc* that any data we want to test for stationarity were generated by an $AR(1)$ process. That is why in practical applications we will mostly see the use of the augmented version of the Dickey-Fuller test. Besides, if it appears appropriate, the augmented version of the test naturally reduces to the simple version of the test.

Imagine a time series $\{y_t\}_{t=1}^T$ generated with the $AR(p)$ process

$$y_t = a_1 y_{t-1} + a_2 y_{t-2} + \cdots + a_{p-2} y_{t-p+2} + a_{p-1} y_{t-p+1} + a_p y_{t-p} + \varepsilon_t .$$

If we add and subtract $a_p y_{t-p+1}$, then we obtain

$$y_t = a_1 y_{t-1} + a_2 y_{t-2} + a_3 y_{t-3} + \cdots + a_{p-2} y_{t-p+2} + (a_{p-1} + a_p) y_{t-p+1} - a_p \Delta y_{t-p+1} + \varepsilon_t .$$

Further if we add and subtract $(a_{p-1} + a_p) y_{t-p+2}$, we obtain

$$y_t = a_1 y_{t-1} + a_2 y_{t-2} + \cdots + (a_{p-2} + a_{p-1} + a_p) y_{t-p+2} - (a_{p-1} + a_p) \Delta y_{t-p+2} - a_p \Delta y_{t-p+1} + \varepsilon_t .$$

We can continue in this way, until we obtain

$$y_t = \left(\sum_{i=1}^p a_i \right) y_{t-1} - \left(\sum_{i=2}^p a_i \right) \Delta y_{t-1} - \cdots$$

$$- \left(\sum_{i=p-2}^p a_i \right) \Delta y_{t-p+3} - \left(\sum_{i=p-1}^p a_i \right) \Delta y_{t-p+2} - a_p \Delta y_{t-p+1} + \varepsilon_t .$$

When we finally subtract y_{t-1} from both sides of the equation, we will obtain

$$\Delta y_t = \gamma y_{t-1} + \sum_{i=2}^p \delta_i \Delta y_{t-i+1} + \varepsilon_t , \text{ where } \gamma = \left(\sum_{i=1}^p a_i - 1 \right), \text{ and } \delta_i = -\sum_{j=i}^p a_j . \quad (3.24)$$

Equation (3.24) resembles equation (3.23) applied in the simple Dickey-Fuller test. Indeed, it is equation (3.23) augmented with the sum $\sum_{i=2}^p \delta_i \Delta y_{t-i+1}$, which controls for autocorrelation in residuals.

The coefficient of interest in our test is again γ. Note that if the coefficient $\gamma = 0$, then $\sum_{i=1}^p a_i = 1$. Similarly, if $\gamma < 0$, then $\sum_{i=1}^p a_i < 1$. In sections 2.4 and 2.5

we explained that if $\sum_{i=1}^{p} a_i = 1$, then the generated time series $\{y_t\}_{t=1}^{T}$ contains a unit root. On the other hand, $\sum_{i=1}^{p} a_i < 1$ is a necessary condition for the stationarity of the generated time series $\{y_t\}_{t=1}^{T}$. Therefore, to test for the presence of a unit root (or for stationarity), we can perform the *ADF* test in the same fashion as the simple version of the test. The difference is only in the estimated equation. Similar to the simple version, the augmented version allows the inclusion of the intercept or intercept plus trend coefficients in order to test for *stationarity*, *level stationarity*, and *trend stationarity*. The critical values for the *ADF* test are the same as the critical values for the simple version of the test. In their paper Dickey and Fuller (1981) show why this is the case.

To perform the augmented Dickey-Fuller test on a time series $\{y_t\}_{t=1}^{T}$ we proceed in a way analogous to the simple version of the test. Depending on whether we want to test for stationarity, level stationarity, or trend stationarity, we use OLS to estimate one of these equations:

Model A: $\Delta y_t = \gamma y_{t-1} + \sum_{i=1}^{K} \rho_i \Delta y_{t-i} + \varepsilon_t$,

Model B: $\Delta y_t = \mu + \gamma y_{t-1} + \sum_{i=1}^{K} \rho_i \Delta y_{t-i} + \varepsilon_t$, or

Model C: $\Delta y_t = \mu + \beta t + \gamma y_{t-1} + \sum_{i=1}^{K} \rho_i \Delta y_{t-i} + \varepsilon_t$.

Note that compared to equation (3.24) we have indexed the sums in a more compact way. We compute the t-statistics of the γ estimator

$$t_{DF} = \frac{\hat{\gamma}}{Se(\hat{\gamma})}.$$

The *t*-statistics enable us to test the hypothesis

H_0: $\gamma = 0$ of a unit root time series

against the alternative

H_A: $\gamma < 0$ of a stationary time series.

The *t*-statistics are compared to the Dickey-Fuller critical values in the same way as with the simple Dickey-Fuller test. The critical values are also the same and, as already mentioned, are tabulated in the Appendix B in Table 2 for the three models A, B, and C and for different time spans *T*.

By including lagged differences in the estimated equation, we correct for possible autocorrelation in the residuals. However, in reality, we do not know the true data generating process. That is, we do not know the true order *p* of the estimated $AR(p)$ process. Instead we must estimate the most appropriate number of lags p. The reliable procedure for determining the appropriate number of lags is a non-parametric method developed by Campbell and Perron (1991) and Ng and Perron (1995). We initially set the maximum number of lags K at a value K_{MAX} (e.g. K_{MAX} equals a number that is reasonable with respect to frequency of our data)[10] and check the statistical significance of the coefficient on the highest lag using a simple t-test. If it is insignificant at the 10% level, we reduce the number of lags by one and proceed in this way until achieving statistical significance. Eventually, if our priors suggest it, we can estimate the equation with a given preferred number of lags. A general parsimony principle applies here: the power of the test decreases with the more lags used to correct for the autocorrelation in residuals.[11]

3.4.3 PHILLIPS-PERRON TEST

The ADF test is probably the most common procedure used in applied research to test for the presence of unit roots. Therefore, it shall not surprise us that many extensions and modifications of this test were developed over time. Dickey and Pantula (1987) proposed an extension of the test if more than one unit root is suspected. Dickey, Bell, and Miller (1986) and Hylleberg et al. (1990) adapted the Dickey-Fuller test to allow testing for seasonal unit roots.[12] Phillips and Perron (1988) proposed a modification of the Dickey-Fuller (DF) test that allows for a weak dependence and heterogeneous distribution of the error terms. The *Phillips-Perron test* (*PP* test) has been frequently used and has become a standard item in software packages.

Phillips (1987) and Phillips and Perron (1988) have developed a more comprehensive theory of unit root non-stationarity. The PP tests are similar to ADF tests, but they incorporate a correction factor to the DF procedure to allow for autocorrelated residuals. In essence Phillips and Perron (1988) have introduced a t-ststistic (t_{PP}) on the unit-root coefficient in a Dickey-Fuller (1979) regression (3.23) that is corrected for autocorrelation and heteroskedasticity:

$$t_{PP} = \frac{\hat{\sigma}_\varepsilon}{\hat{\sigma}} t_{DF} - \frac{1}{2}\left(\hat{\sigma}^2 - \hat{\sigma}_\varepsilon^2\right)\left[\hat{\sigma}\left(T^{-2}\sum_{t=2}^{T}\left(y_{t-1} - \bar{y}_{-1}\right)^2\right)^{1/2}\right]^{-1},$$

---

10   K_{MAX} differs with monthly, quarterly or yearly data. The starting number of lags can be set based on a plausible seasonal pattern. As a general rule we can say that the higher the frequency of the data, the higher the number of lags to begin with.

11   There is ample use of the ADF as a basic tool in the empirical literature dealing with transition, post-transition, and integration issues. To name a few references, ADF has been used as an analytical tool by Bekő (2003), Bulíř (2005), Feridun (2006), Festić et al. (2011), Fukač (2005), Holmes and Otero (2010), Horská (2002), Kapounek and Lacina (2011), and Stavárek (2005), among others.

12   For a brief review of these extensions see Enders (2009).

where $\bar{y}_{-1} = (T-1)^{-1} \sum_{t=1}^{T-1} y_t$, $\hat{\sigma}_\varepsilon^2 = T^{-1} \sum_{t=1}^{T} \hat{\varepsilon}_t^2$ is an estimate of

$\sigma_\varepsilon^2 = \lim_{T \to \infty} T^{-1} \sum_{t=1}^{T} E\left[\varepsilon_t^2\right]$ and $\hat{\sigma}^2 = T^{-1} \sum_{t=1}^{T} \hat{\varepsilon}_t^2 + 2T^{-1} \sum_{j=1}^{T} w_{jl} \sum_{t=j+1}^{T} \hat{\varepsilon}_t \hat{\varepsilon}_{t-j}$

is an estimate of $\sigma^2 = \lim_{T \to \infty} E\left[T^{-1} \left(\sum_{t=1}^{T} \varepsilon_t \right)^2 \right]$.

The triangular set of weights $w_{jl} = \{1 - j/(l+1)\}$ guarantees that the variance estimate $\hat{\sigma}^2$ is positive (Newey-West estimator; Newey and West, 1987).[13]

When performing the test the number of covariances of residuals in the variance estimate $\hat{\sigma}^2$ is determined by using the simple rules. This means that the number of lags l is set to $4(T/100)^{0.25}$ as suggested by Schwert (1989) or simply to $T^{0.25}$ as suggested by Diebold and Nerlove (1990) to work well in practice. After obtaining the value of the Newey and West (1987) estimator, the *PP* statistics can be computed; it is modified accordingly depending on whether (3.23) contains also intercept and trend. The *PP* statistics follows the tabulated Dickey-Fuller distribution. If the *PP* statistics is statistically significant we are able to reject the null of a unit root, even in the presence of serial correlation and/or heteroskedasticity. The test usually gives the same conclusions as the *ADF* test, though.[14]

3.4.4 SHORTCOMINGS OF THE STANDARD UNIT ROOT TESTS

A seminal paper that applies the *ADF* test is that of Nelson and Plosser (1982). They test for the trend stationarity (using model C) of fourteen U.S. macroeconomic time series. The data time spans begin between 1860 and 1909, depending on the individual time series, and end in 1970. They reject the H_0 of a unit root only in the case of the unemployment rate. This result is fairly striking, because it implies that random shocks have a permanent effect.

The results of Nelson and Plosser (1982) foreshadow the major shortcoming of the *ADF* test – its *low power*. The test is not able to distinguish between unit root and near-unit root time series. With near unit root time series we are typically not able to reject the H_0 of a unit root. This means that the test has a high chance of an error of the second type, that is, the probability of not rejecting a false H_0. The power of the *ADF* test can somehow be increased if it is implemented on panel data, that is, if we jointly test several time series for the presence of a unit root. Modifications of the *ADF* test that allow testing for unit roots in panel data will be briefly presented in section 5.

---

13 A similar approach is described in section 3.4.5 where a different unit-root test is introduced. The weights are also known as the so-called Bartlett spectral window.

14 Stavárek (2005) combines *ADF* and *PP* tests in an analysis of exchange rates in a mix of old and new EU countries and simultaneously obtains customary results to conclude that nominal exchange rates are nonstationary in levels but stationary in first differences.

Many time series contain clear structural changes. There can be breaks in both the trend and the intercept of a time series. Such structural changes are, aside from the low power of the test, often the reason why the *ADF* or *PP* tests often result in a time series being labeled as non-stationary. The *ADF* test does not control for changes in the intercept or trend of the time series tested. Therefore, a time series with a structural change is typically found to be non-stationary. Unit root (or stationarity) tests that allow controlling for structural changes will be presented in section 3.5. Using such tests, a time series marked by the *ADF* or *PP* tests as non-stationary can be found to be broken trend stationary instead.

3.4.5 *KPSS* TEST

A possible response to the weakness of the *ADF* test is the *KPSS* test that owes its name to the initials of Kwiatowski, Phillips, Schmidt, and Shin (1992). Although the technical approach of this test is completely different from that of the Dickey-Fuller test, the main difference should be seen in the transposition of the null and the alternative hypothesis. With the *KPSS* test the null hypothesis H_0 claims that the time series is stationary against the alternative H_A of the presence of a unit root. The question of stationarity is approached from the opposite way than the *ADF* test does. This approach responds to the problem of the low test power of the *ADF* test. A near unit root time series that was typically found non-stationary with the *ADF* test can be correctly found stationary using the *KPSS* test.

However, we should be aware that any results of statistical testing are just probabilistic and should not be confused with certain statements. There is always a non-zero chance that we are wrong. Therefore, ideal in unit root testing is to combine both the *ADF* and *KPSS* tests. If a time series is found stationary with the *ADF* test, then it will be most likely found stationary also when using the *KPSS* test and we can believe that it should be stationary, indeed. If a time series is found non-stationary using the *KPSS* test, then we can be fairly sure that it will be found non-stationary also with the *ADF* test and we can believe that it should be non-stationary, indeed. However, it can happen quite often that a time series that was found non-stationary using the *ADF* test will be marked as stationary with the *KPSS* test. In such cases we should be very careful with our final conclusion. We can check how strong the evidence is for stationarity in the *KPSS* case and for non-stationarity in the *ADF* case and decide accordingly. Of course, we can also leave the question of stationarity of such time series unresolved.

The *KPSS* test approach assumes that a time series $\{y_t\}_{t=1}^{T}$ tested for trend stationarity can be decomposed in the sum of a deterministic trend βt, a random walk r_t, and a stationary error ε_t:

$$y_t = \beta t + r_t + \varepsilon_t, \ r_t = r_{t-1} + u_t, \tag{3.25}$$

where u_t are normal i.i.d. with a zero mean and variance σ_u^2 ($u_t \sim N(0, \sigma_u^2)$). The initial value r_0 is treated as fixed and serves the role of an intercept. The stationary error ε_t is allowed to be generated with any general *ARMA* process, that is, it can have a rich autocorrelation structure. Similar to the *ADF* test, the possibility to control for an arbitrary autocorrelation structure of ε_t is very important, because most economic time series are highly dependent on time and, hence, have a rich autocorrelation structure. If we want to test for level stationarity, then the term βt is simply left out from equation (3.25).

The specification described by equation (3.25) implies that the H_0 of the stationarity of y_t is equivalent to the hypothesis of $\sigma_u^2 = 0$ that ensures that $r_t = r_0$ for all t (r_0 is a constant intercept). Analogically, the H_A of the presence of a unit root is equivalent to the hypothesis that $\sigma_u^2 \neq 0$. To test the hypothesis

H_0: $\sigma_u^2 = 0$ (stationary time series)

against the alternative

H_A: $\sigma_u^2 \neq 0$ (unit root or non-stationary time series)

the authors derive a one-sided *LM* statistics. They also compute its asymptotic distribution and simulate asymptotic critical values. The theoretical details are beyond the scope of this text. Here, we will only outline an algorithm to perform the test.

To perform the KPSS test on a time series $\{y_t\}_{t=1}^T$ we use OLS to estimate one of the following equations:

A: $y_t = a_0 + e_t$
B: $y_t = a_0 + \beta t + e_t$.

If we want to test for level stationarity, we estimate equation A. If we intend to test for trend stationarity, we choose equation B. Using the residuals e_t from the estimated equation we compute the *LM* statistics. The *LM* statistics, denoted as η_μ in the case of the level stationarity test and as η_τ in the case of the trend stationarity test, is given by the expression

$$\eta_{\mu/\tau} = T^{-2} \frac{1}{s^2(l)} \sum_{t=1}^{T} S_t^2, \text{ where}$$

$$S_t = \sum_{i=1}^{t} e_i \text{ and}$$

$$s^2(l) = T^{-1}\sum_{t=1}^{T} e_t^2 + 2T^{-1}\sum_{s=1}^{l} w(s,l)\sum_{t=s+1}^{T} e_t e_{t-s}, \text{ where}$$

$$w(s,l) = 1 - s/(l+1).$$

In the equations above, S_t is the partial sum process of the residuals e_t from the estimated equation A or B; $s^2(l)$ is the estimator of the long-run variance of the residuals e_t; and $w(s,l)$ is the so-called Bartlett spectral window.[15] The variance estimator $s^2(l)$ depends on the parameter l and as l increases above 0 the estimator $s^2(l)$ begins to control for possible autocorrelation in the residuals e_t. Finally, the *LM* statistics η_μ or η_τ is compared to the critical values given in Table 3 in Appendix B. If the *LM* statistics exceeds the appropriate critical value, then we reject the H_0 of a stationary time series in favor of the H_A of a unit root or non-stationary time series. Otherwise we cannot reject the H_0 of a stationary time series. The critical values are asymptotic and thus most appropriate for large samples. Nevertheless, in practice they are used also for samples of a moderate size. Moreover, the critical values do not depend on the parameter l. However, the *LM* statistics will depend on the parameter l. The authors do not propose any general algorithm for the choice of the appropriate parameter l. Typically the test is run for l ranging from 0 to 8. As l increases we are less likely to reject the H_0 of stationarity, which is partly the result of the decreasing power of the test. This can give rather ambiguous results. However, in general it can be said that if the H_0 of a stationary time series is not rejected even for low values of l (0, 1, or 2), we conclude that the tested time series is stationary.

Kwiatowski et al. (1992) applied their test to the Nelson and Plosser (1982) data. In agreement with Nelson and Plosser (1982) they find the unemployment rate to be stationary; however, in their case they detected level instead of trend stationarity. Also in agreement, four of the total fourteen time series were found to contain unit roots. With other time series they obtained either mixed results or results that contradict those of Nelson and Plosser (1982). In such cases they conclude that the time series are not sufficiently informative to decide about the unit root presence.

A combination of the *ADF* and *KPSS* tests suggested as a way to eliminate some shortcomings in unit root testing can be found in Fukač (2005), who surveys the question whether inflation expectations surveys yield macroeconomically relevant information. By combining both the *ADF* and *KPSS* tests he is able

---

15   In this application a spectral window is used to estimate a spectral density of errors for a specific interval (window) that moves over the entire range of a series. Data outside the interval are ignored as a window function is a function that is zero-valued outside of some chosen interval (window).

to claim that residuals from the regression of the interest rate on inflation and its surveyed expectations are stationary. The stationarity of residuals is a crucial condition here as they contain the unobservable real interest rate and the risk premium. If the former variable alone contained a unit root, its effect might result in a spurious regression. Since this is not the case, estimates from the regression are unbiased and consistent, although inefficient. It is found that surveyed inflation expectations are not statistically different from market expectations, and even though they do not have predictive power for actual inflation they do have it for the interest rate. Thus, measurements of financial market inflation expectations conducted by the Czech National Bank yield macroeconomically relevant data.[16]

3.5 UNIT ROOTS AND STRUCTURAL CHANGE

We already mentioned that time series containing structural changes can appear non-stationary if tested with the *ADF* test. The *ADF* test does not allow for exogenous changes in the intercept or trend of the time series. Therefore, if such changes are present, the *ADF* test will most likely suggest the presence of a unit root. In general, this would be the case with all unit root tests that do not explicitly model exogenous structural changes. The reason for this lies in the permanent nature of such structural changes. If a permanent change in intercept or trend is not removed from the noise function, that is, if it is not explicitly modeled, then the unit root test will regard it as a current shock realization with a permanent effect. Shocks have permanent effects only in time series that contain unit roots. Therefore, the results of the test will be biased towards finding unit roots, even though the tested time series might be stationary with an exogenous structural change (that is, *broken trend stationary*).

In this section we present two unit root tests that allow for an exogenous structural change in the tested time series. The first test was developed by Perron (1989). The second test was proposed by Zivot and Andrews (1992). The major difference between these two tests lies in the way they regard the date of the exogenous structural change. While Perron's test takes this date as given, Zivot and Andrews propose a modification of Perron's test in which the date of the structural change is estimated.

---

16   Recent applications of the *KPSS* test in the context of Central and Eastern European-targeted research can be found in Hurník and Navrátil (2005) and Vošvrda and Žikeš (2004).

3.5.1 PERRON'S TEST

Perron (1989) proposed his unit root test in response to the results of Nelson and Plosser (1982). Using the *ADF* test, Nelson and Plosser (1982) found a unit root in most U.S. macroeconomic time series. Perron (1989) questioned this result. Using his unit root test he found that most macroeconomic time series do not contain a unit root. Instead, they are stationary with only two shocks that had a permanent effect: the Great Crash of 1929 and the first oil price shock of 1973.

   Perron's test allows testing for the broken trend stationarity of a time series $\{y_t\}_{t=1}^{T}$. It tests the null hypothesis that the series has a unit root with drift and that an exogenous structural break occurs at the break time $T_B \in (1,T)$ against the alternative hypothesis that the time series is stationary around a deterministic time trend with an exogenous change in the trend function at time T_B. Perron's test considers three alternative modifications, which we will denote as *models A, B,* and *C*. Model A permits one exogenous change in the intercept at time T_B. Model B allows for one exogenous change in the linear trend coefficient at time T_B. Finally, model C allows for a combination of an exogenous change in the intercept and the linear trend coefficient at time T_B. Such changes in the trend function of a time series are illustrated in Figure 3.2.

   We define dummy variables indicating the above changes as $D(T_B)_t = 1$ if $t = T_B + 1$ and 0 otherwise; $DU_t = 1$ if $t > T_B$ and 0 otherwise; and $DT_t = t - T_B$ if $t > T_B$ and 0 otherwise. Then models A, B, and C have the following specifications of the null and alternative hypothesis:

1. *Model A:*

$$H_0 : y_t = \mu + dD(T_B)_t + y_{t-1} + \varepsilon_t,$$

$$H_A : y_t = \mu_1 + \beta t + (\mu_2 - \mu_1)DU_t + \varepsilon_t.$$

2. *Model B:*

$$H_0 : y_t = \mu_1 + (\mu_2 - \mu_1)DU_t + y_{t-1} + \varepsilon_t,$$

$$H_A : y_t = \mu + \beta_1 t + (\beta_2 - \beta_1)DT_t + \varepsilon_t.$$

3. *Model C:*

$$H_0 : y_t = \mu_1 + dD(T_B)_t + (\mu_2 - \mu_1)DU_t + y_{t-1} + \varepsilon_t,$$

$$H_A : y_t = \mu_1 + \beta_1 t + (\mu_2 - \mu_1)DU_t + (\beta_2 - \beta_1)DT_t + \varepsilon_t.$$

In all the equations above ε_t denotes stationary errors generated with a general *ARMA* process. This means that similarly to the *ADF* and *KPSS* tests the models allow for the autocorrelation structure of the $\{y_t\}_{t=1}^{T}$ series.

Figure 3.2: Exogenous changes in trend.

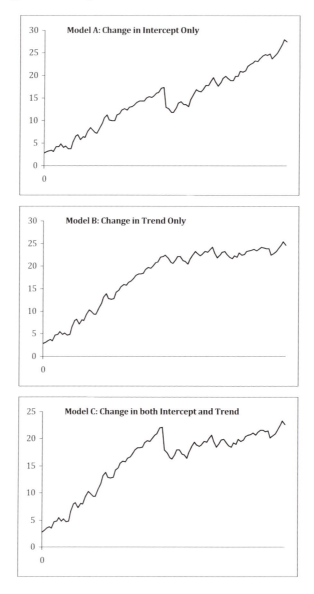

Perron (1989) proposed several alternative ways to perform the test of the above specified H_0 against H_A. He showed that they are asymptotically equivalent and derived asymptotic distribution and critical values for the appropriate test statistics. Here, we will focus only on one of the testing strategies. We will choose the approach that follows the *ADF* test framework and that was finally applied by Perron (1989) on the Nelson and Plosser (1982) data. Moreover, this approach was further extended by Zivot and Andrews (1992) in their unit root test.

To perform Perron's test on a time series $\{y_t\}_{t=1}^{T}$ we estimate one of the following equations:

Model A: $y_t = \mu + \beta t + dD(T_B)_t + \theta DU_t + \alpha y_{t-1} + \sum_{i=1}^{K} \rho_i \Delta y_{t-i} + \varepsilon_t$,

Model B: $y_t = \mu + \beta t + \gamma DT_t + \alpha y_{t-1} + \sum_{i=1}^{K} \rho_i \Delta y_{t-i} + \varepsilon_t$,

Model C: $y_t = \mu + \beta t + dD(T_B)_t + \theta DU_t + \gamma DT_t + \alpha y_{t-1} + \sum_{i=1}^{K} \rho_i \Delta y_{t-i} + \varepsilon_t$.

If we assume an exogenous change in the intercept only, then we use model A; if we expect an exogenous change in the linear trend only, then we use model B; and if we expect both an exogenous change in the intercept and linear trend, then we choose model C. Note that the estimated regressions for models A and C directly nest both the null and alternative hypothesis. This is not the case for model B, where the regressor DU_t is missing. The reason for this is related to the asymptotic distribution of the t-statistics of the coefficient α.[17] For each of the three models A, B, and C the null and the alternative hypotheses can be expressed in terms of the estimated coefficients in the following way:

Model A: $H_0 : \alpha = 1, \beta = 0, \theta = 0, d \neq 0; H_A : \alpha < 1, \beta \neq 0, \theta \neq 0, d = 0$,

Model B: $H_0 : \alpha = 1, \beta = 0, \gamma = 0; H_A : \alpha < 1, \beta \neq 0, \gamma \neq 0$,

Model C: $H_0 : \alpha = 1, \beta = 0, \gamma = 0, d \neq 0, \theta \neq 0; H_A : \alpha < 1, \beta \neq 0, \gamma \neq 0, \theta \neq 0, d = 0$.

In the unit root test with all three models we focus only on the part of the hypothesis concerning the coefficient α:

H_0: $\alpha = 1$,

H_A: $\alpha < 1$.

To test this hypothesis we compute the t-statistics for testing $\alpha = 1$ as

$$t_{\hat{\alpha}} = \frac{\hat{\alpha} - 1}{Se(\hat{\alpha})}$$

and compare it to the asymptotic critical values that were tabulated by Perron (1989). These are given in Table 4 in Appendix B. The critical values differ for

---

17   For details see Perron (1989).

each of the three models and depend also on the so-called sample pre-break fraction that is denoted as $\lambda = T_B/T$. The pre-break fraction takes into account when a possible break occurs with respect to the data time span. If $t_{\hat{\alpha}}$ is lower than the appropriate critical value, then we reject the H_0 in favor of the H_A; otherwise we cannot reject the H_0. Rejecting the null hypothesis of $\alpha = 1$ means that the time series is broken trend stationary. Therefore, once we reject H_0, then the remaining coefficients' t-statistics have simple t-distributions and we can check their significance using the standard t-test. The remaining coefficients should satisfy the requirements given above for the general specification of the alternative hypothesis. For example, if we use model C and, based on critical values, we reject H_0: $\alpha = 1$, then the coefficients β, γ, and θ should be significant and the coefficient d should be insignificant. If this is not at least roughly the case, then we should reconsider our choice of model. Note that the critical values tabulated by Perron (1989) are asymptotic, similarly as the critical values for the *KPSS* test are. This means that they hold for large samples only. However, with some caution we can use them also for moderate samples. We should just bear in mind that the use of the asymptotic critical values with small data samples could lead to an overrejection of the H_0. In other words the asymptotic critical values are not strict enough for small data samples.

Analogically to the *ADF* test, the sums $\sum_{i=1}^{K} \rho_i \Delta y_{t-i}$ control for possible autocorrelation in the residuals. The parameter K is chosen in the same way as already described for the *ADF* test. We start with a value of K equal to K_{MAX} and check the significance of the coefficient ρ_K at the 10% significance level.[18] If significant, then we choose $K = K_{MAX}$; if not, then we decrease K by one and continue in the same fashion, until ρ_K is found to be significant.

We have already mentioned that Perron (1989) revisited the results of Nelson and Plosser (1982). Using his broken trend stationarity test he came to a thoroughly different conclusion. Taking the Great Crash of 1929 as an exogenous structural change, Perron (1989) found broken trend stationarity in ten out of the thirteen time series that were found non-stationary by Nelson and Plosser (1982) using the *ADF* test. Moreover, he found the post-war quarterly U.S. real GNP series also broken trend stationary with the first oil price shock of 1973 taken as an exogenous structural change.

An instructive application of Perron's test is performed by León-Ledesma and McAdam (2004), who quantify the degree of persistence in the unemployment rates of transition countries against the EU over the period 1992–2001. They take into account the existence of structural breaks in unemployment. In

---

18 Perron (1989) chose the value $K_{MAX} = 8$ for all Nelson and Plosser (1982) time series and the value $K_{MAX} = 12$ for the post-war quarterly U.S. real GNP series.

general, they can reject the unit-root hypothesis after controlling for structural changes and business-cycle effects, but they observe the presence of a high and low unemployment equilibria. The speed of adjustment is faster for transition countries than for the EU, although the former tend to move more frequently between equilibria.

A different use of Perron's test from a truly long-term perspective is presented in Cuñado and McAdam (2006), who examine the real convergence hypothesis in some Central and Eastern European countries towards Germany and the U.S. over the period 1950–2003. They find no evidence of real convergence for the whole period. However, when they allow for structural breaks, evidence is found of a catch-up process during the 1990s to 2003 period for Poland, the Czech Republic and Hungary towards Germany and only for Poland towards the US economy.

3.5.2 ZIVOT AND ANDREWS' TEST

Zivot and Andrews (1992) questioned the arbitrary choice of the trend break dates made by Perron (1989). They proposed a modification of Perron's test, where the year of the break is estimated rather than postulated. In this way they transformed Perron's unit root test, which is conditional on a known break point, into an *unconditional broken trend stationarity test*.

Zivot and Andrews (1992) designed their test, similar to Perron (1989), for the three models A, B, C. However, with a time series $\{y_t\}_{t=1}^{T}$ they postulated the *identical* unit root null hypothesis for all three models as:

$$H_0 : y_t = \mu + y_{t-1} + \varepsilon_t .$$

The alternative hypothesis is that the time series $\{y_t\}_{t=1}^{T}$ can be represented by a trend stationary process with a one time break in the intercept (model A), trend (model B), or both trend and intercept (model C). The break occurring at an unknown time is estimated to yield the date that gives the largest weight to the alternative hypothesis. If we denote the estimated pre-break fraction corresponding to this estimated break date T_B as $\hat{\lambda} = T_B / T$, then the alternative hypothesis for the three models A, B, and C can be specified as:

Model A: $H_A : y_t = \mu_1 + \beta t + (\mu_2 - \mu_1)DU_t(\hat{\lambda}) + \varepsilon_t$,

Model B: $H_A : y_t = \mu + \beta_1 t + (\beta_2 - \beta_1)DT_t(\hat{\lambda}) + \varepsilon_t$,

Model C: $H_A : y_t = \mu_1 + \beta_1 t + (\mu_2 - \mu_1)DU_t(\hat{\lambda}) + (\beta_2 - \beta_1)DT_t(\hat{\lambda}) + \varepsilon_t$, where $DU_t(\hat{\lambda})$ and $DT_t(\hat{\lambda})$ are defined as $DU_t(\hat{\lambda}) = 1$ if $t > \hat{\lambda}T$ and 0 otherwise; and $DT_t(\hat{\lambda}) = t - T_B$ if $t > \hat{\lambda}T$ and 0 otherwise. Similarly as in the case of the preceding tests, ε_t denotes stationary errors generated with a general ARMA process.

To perform Zivot and Andrews' test on a time series $\{y_t\}_{t=1}^T$ we use OLS to estimate one of these equations:

Model A: $y_t = \mu + \beta t + \theta DU_t(\lambda) + \alpha y_{t-1} + \sum_{i=1}^{K} \rho_i \Delta y_{t-i} + \varepsilon_t$,

Model B: $y_t = \mu + \beta t + \gamma DT_t(\lambda) + \alpha y_{t-1} + \sum_{i=1}^{K} \rho_i \Delta y_{t-i} + \varepsilon_t$,

Model C: $y_t = \mu + \beta t + \theta DU_t(\lambda) + \gamma DT_t(\lambda) + \alpha y_{t-1} + \sum_{i=1}^{K} \rho_i \Delta y_{t-i} + \varepsilon_t$.

As in Perron's case depending on our priors about the structural change we use model A, B, or C. Note that none of the estimated regressions contains the regressor $D(T_B)_t$ any more. We no longer need this dummy, because it is not contained in $H_0: y_t = \mu + y_{t-1} + \varepsilon_t$, which is common for all three models. Even without the dummy $D(T_B)_t$, the estimated equations for all three models nest both the null and the alternative hypothesis. We estimate the equation of the chosen model for all possible parameters $\lambda = T_B/T$ from a range Λ that is a specified closed subset of the interval $(0,1)$. Zivot and Andrews use $\Lambda = [2/T,(T-1)/T]$. The trimming of the sample prevents searching for a break at the very beginning or end of the data sample. For each λ we compute $t_{\hat{\alpha}}(\lambda)$ – the one sided t-statistics for testing the null unit root hypothesis

$H_0: \alpha = 1$, against the broken trend stationarity alternative

$H_A: \alpha < 1$.

The t-statistics $t_{\hat{\alpha}}(\lambda)$ is defined as in Perron's test with the equation

$$t_{\hat{\alpha}}[\lambda] = \frac{\hat{\alpha}[\lambda] - 1}{Se(\hat{\alpha}[\lambda])}.$$

Again, the sums $\sum_{i=1}^{K} \rho_i \Delta y_{t-i}$ control for possible autocorrelation in the residuals. The parameter K is chosen in the same way as already described for the ADF and Perron tests. We start at the value of K equal to K_{MAX} and check the significance of the coefficient ρ_K at the 10% significance level.[19] If significant, then

---

19   Zivot and Andrews (1992) chose as Perron (1989) the value $K_{MAX} = 8$ for all Nelson and Plosser (1982) time series and the value $K_{MAX} = 12$ for the post-war quarterly U.S. real GNP series.

we choose $K = K_{MAX}$; if not, then we decrease K by one and continue in the same fashion until ρ_K is significant. Using this algorithm we choose an individual K for each of the estimated equations. This means that K can vary as λ varies.

Finally, we choose our estimated $\hat{\lambda}$ so that it minimizes the value of $t_{\hat{\alpha}}(\lambda)$. That is, we choose $\hat{\lambda}$ that gives the greatest value to the alternative hypothesis of a broken trend stationary time series. If we denote the minimized t-statistics as $t_{\hat{\alpha}}[\hat{\lambda}_{inf}]$, then we can write

$$t_{\hat{\alpha}}[\hat{\lambda}_{inf}] = \inf_{\lambda \in \Lambda} t_{\hat{\alpha}}(\lambda),$$

where Λ is a pre-defined closed subset of $(0, 1)$ and true λ is assumed to be unknown.

To complete the test we compare $t_{\hat{\alpha}}[\hat{\lambda}_{inf}]$ with the asymptotic critical values computed by Zivot and Andrews (1992). If $t_{\hat{\alpha}}[\hat{\lambda}_{inf}]$ is lower than the appropriate critical value, then we reject the H_0 of a unit root in favor of the H_A of a broken trend stationary time series. The critical values are given in Table 5 in Appendix B. They differ with models A, B, and C. Note that this time $\hat{\lambda}$ was estimated and not postulated as in Perron (1989). As a result, Zivot and Andrews' (1992) critical values are more stringent in rejecting the H_0 (greater in absolute value) than Perron's critical values are. Generally, this should be the case with any unconditional versus conditional tests.

That is also why, unlike Perron (1989), Zivot and Andrews (1992) are not all that optimistic about the broken trend stationarity of the tested time series. They cannot reject the unit root hypothesis for four of the ten Nelson and Plosser (1982) time series that were found stationary by Perron (1989). Moreover, also the postwar quarterly U.S. real GNP series was found non-stationary with their test. Interesting is that the estimated break dates did not coincide in all cases with the break dates chosen by Perron (1989). The year of the Great Crash of 1929 was estimated as the break year only in eight out of the thirteen cases and the year 1973 of the first price shock was not estimated as a break year at all.

Zivot and Andrews (1992) also investigated the behavior of their test under finite samples. The simple specification of their null hypothesis enabled them to use Monte Carlo simulations to compute finite sample critical values for their test statistics $t_{\hat{\alpha}}[\hat{\lambda}_{inf}]$. Not surprisingly, these finite sample critical values were found to be larger in absolute value, that is, less likely to allow the rejection of the H_0 than the asymptotic critical values. Using these finite sample critical values they were not able to reject the H_0 for three additional time series. We do not include the finite sample critical values here, because Zivot and Andrews (1992) computed them only for the sample sizes of the actually tested time series. Therefore, in a general case they would be of limited use.

The pressing notion that a failure to account for the breaks can produce misleading tests and result in an incorrect inference is part of the background motivation of Chaudhuri and Wu (2003), who examine whether the stock-price indices of seventeen emerging markets can be characterized as random walk (unit root) or mean reversion processes. They implement the Zivot and Andrews (1992) sequential test for a random walk that explicitly takes into account the effects of structural changes in the stock prices of seventeen emerging markets. For ten countries, the null hypothesis of a random walk can be rejected at the 1% or 5% significance level. Further, for fourteen countries, the stock markets exhibit significant structural breaks, which appear either in the intercept, in the time trend, or in both. These structural changes, as identified by the test, are in general consistent with their corresponding market liberalization dates and/or can be explained by other major economic events in the underlying economies.

3.6 DETECTING A STRUCTURAL CHANGE

Testing the homogeneity of a dynamic process or the stability of a model's coefficients is standard econometric procedure. This issue, identified as a change-point problem, is covered by a sizable body of research (Banerjee, Lumsdaine, and Stock, 1992; Chu and White, 1992; Perron and Vogelsang, 1992; Andrews, 1993; Andrews and Ploberger, 1994; and Vogelsang and Perron, 1998; to name just a few of the earlier works). The goal of the testing is to ascertain whether a structural change or break has occurred somewhere in the sample and, if so, to estimate the time of its occurrence. The reason for finding a true structural break is that estimates obtained from a model, which does not account for a break if one truly occurs, would be meaningless and implications based on the estimates would be incorrect.

Structural change is covered in a considerable amount of literature, which predominantly focuses on various macroeconomic fundamentals including aggregate output, international trade, employment, money, and interest rates.[20] The research on structural breaks in exchange rates is less frequent.[21] In any event, a rich literature on the econometrics of structural change has developed over the years. Summaries of recent advances can be found in special issues of the *Journal of Econometrics* edited by Dufour and Ghysels (1996) and Banerjee and Urga (2005).

---

20 Perron (1989) and Zivot and Andrews (1992) present exogenous and endogenous approaches, respectively, to account for a structural break. Stock and Watson (1996), Ben-David and Papell (1997, 1998), Kim and Nelson (1999), Papell, Murray, and Ghiblawi (2000), Ewing and Wunnava (2001), Henry and McAdam (2001), Krolzig (2001), Ozmen and Parmaksiz (2003a,b), and Mills and Wang (2003) apply various techniques to explore the issue of structural breaks on particular macroeconomic fundamentals.

21 Edison and Fisher (1991), Antzoulatos and Yang (1996), Wu (1997), Kim and Tsurumi (2000), Wu, Tsai, and Chen (2004), Zettelmeyer (2004), Dibooglu and Kutan (2001), Kočenda (2005).

In the previous section we have presented unit root tests that enable controlling for one structural change, model a change explicitly and exclude it from the noise function. In this section we will focus on the search for the break points endogenously. The tests presented in this section will be in a certain sense similar to the test of Zivot and Andrews (1992), who also estimated the break year instead of taking it as given. However, this time we will ignore the issue of testing for unit roots.

3.6.1 SINGLE STRUCTURAL CHANGE

The test proposed by Vogelsang (1997) enables a decision whether there is a single break in the trend function of a given time series and if so, it also enables an estimation of the break date. It focuses only on structural change and ignores the unit root issue (even though, as we will see later, the critical values will differ for stationary and non-stationary time series). The procedure's advantage lies in its not imposing restrictions on the nature of data since it allows for both stationary and unit root errors. Also, it can be applied to regressors that are a general polynomial function of time. Moreover, it does not impose any parametric specifications on the distribution of errors, except the existence of the fourth moment, which is a standard assumption. In this respect the procedure is superior to those developed earlier. A potential weakness is that it allows only for a single break in the trend function. Tests that allow for multiple structural changes are the topic of the next section.

Vogelsang (1997) assumes the following data generating process for a time series $\{y_t\}_{t=1}^{T}$ with a break in the trend function at an unknown time T_B^C:

$$y_t = \theta_0 + \sum_{i=1}^{p} \theta_i t^i + \gamma_0 DU_t + \sum_{i=1}^{p} \gamma_i DT_t^i + v_t \text{ and } A(L)v_t = \varepsilon_t, \qquad (3.26)$$

where $DU_t = 1$ if $t > T_B^C$ and 0 otherwise, $DT_t = t - T_B^C$ if $t > T_B^C$ and 0 otherwise, and $A(L) = 1 - a_1 L - \cdots - a_{K+1} L^{K+1}$. The autoregressive polynomial $A(L)$ is assumed to have at most one real valued root on the unit circle and all others strictly outside the unit circle. The error process ε_t is assumed to be i.i.d. $(0, \sigma_\varepsilon^2)$ with a finite fourth moment. We see that similar to the Perron (1989) and Zivot and Andrews (1992) tests the errors are allowed to be generated by a general (invertible) ARMA process. Moreover $\{y_t\}_{t=1}^{T}$ can be both broken trend stationary or a unit root process, depending on whether $A(L)$ has or does not have one real valued root on the unit circle. The trend function can be a general polynomial of the order p. Given the parameterization of equation (3.26) the null hypothesis of no trend break is given by

$H_0 : \gamma_i = 0$ for all $i = 0,1,2,...,p$.

The alternative is specified as

H_A: $\gamma_i \neq 0$ for at least one i,

which means that at least one of the trend polynomials or the intercept contains a break.

In order to perform the test it is appropriate to adjust equation (3.26) using *ADF* factorization. Remember that in the case of the *ADF* test we have rewritten the autoregressive equation $A(L)y_t = \varepsilon_t$ as $\Delta y_t = \pi y_{t-1} + \sum_{i=1}^{K} \rho_i \Delta y_{t-i} + \varepsilon_t$. Similarly, we can apply *ADF* factorization on the equation $A(L)v_t = \varepsilon_t$ and obtain

$$\Delta v_t = \pi v_{t-1} + \sum_{i=1}^{K} \rho_i \Delta v_{t-i} + \varepsilon_t,$$

with $\pi = \sum_{j=1}^{K+1} a_j - 1$ and $\rho_i = -\sum_{j=i+1}^{K+1} a_j$. Using this, equation (3.26) can be rewritten as

$$\Delta y_t = \beta_0 + \sum_{i=1}^{p} \beta_i t^i + \delta_0 DU_t + \sum_{i=1}^{p} \delta_i (DT_t)^i + \sum_{i=1}^{K} \eta_i D(T_B^C + i)_t + \pi y_{t-1} + \sum_{i=1}^{K} \rho_i \Delta y_{t-i} + \varepsilon_t,$$

where $D(T_B^C + i)_t$ are the so-called one-time crash dummies that equal 1 if $t = T_B^C + i$ and 0 otherwise. The newly defined coefficients β_i, δ_i, and η_i must satisfy

$$\beta_0 + \sum_{i=1}^{p} \beta_i t^i = \theta_0 + A(L) \sum_{i=1}^{p} \theta_i t^i$$

and

$$\sum_{i=1}^{p} \delta_i (DT_t)^i + \sum_{i=1}^{K} \eta_i D(T_B^C + i)_t = A(L)\gamma_0 DU_t + A(L) \sum_{i=1}^{p} \gamma_i DT_t^i.$$

The one-time crash dummies $D(T_B^C + i)_t$ are asymptotically negligible and can be dropped from the final model.

To perform Vogelsang's test on a time series $\{y_t\}_{t=1}^{T}$ we apply the *OLS* method to estimate the equation

$$\Delta y_t = \beta_0 + \sum_{i=1}^{p} \beta_i t^i + \delta_0 DU_t + \sum_{i=1}^{p} \delta_i (DT_t)^i + \pi y_{t-1} + \sum_{i=1}^{K} \rho_i \Delta y_{t-i} + \varepsilon_t \qquad (3.27)$$

for all possible break dates $T_B = \lambda T$ with $\lambda \in [\lambda^*, 1 - \lambda^*]$, where $\lambda^* > 0$. Note that $[\lambda^*, 1 - \lambda^*]$ is, similarly as in the test of Zivot and Andrews (1992), a closed subset of the interval (0,1). The trimming parameter λ^* specifies a portion of the whole time span T at the beginning and at the end that is not allowed to contain the true break date T_B^C.

With $\lambda \in [\lambda^*, 1 - \lambda^*]$ the possible break dates T_B are chosen from a discrete set $\Lambda = [T_B^*, T_B^* + 1, ..., T - T_B^*]$, where $T_B^* = \lambda^* T$. With each of the estimated equations, which differ in the assumed break date T_B, we compute the appropriate F-statistics $F(T_B/T)$ for testing the joint hypothesis that $\delta_i = 0$ for $i = 0,1,...,p$. Recall that the F-statistics is computed as

$$F(T/T) = \frac{(SSR_R - SSR_U)/j}{SSR/(T-s)},$$

where SSR_R and SSR_U denote the sum of squared residuals from the restricted and unrestricted regression, j stands for the number of restrictions, and s denotes the number of regression parameters in the unrestricted equation; in our case $j = p + 1$ and $s = 2(p + 1) + K + 1$. Using the F-statistics $F(T_B/T)$ we can compute the three different test statistics proposed by Vogelsang. These are the *MeanF*, *ExpF*, and *SupF* statistics defined as

$$MeanF = T^{-1} \sum_{T_B \in \Lambda} (p+1) F(T_B/T),$$

$$ExpF = \log \left[T^{-1} \sum_{T_B \in \Lambda} \exp \left(\frac{1}{2}(p+1) F(T_B/T) \right) \right], \text{ and}$$

$$SupF = \sup_{T_B \in \Lambda} (p+1) F(T_B/T).$$

Note that in the expressions above each $F(T_B/T)$ statistics is multiplied by the number of restrictions $(p + 1)$. It is done in order to make the F-statistics converge asymptotically to the *Wald* statistics, which were originally used by Vogelsang (1997). Finally, to test the hypothesis

H_0: of a stable trend function (or of no break in a trend function)

against the alternative

H_A: of a break in at least one of the trend polynomials or in the intercept

we compare the test statistics *MeanF*, *ExpF*, and *SupF* to the asymptotic critical values tabulated by Vogelsang (1997) and given in Table 6 in Appendix B. If the test statistics exceeds the appropriate critical value, we reject the H_0 of the stable trend function in favor of the H_A of a break in at least one of the trend polynomials or the intercept; otherwise, we cannot reject the H_0. We can use any of the three statistics proposed by Vogelsang. The statistics *MeanF* and *ExpF* belong to a class of optimal statistics proposed by Andrews and Ploberger (1994) provided $p = 0$ (no trend) and v_t is stationary. The statistics *ExpF* is designed to have power in detecting large breaks, whereas the *MeanF* statistics is designed to have power in detecting small breaks. The statistics *SupF* is not a member of the class of optimal statistics but has the advantage of providing the most accurate estimate of the true break date.

Obviously, the critical values differ for each of the alternative test statistics. They also differ with the trimming parameter λ^* and with the order of the estimated trend polynomial p. Vogelsang (1997) tabulated the critical values for two choices of the trimming parameter $\lambda^* = 0.01$ (1% trimming) and $\lambda^* = 0.15$ (15% trimming), and for three choices of the trend polynomial $p = 0$ (intercept only), $p = 1$ (intercept and a linear trend coefficient), and $p = 2$ (intercept plus a linear and quadratic trend coefficients). In practical application this is fully sufficient, because a cubic trend ($p = 3$) is barely justifiable in any economic time series model.

Moreover, different critical values should be applied to stationary and unit root time series. Note that the terms stationary and unit root time series refer to the error process v_t from equation (3.26). Thus, we have to distinguish if the tested time series $\{y_t\}_{t=1}^T$ is broken trend stationary or not. With broken trend stationarity we mean stationarity around the chosen type of trend ($p = 0$, 1, or 2) with a break at the true break date. Because we do not know the true break date before running Vogelsang's test, we also do no not know if the time series is broken trend stationary or contains a unit root. Therefore, the choice between stationary and unit root critical values is somewhat problematic. A conservative approach would suggest the use of unit root critical values that are greater, and thus less likely to allow the rejection of the H_0.

Note also that the critical values are asymptotic. This means that they should be used only with large data samples. However, with some caution we can use them also with samples of moderate length. The choice of trimming is fairly deliberate and depends on our expectations about the true break date T_B. If we expect the break to occur in the beginning or end of the sample, then we will prefer 1% trimming. However, with moderate samples and 1% trimming it could happen that $T_B^* = \lambda^* T$ is, after rounding, equal to 0. In such a case we must choose the larger 15% trimming.

Aside from the choice of stationarity, trimming, and statistics, we have to choose two other parameters of the estimated equations (3.27): the order of the trend polynomial p and the number of lagged differences K. The structural change literature provides little guidance regarding the choice of p. Usually, the order of the trend polynomial p is chosen based on our priors and on a visual inspection of the time series tested. The value of $p = 0$ is appropriate if the time series oscillates around a level that can be possibly broken. The value of $p = 1$

or 2 should be chosen if the time series contains a linear or quadratic trend, respectively. Of course, these trends can also be broken.

A more formal algorithm for the choice of p was proposed by Ben-David and Papell (1997).[22] They start with $p = 2$ (quadratic trend). If the no-trend-break H_0 can be rejected, then they report the result. If the H_0 cannot be rejected with $p = 2$, then they perform the test on the model with $p = 1$ (linear trend). If the H_0 can be rejected then they report the results. Otherwise they estimate the model with $p = 0$ (no trend), perform the test and report the results.

Similarly as with the ADF, Perron, and Zivot and Andrews tests, the sum $\sum_{i=1}^{K} p_i \Delta y_{t-i}$ in the estimated equations (3.27) controls for the possible autocorrelation in residuals. Therefore, the parameter K can be again determined using the non-parametric method proposed by Campbell and Perron (1991) and Ng and Perron (1995). We initially set the maximum number of lags K at an appropriate level K_{MAX} and check the statistical significance of the coefficient on the highest lag using a simple two sided t-test. If insignificant at the 10% significance level, we reduce the number of lags by one and proceed in this way until achieving statistical significance. Using this procedure we should determine an individual K for each of the estimated equations (3.27), that is for each break date T_B from the discrete set Λ.[23]

Besides applying the test on the levels of the time series $\{y_t\}_{t=1}^{T}$, Vogelsang (1997) also proposes a version of the test applicable to first differences. Conducting the test on the first differences of $\{y_t\}_{t=1}^{T}$ leads to efficiency gains in the case when the error process v_t from equation (3.26) does contain a unit root. The test is proposed only for the case of $p = 1$. First differencing transforms the estimated equations (3.27) into

$$\Delta y_t = \beta_1 + \delta_1 DU_t + \sum_{i=1}^{K} p_i \Delta y_{t-i} + \varepsilon_t. \tag{3.28}$$

---

22 In light of the substantial movement towards trade liberalization during the post-war period, Ben-David and Papell (1997) attempt to determine if and when countries experienced statistically significant changes in the paths of their export-GDP and import-GDP ratios using the test of Vogelsang (1997). They find that most trade ratios exhibited a structural break in their time paths, post-break trade exceeded pre-break trade for the majority of countries, the coincidence in timing between the import and export breaks does not appear to be particularly strong, and there is little relation between the extent of changes in imports and the extent of changes in exports for most countries.

23 To determine appropriate number of lags K, Vogelsang (1997) used a similar procedure proposed by Perron and Vogelsang (1992). He started with a value of K equal to 10 and using a simple two sided t-test checked the significance of the coefficient on the highest lag at the 5% level, but not the 10% level. If insignificant, he continued in the same fashion as already proposed above. However, if significant, he increased K by one and continued doing so until the coefficient on the highest lag became insignificant or until he reached a value of K equal to 15.

Note that β_0 and δ_0 disappear from the equation upon first differencing. This means that we cannot use the test on first differences to detect breaks in the intercept of a time series.

To perform Vogelsang's test on the first differences we proceed in an analogous way as when performing the test on levels. We apply the OLS method to estimate equation (3.28) for all possible break dates $T_B = \lambda T$ with $\lambda \in [\lambda^*, 1 - \lambda^*]$. With each estimated equation we compute the appropriate F-statistics $F(T_B/T)$ for testing the hypothesis $\delta_1 = 0$. Then we compute the test statistics $MeanF$, $ExpF$, and $SupF$ in the same way as already described. To test the hypothesis H_0 of a stable trend function against the alternative H_A of a break in the intercept or linear trend we compare the test statistics $MeanF$, $ExpF$, and $SupF$ to the appropriate critical values. If the test statistics exceeds the appropriate critical value, we reject the H_0 of the stable trend function in favor of the H_A of a break in the intercept or linear trend; otherwise, we cannot reject the H_0. We use the same critical values as those for the test on levels, which are given in Table 6 in Appendix B. However, it is shown that for the test on first differences we should use the critical values for stationary case. Again we shall mention that this holds only when the error process v_t from equation (3.26) does contain a unit root.

Vogelsang (1997) applied both versions (on levels and on differences) of his test to a large set of data that included among others the Nelson and Plosser (1982) time series. He considered only the presence of an intercept and a linear trend (e.g. up to $p = 1$). He was able to detect trend breaks in many of the tested time series and concluded that the assumption of a stable linear trend will often lead to misspecified univariate time series models.

An application of the methodology is given in Kočenda (2005) with the aim to endogenously search for the single most significant structural break in exchange rates of the CEE countries. It was hypothesized that structural breaks in exchange rates are driven by exchange rate policies and that such a hypothesis could not be rejected in general. The findings show that for the majority of transition countries a break in exchange rate occurred before or exactly coincided with a major change in the exchange rate regime. The latter case supports the hypothesis, even though for some countries a structural break in exchange rate happened several months before the exchange regime was revised. A policy step, in the form of a regime change or realignment that took place some time after the break, was to accommodate a structural break that had happened already. The step thus brings the administration of a regime in line with the actual development of a nominal exchange rate. Thus, empirical findings show that in some cases reality defies conventional wisdom and apparent policy steps may not coincide with structural breaks. Since changes generally led toward greater flexibility, such a move may be interpreted as a response to increasing volatility of shocks attributable to an increase in the degree of international capital mobility.

In another application, Hanousek and Kočenda (2011a) use Vogelsang's test as an intermediate step to first find breaks in the time series of fiscal variables and then to test for the effect of corruption and economic freedom on the dynamics of public investment and public finance in the new members of the European Union. As advocated earlier in this section (Section 3.6), if the existence of a structural break is not appropriately accounted for, then the interpretation of the estimates would lead to incorrect and misleading implications.

3.6.2 MULTIPLE STRUCTURAL CHANGE

When we consider a model that captures an underlying process in a data set, it is natural to discriminate among models and avoid those with unnecessary parameters since these models should be considered as misspecified. In a similar spirit, a model that accounts for a structural change should be considered misspecified when in fact more than one break is present in the data. Detecting the number of structural breaks thus becomes important since ignoring multiple breaks may lead to false conclusions. On the other hand, the search for structural changes in the trend function of a time series should be pursued sensibly. As the number of potential breaks increases in excess, then a pressing question appears: "What is left from a trend and where is it after all?" In this part we turn our attention to methods designed to identify multiple breaks.

Bai and Perron (1998) consider theoretical issues related to multiple structural changes occurring at unknown times in the linear regression model estimated by least squares.[24] The main aspects of their contribution are the properties of the estimator, including the estimates of the break dates. They devise a test that allows for an inference to be made about the presence of structural change and the actual number of breaks in a general case of a partial structural change model where not all parameters are subject to shift. In a later work Bai and Perron (2003a) extend their idea to consider practical issues for the empirical applications of the procedure. They first address the problem of the estimation of the break dates and present an efficient algorithm to obtain global minimizers of the sum of squared residuals. This algorithm is based on the principle of dynamic programming and requires at most a least-squares operation of order $O(T^2)$ for any number of breaks. This method can be applied to both pure and partial structural change models. Then, they consider the problem of forming confidence intervals for the break dates under various hypotheses about the structure of the data and the errors across segments. Further, they address the issue of testing for structural changes under very

---

24   Bai (1999) considers a likelihood ratio test for multiple structural change.

general conditions on the data and the errors, as well as the issue of estimating the number of breaks. The asymptotic distributions of the tests depend on a trimming parameter ε and critical values were tabulated in Bai and Perron (2003a) for $\varepsilon = 0.05$.[25] As discussed in Bai and Perron (2006), larger values of ε are needed to achieve tests with a correct size in finite samples, when allowing for heterogeneity across segments or serial correlation in the errors. Bai and Perron (2003b) supplement the set of critical values available with other values of the trimming parameter ε to enable proper empirical applications. The code needed to run the test for multiple structural changes is available for non-profit academic use at http://people.bu.edu/perron. This section draws heavily from Bai and Perron (1998, 2003a, b) and for the sake of consistency follows the same notation.

The test for multiple structural change develops in the following way. Consider a multiple linear regression with m breaks, hence $m + 1$ regimes:

$$y_t = x_t'\beta + z_t'\delta_j + u_t \quad t = T_{j-1} + 1,..., T_j \tag{3.29}$$

for $j = 1,..., m + 1$. In this model, y_t is the observed dependent variable at time t; x_t ($p \times 1$) and z_t ($q \times 1$) are vectors of covariates and β and δ_j ($j = 1,..., m + 1$) are the corresponding vectors of coefficients; u_t is the error term. The indices $(T_1,..., T_m)$, or the break points, are explicitly treated as unknown and conventionally, $T_0 = 0$ and $T_{m+1} = T$. The purpose is to estimate the unknown regression coefficients together with the break points when T observations on (y_t, x_t, z_t) are available. The specification depicts a partial structural change model since the parameter vector β is not subject to shifts and is estimated using the entire sample of data. When $p = 0$, the specification becomes a pure structural model in which all coefficients are subject to change. The variance of the error term may change over time and does not need to be constant.[26]

The system of multiple linear regression in (3.29) may be rewritten in matrix notation as

$$Y = X\beta + \bar{Z}\delta + U, \tag{3.30}$$

where $Y = (y_1,..., y_T)'$, $X = (x_1,..., x_T)'$, $U = (u_1, ..., u_T)'$, $\delta = (\delta'_1, \delta'_2,..., \delta'_{m+1})'$, and $\bar{Z}$ is the matrix that diagonally partitions Z at $(T_1,..., T_m)$, i.e. $\bar{Z} = diag(Z_1,...Z_{m+1})$ with $Z_i = (Z_{T_{i-1}+1},...Z_{T_i})'$. The true value of a parameter is denoted with a 0 superscript. Hence, $\delta^0 = (\delta_1^{0'},...,\delta_{m+1}^{0'})'$ and $(T_1^0,...,T_m^0)$ denote true values of

---

the parameters δ and break points T. The matrix $\bar{Z}^0$ diagonally partitions Z at $(T_1^0,...,T_m^0)$. Thus, the true data generating process is assumed to be

$$Y = X\beta^0 + \bar{Z}^0\delta^0 + U. \tag{3.31}$$

As stated earlier, the purpose is to estimate the unknown regression coefficients together with the break points. The estimation procedure is based on the least-squares principle. For each m-partition $(T_1,..., T_m)$, the corresponding estimates of β and δ_j are obtained by minimizing the sum of squared residuals:

$$(Y - X\beta - \bar{Z}\delta)'(Y - X\beta - \bar{Z}\delta) = \sum_{i=1}^{m+1} \sum_{t=T_{i-1}+1}^{T_i} [y_t - x_t'\beta - z_t'\delta_i]^2. \tag{3.32}$$

In order to perform the analysis, some restrictions on the possible values of the break dates need to be imposed. Specifically, each of the break dates must be asymptotically distinct and bounded from the boundaries of the sample. To ensure this, denote $\lambda_i = T_i / T$ $(i = 1,..., m)$ as break fractions of the sample. Further, define a set Λ_ε for the trimming parameter ε (an arbitrary positive number), which imposes a minimal length h for a segment of break $(\varepsilon = h/T)$ as

$$\Lambda_\varepsilon = \{(\lambda_1,...,\lambda_m); |\lambda_{i+1} - \lambda_i| \geq \varepsilon, \lambda_1 \geq \varepsilon, \lambda_m \leq 1 - \varepsilon\}. \tag{3.33}$$

Let $\hat{\beta}(\{T_j\})$ and $\hat{\delta}(\{T_j\})$ stand for the estimates based on the given m-partition $(T_1,..., T_m)$, denoted $\{T_j\}$. After these are substituted in the objective function, the resulting sum of squared residuals is denoted as $S_T(T_1,..., T_m)$. Then, with the minimization taken over all partitions $(T_1,..., T_m)$ such that $T_i - T_{i-1} \geq h = T_\varepsilon$, the estimated break points are

$$(\hat{T}_1,...,\hat{T}_m) = \arg\min_{(\lambda_1,...,\lambda_m) \in \Lambda_\varepsilon} S_T(T_1,...,T_m). \tag{3.34}$$

Regression parameter estimates are those associated with the m-partition $\{\hat{T}_j\}$. A detailed method to efficiently compute such estimates is based on a dynamic programming algorithm described in Bai and Perron (2003a).

Bai and Perron (1998) considered three distinctive approaches in testing for multiple structural changes. The first approach is in testing the hypothesis of no break against that of a fixed number of breaks. The second approach keeps the number of breaks unknown and this is confronted with the null of no break. The third test is of ℓ versus $\ell + 1$ breaks.

1. No break vs. known number of breaks – Supremum F-test
The basis for discriminating between the hypotheses of no break ($m = 0$) or a fixed known number of breaks ($m = k$) is a sup F-test. Let R be the conventional matrix such that $(R\delta)' = (\delta_1' - \delta_2',..., \delta_k' - \delta_{k+1}')$. Then define

$$F_T(\lambda_1,...,\lambda_k;q) = \frac{1}{T}\left(\frac{T-(k+1)q-p}{kq}\right)\hat{\delta}'R'(R\hat{V}(\hat{\delta})R')^{-1}R\hat{\delta},$$

where, in the least constrained version, $\hat{V}(\hat{\delta})$ is an estimate of the covariance matrix of $\hat{\delta}$ robust to serial correlation and heteroskedasticity. Thus, $\hat{V}(\hat{\delta})$ is a consistent estimate of

$$V(\hat{\delta}) = p\lim_{T\to\infty}T(\bar{Z}'M_X\bar{Z})^{-1}\bar{Z}'M_X\Omega M_X\bar{Z}(\bar{Z}'M_X\bar{Z})^{-1}, \qquad (3.35)$$

where $M_X = I - X(X'X)^{-1}X'$. A consistent estimate may take a different form if some restrictions are imposed on the nature of the heterogeneity across data segments and/or serial correlation in errors.[27]

The test itself is designed in the spirit of Andrews (1993) as a supremum F-test:

$$\sup F_T(k;q) = F_T(\hat{\lambda}_1,...,\hat{\lambda}_k;q), \qquad (3.36)$$

where $(\hat{\lambda}_1,...,\hat{\lambda}_k)$ minimizes the global sum of squared residuals under specific trimming, which is equivalent to maximizing the F-test under the assumption of spherical errors. This approach asymptotically equals maximizing the F-test in (3.34) since the estimated break dates are consistent even in the presence of serial correlation.

Depending on the assumptions made with respect to the distribution of the data and errors across segments, different versions of the test can be obtained. Such differences relate to variations of how the construction of the estimate $V(\hat{\delta})$ given by (3.35) is specified. Bai and Perron (1998) presented the critical values for the single trimming parameter $\varepsilon = 0.05$. However, a larger value of the trimming parameter is needed when heterogeneity across segments or correlation in the errors are present. Bai and Perron (2003b) obtain via simulation additional critical values for $\varepsilon = 0.05, 0.10, 0.15, 0.20,$ and 0.25.[28] The number of breaks allowed is a function of the trimming parameter value. For $\varepsilon = 0.10$ the maximum number of breaks $k = 8$, since allowing for nine breaks restricts estimates to exactly $\hat{\lambda}_1 = 0.1$, $\hat{\lambda}_2 = 0.2$ up to $\hat{\lambda}_9 = 0.9$. In a similar fashion the maximum number of breaks is five for $\varepsilon = 0.15$, three for $\varepsilon = 0.20$ and two for $\varepsilon = 0.25$. For $\varepsilon = 0.05$ the maximum value of k is 9. The critical values allow hypothesis testing at a significance of 10, 5, 2.5, and 1% and are tabulated for up to $q = 10$ regressors.[29]

27 For example, imposing the same variance and no autocorrelation in the errors results in a consistent estimate taking the form $V(\hat{\delta}) = p\lim_{T\to\infty}T(\bar{Z}'M_X\bar{Z})^{-1}$. In such a case the distribution of the regressors is allowed to differ across data segments, though.

28 See Bai and Perron (2003b) for details on simulations.

29 The complete set of critical values is available at http://people.bu.edu/perron.

2. No break vs. unknown number of breaks – Double maximum tests

Quite frequently researchers do not want to impose a specific number of breaks but need to investigate the issue of multiple structural change without specifying the number of breaks *ex ante*. Bai and Perron (1998) developed two tests for such a purpose. The null hypothesis of no structural break is set against the alternative with an unknown number of breaks that is bounded by an upper limit *M*.

The two tests are labeled *double maximum tests*. Since the number of breaks is *a priori* unknown, both versions of the test incorporate weights that may be understood as if imposing some prior knowledge on the likelihood for a different number of breaks. The simplest solution in such a case is to set all weights equal to unity. Such an approach yields an equally weighted (unity) double maximum test defined as

$$UD\max F_T(M,q) = \max_{1 \le m \le M} F_T(\hat{\lambda}_1, ..., \hat{\lambda}_m; q), \tag{3.37}$$

where $\hat{\lambda}_j = \hat{T}_j / T$ (*j* = 1,..., *m*) are the estimates of the break points using the global minimization of the sum of squared residuals assuming segments of minimal length $h = \varepsilon T$. The limiting distribution of the test is given as $\max_{1 \le m \le M} \sup_{(\lambda_1, ..., \lambda_m) \in \Lambda_\varepsilon} F(\lambda_1, ..., \lambda_m; q)$. For a fixed *m*, $F(\lambda_1, ..., \lambda_m; q)$ is the sum of *m* dependent chi-square random variables with *q* degrees of freedom, each one divided by *m*. Division by *m* can be viewed as scaling since as the number of breaks *m* increases the given data sample becomes less informative with respect to the hypothesis. As *m* increases, the critical values decrease, which implies that the marginal *p*-values decrease with *m* and may result in a lower power of the test as the number of breaks becomes large.

This shortcoming can be alleviated by considering a set of weights such that the marginal *p*-values are equal across values of *m*. This implies weights that depend on *q* and the significance level of the test *α*. More precisely, let *c*(*q*, *α*, *m*) be the asymptotic critical values of the test $F_T(\hat{\lambda}_1, ..., \hat{\lambda}_m; q)$ for a significance level *α*. Then, the weights are defined as $a_1 = 1$ and for *m* > 1 as $a_m = c(q, \alpha, 1) / c(q, \alpha, m)$. The version of the weighted double maximum test is then defined as

$$WD\max F_T(M,q) = \max_{1 \le m \le M} \frac{c(q,\alpha,1)}{c(q,\alpha,m)} F_T(\hat{\lambda}_1, ..., \hat{\lambda}_m; q) \tag{3.38}$$

$$\Rightarrow \max_{1 \le m \le M} \frac{c(q,\alpha,1)}{c(q,\alpha,m)} \sup_{(\lambda_1, ..., \lambda_m) \in \Lambda_\varepsilon} F(\lambda_1, ..., \lambda_m; q). \tag{3.39}$$

The critical values were tabulated by Bai and Perron (1998) and Bai and Perron (2003b) for $\varepsilon = 0.05$ and 0.10 when the upper bound on the number of breaks

M is 5, for $\varepsilon = 0.15$ (M = 5), for $\varepsilon = 0.20$ (M = 3), and for $\varepsilon = 0.25$ (M = 2); q ranges from 1 to 10.[30]

3. Test of ℓ versus $\ell + 1$ breaks

This is a test of the null hypothesis of ℓ breaks against the alternative that an additional break exists (ℓ versus $\ell + 1$ breaks). The test consists of an application of ($\ell + 1$) tests of the null hypothesis of no structural break against the alternative of a single break. It is applied to each data segment containing observations $\hat{T}_{i-1} + 1$ to $\hat{T}_i$ ($i = 1,..., \ell + 1$) using the previous notation $\hat{T}_0 = 0$ and $\hat{T}_{i+1} = T$. The test is defined by

$$F_T(\ell+1\mid\ell)=\left\{S_T\left(\hat{T}_1,...,\hat{T}_\ell\right)- \min_{1\le i\le\ell+1}\inf_{\tau\in\Lambda_{i,\eta}} S_T\left(\hat{T}_1,...,\hat{T}_{i-1},\tau,\hat{T}_i,...,\hat{T}_\ell\right)\right\}/\hat{\sigma}^2, \quad (3.40)$$

where $\Lambda_{i,\eta} = \left\{\tau; \hat{T}_{i-1} + \left(\hat{T}_i - \hat{T}_{i-1}\right)\eta \le \tau \le \hat{T}_i - \left(\hat{T}_i - \hat{T}_{i-1}\right)\eta\right\}$ and $\hat{\sigma}^2$ is a consistent estimate of σ^2 under the null hypothesis. It should be noted that for $i = 1$, the resulting sum of squared residuals $S_T\left(\hat{T}_1,...,\hat{T}_{i-1},\tau,\hat{T}_i,...,\hat{T}_\ell\right)$ is understood as $S_T\left(\tau,\hat{T}_1,...,\hat{T}_\ell\right)$ and for $i = \ell + 1$ as $S_T\left(\hat{T}_1,...,\hat{T}_\ell,\tau\right)$. Once the sum of squared residuals are calculated over all segments where an additional break is included we can compare their minimal values for the purpose of hypothesis testing. If the minimal value of SSR for the ($\ell + 1$) breaks is sufficiently smaller that the minimal value of SSR for the model with ℓ breaks, then the null hypothesis of ℓ breaks is rejected in favor of the ($\ell + 1$) model.

Bai and Perron (1998) provided asymptotic critical values for trimming with $\varepsilon = 0.05$ for q ranging from 1 to 10 and ℓ ranging from 0 to 9. Bai and Perron (2003b) provided additional critical values for trimming with $\varepsilon = 0.10$, 0.15, 0.20, and 0.25. Restrictions on the number of breaks for different values of trimming, as in the case of the preceding supremum F-test, do not apply.[31]

With respect to the size and power of the tests described above, Bai and Perron (2006) presented an extensive simulation analysis. Following its results a practical tactic emerges on how to employ these procedures. We begin with the UDmax or WDmax tests to see if at least one break is present. If these tests point toward the presence of at least one break, then we employ a sequence of the supF($\ell + 1 \mid \ell$) statistics constructed using global minimizers for the break dates to find out what the number of breaks is in the sample. When adopting this approach we ignore the test of one versus no break (F(1 | 0)) and select m

30 The complete set of critical values is available at http://people.bu.edu/perron.
31 The complete set of critical values is available at http://people.bu.edu/perron.

such that the tests $\sup F(\ell + 1 \mid \ell)$ are insignificant for $\ell \geq m$). Bai and Perron (2006) claim that this strategy leads to the best results and they recommend it for empirical applications.

Further, Bai and Perron (2003b) make the following recommendations with respect to testing. First, the researcher should make sure that the specifications are such that the size of the test is adequate under the hypothesis of no break. If serial correlation and/or heterogeneity in the data or errors across segments are not allowed in the estimated regression model (and not present in the data generating process), using any value of the trimming ε will lead to tests with adequate sizes. However, if such features are allowed, a higher trimming is needed. With a sample of $T = 120$, the trimming parameter $\varepsilon = 0.15$ should be enough for heterogeneity in the errors or the data. If serial correlation is allowed, $\varepsilon = 0.20$ may be needed. The trimming parameters could be reduced if a longer time series is available and increased for shorter data samples. The appropriate choice of the critical values for various trimming parameters should be used in practice.

Gilman and Nakov (2004) is a compelling example of an application of this technique to applied research that deals with structural breaks present in real-world data. They present a model in which the exogenous money supply causes changes in the inflation rate and the output growth rate. Shifts in the model's credit sector productivity cause shifts in the income velocity of money that can break the otherwise stable relationships among money, inflation, and output growth. They test the model on two (at that time) EU accession countries, Hungary and Poland, by using a vector autoregressive system (see sections 4.1 and 4.2 for details) that incorporates multiple structural breaks. The breaks are endogenously determined by the Bai and Perron (1998, 2003a) methodology. Three structural breaks are found for each country that are linked to changes in velocity trends and to the breaks found in the other country. Such an outcome gives supportive evidence for accounting for structural changes in the data before employing standard techniques.

Another example of applying the methodology is the analysis of Camarero, Carrion-i-Silvestre and Tamarit (2005), who, by using unit root tests that account for the presence of level shifts, test for hysteresis effects versus the natural rate hypothesis on the unemployment rates of the ten new member countries of the EU. They find that the time series properties of the variables are compatible with a changing natural rate. They use a univariate approach to measure the non-accelerating inflation rate of unemployment (NAIRU) as the local mean of unemployment between structural changes. Further, from the point estimates of the breakpoints, two groups of countries can be formed in terms of the number of breaks. The first one consists of small countries (including the Baltic states and Malta) and of Poland, which display three or four structural changes. The second group includes medium-size economies

(Czech Republic, Hungary, Slovakia, and Slovenia) that only experience one or two breaks. The estimated breaks are associated with political or institutional events of relevance in the transition process. Some of these events are common to all the countries, whereas others are idiosyncratic. For example, the degree of openness is larger for the small economies, so they are more exposed to external shocks and therefore exhibit more breaks. In the case of Poland, the higher number of breaks is due to the special transition strategy followed from the very beginning of the 1990s. In any event, structural breaks in the NAIRU of transition countries can be with a high degree of confidence associated with institutional changes coming from the implementation of market-oriented re-forms.

Further, the combination of techniques introduced in sections 3.4–3.6 has been exploited by Uctum, Thurston, and Uctum (2006) who assess fiscal performances in G7 and selected Latin American and Asian countries. In the paper questions related to fiscal performance and sustainability are consid-ered. The authors find that traditional *ADF* tests of sustainability overwhelm-ingly fail to reject the non-stationarity of public debt in the troubled areas of the world. However, these tests suffer a major weakness as they are sensitive to structural breaks, which bias results towards not rejecting unit roots. For this reason the authors control for structural breaks by using Bai and Per-ron (1998, 2003a) methodology; it is found that the outcomes change drasti-cally for a majority of countries. In sum, they find that: (i) The traditional unit root tests often overlook the corrective actions taken by many governments. Controlling for structural breaks changes the non-stationarity results dra-matically among the countries. (ii) The estimation of a reaction function for governments, expanded by incorporating structural breaks, provides further evidence for significant active anti-debt policies among G7 countries, and to a lesser extent in the other regions.

Finally, testing for multiple structural changes has recently taken also mul-tivariate approach. Relevant techniques are covered for example by Perron and Qu (2007), and Kejriwal and Perron (2010). A detailed coverage of these tech-nique is beyond the scope of this text, though.

3.7 NON-LINEAR STRUCTURE AND CONDITIONAL HETEROSKEDASTICITY

In the preceding sections we presented various univariate time series models and tests. Although often quite diverse in their nature, all the presented models have one common feature. We have always assumed the variance of the error term conditional on the information revealed before the time t realizations (at the time $t-1$), denoted as $var_{t-1}[\varepsilon_t] = E_{t-1}[\varepsilon_t^2]$, to be constant and equal to the unconditional variance of ε_t, denoted as $var[\varepsilon_t] = E[\varepsilon_t^2]$. In the following sections devoted to non-linear structure and conditional heteroskedasticity this assumption will be relaxed. Instead of a constant conditional variance we will assume that the conditional variance is governed by an *autoregressive*, possibly combined with a *moving average*, process. This means that besides the parameters of the mean equation that govern the behavior of y_t, we will have to also estimate the parameters of the *AR* or *ARMA* process that will govern the behavior of the conditionally heteroskedastic errors. This richer specification of the model does not occur at no cost. Instead of *OLS* we will need to apply the *maximum likelihood estimation* (*MLE*) procedure to estimate the autoregressive conditional heteroskedastic (*ARCH*) models. The *MLE* estimation requires distributional assumptions to be imposed on the error process ε_t. Such assumptions are obviously much stronger than the orthogonality condition needed for the *OLS* estimates to be unbiased and consistent.

ARCH models are very useful, particularly in the field of finance. Financial time series are prone to exhibit periods of high and low volatility. Exactly such behavior can be modeled using conditional heteroskedastic disturbances. Moreover, it is the variance of financial time series that is of a great importance. If you consider a time series of asset returns, then the returns are represented by the mean, and the risk associated with holding a particular asset is measured by the variance of the series. The optimal portfolio is often chosen within the mean-variance framework, as for example in the Capital Asset Pricing Model (*CAPM*) of Sharpe (1964), Lintner (1965), and Mossin (1966). Therefore, the capacity of *ARCH* models to model and predict the changing variance of financial time series is of great importance. This is even more true when this type of model is used by analytical departments of financial firms where vast amounts of money are at stake, unlike in purely academic exercises. As a result, we typically see time series of asset returns, exchange rates, or other high frequency data estimated with *ARCH* models. Nevertheless, *ARCH* models began to be used in other areas as well due to their popularity in finance. After all, in the seminal paper by Engle (1982), where *ARCH* models were introduced, the author used an *ARCH* model to estimate a time series of U.K. inflation.

Below, we will first review the concept of conditional and unconditional expectations and then introduce a simple *ARCH* model and its generalized extensions (*GARCH* models). Following this, we will present procedures and tests that enable the detection of conditional heteroskedasticity, propose an algorithm that enables the detection of conditional heteroskedasticity and then identify and estimate the most parsimonious *ARCH* or *GARCH* model. Finally, we will briefly list various popular extensions and modifications of *ARCH* models.

3.7.1 CONDITIONAL AND UNCONDITIONAL EXPECTATIONS

Understanding the difference between conditional and unconditional expectations is crucial for understanding *ARCH* models. For simplicity, let us focus on
the conditional and unconditional expectations of y_t time series governed by
a simple *AR*(1) process. The identical technique can be used to form conditional and unconditional expectations of the variance of an *ARCH* error term ε_t.
   Consider the following *AR*(1) process:

$$y_t = a_0 + a_1 y_{t-1} + \varepsilon_t ,$$

with $0 < a_1 < 1$ and ε_t independent disturbances with mean 0 and variance
σ^2. Clearly y_t depends only on its past values and on the current realization
of ε_t. Thus, the information needed to form conditional expectations is only
that of the past values of y_t. Moreover, with an *AR*(1) process the information
about all past realizations of y_t is fully comprised in the realization of y_{t-1}.
The conditional expectation of the mean and variance of y_t can therefore be
written as

$$E_{t-1}[y_t] = E[y_t \mid y_{t-1}, y_{t-2}, ...] = E[y_t \mid y_{t-1}] = E[a_0 + a_1 y_{t-1} + \varepsilon_t] = a_0 + a_1 y_{t-1},$$

$$var_{t-1}[y_t] = E[(y_t - E(y_t))^2 \mid y_{t-1}] = E[(y_t - (a_0 + a_1 y_{t-1}))^2 \mid y_{t-1}] = E[\varepsilon_t^2] = \sigma^2 .$$

With unconditional expectations the situation is quite different. When forming
unconditional expectations, we must act as if the only information we have is
that about the mean and variance of the error process ε_t, whose realizations are
independent. We do not know anything about the past realizations of y_t. Therefore, to form unconditional expectations we must first solve the *AR*(1) equation
in terms of ε_t. The unconditional expectation of the mean and variance of y_t can
be written as

$$E[y_t] = E[(1 - a_1 L)^{-1}(a_0 + \varepsilon_t)] = E\left[a_0 / (1 - a_1) + \sum_{i=0}^{\infty} a_1^i \varepsilon_{t-i} \right] = a_0 / (1 - a_1),$$

$$var[y_t] = E[(y_t - E(y_t))^2] = E\left[\left(\sum_{i=0}^{\infty} a_1^i \varepsilon_{t-i} \right)^2 \right] = \sigma^2 / (1 - a_1^2).$$

Note that in the computation of unconditional variance we have used the fact
that errors ε_t are independent and thus uncorrelated across time. In the expressions for the unconditional mean and variance of y_t we had to use all the past
realizations of ε_t. That is why the unconditional expectations are sometimes

also called *long run expectations.* Based on the above, it is clear that there are differences in the values of the two variances.[32]

3.7.2 ARCH MODEL

The basic type of *ARCH* model was proposed by Engle (1982). In the simplest case, denoted as *ARCH*(1), Engle modeled the residuals ε_t from an *ARMA* model of y_t with the following equation

$$\varepsilon_t = v_t \sqrt{\alpha_0 + \alpha_1 \varepsilon_{t-1}^2} , \tag{3.41}$$

where v_t are independently normally distributed with mean 0 and variance $\sigma_v^2 = 1$, and independent of ε_{t-1}. The constants α_0 and α_1 satisfy the conditions $\alpha_0 > 0$, and $0 \le \alpha_1 < 1$.

Using equation (3.41) the unconditional expectations of ε_t are:

$$E[\varepsilon_t] = E\left[v_t \sqrt{\alpha_0 + \alpha_1 \varepsilon_{t-1}^2}\right] = 0,$$

$$cov[\varepsilon_t \varepsilon_{t-i}] = E[\varepsilon_t \varepsilon_{t-i}] = E\left[v_t v_{t-i} \sqrt{\alpha_0 + \alpha_1 \varepsilon_{t-1}^2} \sqrt{\alpha_0 + \alpha_1 \varepsilon_{t-i-1}^2}\right] = 0,$$

$$var[\varepsilon_t] = E[\varepsilon_t^2] = E\left[v_t^2(\alpha_0 + \alpha_1 \varepsilon_{t-1}^2)\right] = \alpha_0 / (1 - \alpha_1).$$

The first equation holds because $E[v_t] = 0$. Since $E[v_t v_{t-i}] = 0$ we obtain the second equation. Finally, because $E\left[v_t^2\right] = \sigma_v^2 = 1$ and the unconditional variances of ε_t^2 and ε_{t-1}^2 must equal, we obtain the third equation. Thus, we see that the unconditional expectations are the same as those of white noise disturbances: unconditional mean and covariances are equal to zero and the unconditional variance is finite and constant over time. This is also the reason why *ARCH* disturbances remain covariance stationary.

The conditional expectations of ε_t are:

$$E_{t-1}[\varepsilon_t] = E_{t-1}\left[v_t \sqrt{\alpha_0 + \alpha_1 \varepsilon_{t-1}^2}\right] = 0,$$

$$cov_{t-1}[\varepsilon_t \varepsilon_{t-i}] = E_{t-1}[\varepsilon_t \varepsilon_{t-i}] = E_{t-1}\left[v_t v_{t-i} \sqrt{\alpha_0 + \alpha_1 \varepsilon_{t-1}^2} \sqrt{\alpha_0 + \alpha_1 \varepsilon_{t-i-1}^2}\right] = 0,$$

---

32 Differences in the values of the conditional and unconditional variance are important in applied research, but even more so in financial analysis performed by financial and investment companies due to the large amounts of money that are involved.

$$var_{t-1}[\varepsilon_t] = E_{t-1}[\varepsilon_t^2] = E_{t-1}\left[v_t^2(\alpha_0 + \alpha_1\varepsilon_{t-1}^2)\right] = \alpha_0 + \alpha_1\varepsilon_{t-1}^2.$$

Because $E[v_t] = 0$ and $E[v_t v_{t-i}] = 0$, then also the conditional mean and covariances are equal to 0. However, the conditional variance of ε_t, which we will denote as $h_t = E_{t-1}[\varepsilon_t^2]$, is equal to $\alpha_0 + \alpha_1\varepsilon_{t-1}^2$. Thus, the only difference between white noise disturbances and $ARCH(1)$ disturbances lies in their conditional variance. With $ARCH(1)$ disturbances generated by equation (3.41) the conditional variance h_t follows something like an $AR(1)$ process. Note that it is not exactly an $AR(1)$ process, because $\varepsilon_{t-1}^2 \neq h_{t-1}$; the first is a concrete realization of a random variable, while the second is its conditional mean.

We have already mentioned that the coefficients α_0 and α_1 must satisfy the conditions $\alpha_0 > 0$ and $0 \le \alpha_1 < 1$. The conditions $\alpha_0 > 0$ and $\alpha_1 \ge 0$ ensure that the conditional variance is always greater than 0. Moreover, the condition $\alpha_1 < 1$ is needed for the "quasi" autoregressive process $h_t = E_{t-1}[\varepsilon_t^2] = \alpha_0 + \alpha_1\varepsilon_{t-1}^2$ to be stable. If α_1 was greater than 1, then with non-zero probability the conditional variance would explode to infinity. With $\alpha_0 > 0$ and $0 \le \alpha_1 < 1$ an $ARCH(1)$ process implies that a large realization of the disturbance ε_t will most likely be followed by a large realization of ε_{t+1}. Similarly, a small disturbance will probably be followed by another small disturbance. This is why $ARCH$ models are suitable for modeling time series that exhibit periods of large and small volatility.[33]

So far we have discussed only the properties of $ARCH(1)$ disturbances. An important question also is how the presence of $ARCH(1)$ disturbances changes the properties of the $\{y_t\}$ sequence. For simplicity we will assume an $AR(1)$ model of y_t with $ARCH(1)$ disturbances. Formally such a model can be written as

$$y_t = a_0 + a_1 y_{t-1} + \varepsilon_t,$$

$$\varepsilon_t = v_t\sqrt{\alpha_0 + \alpha_1\varepsilon_{t-1}^2}.$$

The conditional mean and variance of y_t is

$$E_{t-1}[y_t] = a_0 + a_1 y_{t-1},$$

$$var_{t-1}[y_t] = E_{t-1}[(y_t - (a_0 + a_1 y_{t-1}))^2] = E_{t-1}[\varepsilon_t^2] = \alpha_0 + \alpha_1\varepsilon_{t-1}^2.$$

To obtain the unconditional mean and variance we must, similarly as in section 3.7.1., solve the $AR(1)$ equation for y_t in terms of ε_t. Solving the $AR(1)$ equation

---

33   Mandelbrot (1963) introduced several facts that characterize many economic and especially financial time series: 1. series of prices are leptokurtic, 2. the variance of series of prices changes over time, 3. large price changes occur often, contrary to predictions, and 4. successive price changes exhibit recognizable patterns.

we obtain $y_t = a_0 / (1 - a_1) + \sum_{i=0}^{\infty} a_1^i \varepsilon_{t-i}$ and for unconditional expectations we can write

$$E[y_t] = E\left[a_0 / (1 - a_1) + \sum_{i=0}^{\infty} a_1^i \varepsilon_{t-i} \right] = a_0 / (1 - a_1),$$

$$var[y_t] = E\left[\left(\sum_{i=0}^{\infty} a_1^i \varepsilon_{t-i} \right)^2 \right] = \sum_{i=0}^{\infty} a_1^{2i} E[\varepsilon_{t-i}^2] = \frac{E[\varepsilon_t^2]}{1 - a_1^2} = \frac{[\alpha_0 / (1 - \alpha_1)]}{1 - a_1^2}.$$

This means that the conditional and unconditional mean of y_t are the same as with a simple $AR(1)$ model without $ARCH(1)$ errors. The conditional variance is the same as that of the $ARCH(1)$ errors. However, with the unconditional variance the $AR(1)$ equation for y_t and the $ARCH(1)$ equation for ε_t interact. As a result the unconditional variance increases with a_1^2, α_0, and α_1.

Until now, we have for simplicity considered only an $ARCH(1)$ model. Engle (1982) proposed a general $ARCH(q)$ model of the residuals ε_t from any linear regression. Because we focus on univariate time series analysis here, instead of the whole set of linear regressions we will consider only $ARMA(P,Q)$ models. A general $ARMA(P,Q) - ARCH(p)$ model can be written as

$$y_t = a_0 + \sum_{i=1}^{P} a_i y_{t-i} + \sum_{i=0}^{Q} b_i \varepsilon_{t-i},$$

$$\varepsilon_t = v_t \sqrt{\alpha_0 + \sum_{i=1}^{p} \alpha_i \varepsilon_{t-i}^2}, \tag{3.42}$$

$$v_t \sim i.i.d.N(0,1), \; \alpha_0 > 0, \; \alpha_i \geq 0 \text{ for all i}, \; \sum_{i=1}^{p} \alpha_i < 1.$$

The $ARCH(p)$ errors ε_t defined in (3.42) have, similar to $ARCH(1)$ errors, zero conditional and unconditional mean and all covariances. The conditional variance of ε_t denoted as h_t is

$$h_t = E_{t-1}[\varepsilon_t^2] = E_{t-1}\left[v_t^2 (\alpha_0 + \sum_{i=1}^{p} \alpha_i \varepsilon_{t-i}^2) \right] = \alpha_0 + \sum_{i=1}^{p} \alpha_i \varepsilon_{t-i}^2.$$

The unconditional variance of ε_t is

$$E[\varepsilon_t^2] = E\left[v_t^2 (\alpha_0 + \sum_{i=1}^{p} \alpha_i \varepsilon_{t-i}^2) \right] = \frac{\alpha_0}{1 - \sum_{i=1}^{p} \alpha_i}.$$

We see that the unconditional variance is finite and constant and the conditional variance follows an $AR(p)$-like process. The conditions $\alpha_0 > 0$ and $\alpha_i \geq 0$

ensure that the conditional variance h_t is always greater than 0. The condition $\sum_{i=1}^{P}\alpha_i < 1$ is a sufficient and necessary condition for the stability of the conditional variance equation $h_t = \alpha_0 + \sum_{i=1}^{P}\alpha_i\varepsilon_{t-i}^2$. So, if $\sum_{i=1}^{P}\alpha_i \geq 1$, then there exists a non-zero probability that the conditional variance h_t will explode to infinity. Recall sections 2.4. and 2.5. about stability and stationarity conditions to see that given $\alpha_i \geq 0$ for all i, all the roots of the inverse characteristic equation $1 - A(L) = 1 - \sum_{i=1}^{P}\alpha_i L^i = 0$ will lie outside the unit circle, if and only if $\sum_{i=1}^{P}\alpha_i < 1$.

All the parameters of an $ARMA(P,Q) - ARCH(p)$ model are estimated jointly using the *maximum likelihood estimation* (*MLE*) procedure, which is incorporated in most statistical software packages. To form the log likelihood function we use the fact that the $ARCH(p)$ errors ε_t from the estimated equation (3.42) are conditionally normal with mean 0 and variance h_t, that is: $\varepsilon_t \mid \varepsilon_{t-1}, \varepsilon_{t-2}, \ldots,$ $\varepsilon_{t-p} \sim N(0, h_t)$. With T observations the joint density is a product of all conditional densities, thus the log likelihood function is a sum of the conditional normal log likelihoods l_t. Instead of the sum we can maximize the average of l_t denoted as l and defined as

$$l = \frac{1}{T}\sum_{t=1}^{T}l_t,$$

where $l_t = -\frac{1}{2}\log h_t - \frac{1}{2}\varepsilon_t^2 / h_t$.

The average log likelihood l is a function of the regression parameters $\left[\{a_i\}_{i=0}^{P}, \{b_j\}_{j=0}^{Q}, \{\alpha_k\}_{k=0}^{P}\right]$. The *MLE* parameters' estimates are the values of the parameters that maximize the average log likelihood l.

3.7.3 GARCH MODEL

In *ARCH* models a relatively long lag p is often needed. To avoid problems with negative variance, which would occur if the conditions imposed on coefficients α in equation (3.42) were violated, a fixed lag structure is typically imposed. For example Engle (1982) estimated the U.K. inflation time series using an $ARCH(4)$ model with the parameters restricted to having a fixed ratio $\alpha_1 : \alpha_2 :$ $: \alpha_3 : \alpha_4 = 4 : 3 : 2 : 1$. He modeled the conditional variance with the following equation: $h_t = E_{t-1}[\varepsilon_t^2] = \alpha_0 + \alpha_1(0.4\varepsilon_{t-1}^2 + 0.3\varepsilon_{t-2}^2 + 0.2\varepsilon_{t-3}^2 + 0.1\varepsilon_{t-4}^2)$.

To allow for both a longer memory and a more flexible lag structure a natural extension of the *ARCH* class of models was proposed by Bollerslev (1986) who termed the new class of models *generalized autoregressive conditional heteroskedastic models (GARCH)*. A general *ARMA(P,Q) – GARCH(p,q)* model can be written as

$$y_t = a_0 + \sum_{i=1}^{P} a_i y_{t-i} + \sum_{i=0}^{Q} b_i \varepsilon_{t-i},$$

$$\varepsilon_t = v_t \sqrt{\alpha_0 + \sum_{i=1}^{p} \alpha_i \varepsilon_{t-i}^2 + \sum_{i=1}^{q} \beta_i h_{t-i}},$$
(3.43)

where $v_t \sim$ i.i.d. N(0,1), $\alpha_0 > 0$, $\alpha_i \geq 0$, $\beta_i \geq 0$, for all i, $\sum_{i=1}^{p} \alpha_i + \sum_{i=1}^{q} \beta_i < 1$.

The difference from the *ARCH(p)* model defined in the previous section is in the term $\sum_{i=1}^{q} \beta_i h_{t-i}$ included in the expression for ε_t. As a result the conditional variance h_t of the error term ε_t is

$$h_t = E_{t-1}[\varepsilon_t^2] = E_{t-1}\left[v_t^2(\alpha_0 + \sum_{i=1}^{p} \alpha_i \varepsilon_{t-i}^2 + \sum_{i=1}^{q} \beta_i h_{t-i}) \right] = \alpha_0 + \sum_{i=1}^{p} \alpha_i \varepsilon_{t-i}^2 + \sum_{i=1}^{q} \beta_i h_{t-i}. (3.44)$$

This means that the conditional variance is not only a function of the past realizations of ε_t^2 but also of the past conditional variances h_t. Again, the restrictions $\alpha_0 > 0$, $\alpha_i \geq 0$, and $\beta_i \geq 0$ ensure that the conditional variance is always greater than zero and the restriction $\sum_{i=1}^{p} \alpha_i + \sum_{i=1}^{q} \beta_i < 1$ is a sufficient and necessary condition for the stability of the conditional variance equation (3.44). If $\sum_{i=1}^{p} \alpha_i + \sum_{i=1}^{q} \beta_i \geq 1$, then there exists a non-zero probability that the conditional variance h_t will explode to infinity. The role of the condition $\sum_{i=1}^{p} \alpha_i + \sum_{i=1}^{q} \beta_i < 1$ becomes even more apparent when we write the expression for the unconditional variance:

$$E[\varepsilon_t^2] = E\left[v_t^2(\alpha_0 + \sum_{i=1}^{p} \alpha_i \varepsilon_{t-i}^2 + \sum_{i=1}^{q} \beta_i h_{t-i}) \right] = \frac{\alpha_0}{1 - \sum_{i=1}^{p} \alpha_i - \sum_{i=1}^{q} \beta_i}.$$

We obtain this expression because for unconditional expectations of a stationary process it must hold that $E[\varepsilon_t^2] = E[\varepsilon_{t-i}^2]$ and because $E[h_t] = E[E_{t-1}[\varepsilon_t^2]] = E[\varepsilon_t^2]$.

Clearly, if $\sum_{i=1}^{p}\alpha_i+\sum_{i=1}^{q}\beta_i\geq 1$, then the unconditional variance $E[\varepsilon_t^2]$ would either go to infinity or be negative, which is not plausible.

With $\alpha_i\geq 0$ and $\beta_i\geq 0$ the condition $\sum_{i=1}^{p}\alpha_i+\sum_{i=1}^{q}\beta_i<1$ implies $\sum_{i=1}^{q}\beta_i<1$. This means that all the roots of the inverse characteristic equation $1-B(L)=1-\sum_{i=1}^{q}\beta_iL^i=0$ will lie outside the unit circle. Therefore, if we define $A(L)=\sum_{i=1}^{p}\alpha_iL^i$, we can adjust equation (3.44) to

$$h_t=(1-B(L))^{-1}\alpha_0+(1-B(L))^{-1}A(L)\varepsilon_t^2$$

$$=(1-B(L))^{-1}\alpha_0+D(L)\varepsilon_t^2$$

$$=\frac{\alpha_0}{1-\sum_{i=1}^{q}\beta_i}+\sum_{i=1}^{\infty}\delta_i\varepsilon_{t-i}^2,\text{ where }D(L)=\sum_{i=1}^{\infty} L=(1-B(L)) A(L).$$

Thus, a *GARCH(p,q)* model can be represented with an infinite *ARCH(∞)* model with the lag distributed according to the equation $D(L)=\sum_{i=1}^{\infty}\delta_iL^i=(1-B(L))^{-1}A(L)$.

GARCH models indeed have a longer memory and a more flexible lag structure than *ARCH* models. An analogy to *AR* and *ARMA* models is quite obvious. Any invertible *ARMA* model also has an infinite *AR* representation. Clearly, the principle of parsimony will often lead us to the choice of *GARCH* models with fewer parameters over *ARCH* models with many parameters. In a similar way we would often choose a simple *ARMA* model over an overparameterized *AR* model.

In fact, we will see that the analogy between *ARCH* and *GARCH* models and *AR* and *ARMA* models can become even more apparent. By defining $\omega_t=\varepsilon_t^2-h_t$ we can rewrite equation (3.44) in the following way:

$$\varepsilon_t^2=\alpha_0+\sum_{i=1}^{m}(\alpha_i+\beta_i)\varepsilon_{t-i}^2+\omega_t-\sum_{i=1}^{q}\beta_i\omega_{t-i}, \tag{3.45}$$

where m = max(q,p) and ω_t disturbances are serially uncorrelated with mean 0 and variance h_t, because $\omega_t=\varepsilon_t^2-h_t=v_t^2h_t-h_t=(v_t^2-1)h_t$ (note that $(\frac{\omega_t}{h_t}+1)\sim\chi_1^2$). Thus, with a *GARCH(p,q)* model the squared disturbances ε_t^2 follow an *ARMA(m,q)* process with uncorrelated but heteroskedastic innovations ω_t. Similarly, with an *ARCH(p)* model q is equal to 0 and the squared disturbances ε_t^2 follow an *AR(p)* process.

All the parameters of an *ARMA(P,Q)* – *GARCH(p,q)* model are estimated jointly using the *maximum likelihood estimation* (*MLE*) procedure exactly in the same fashion as *ARCH* models, described in the previous section. Most statistical software packages contain a routine for the maximum likelihood estimation of such models (more on this issue in section 3.7.4).

To conclude, a standard *GARCH(p,q)* model is in the applied literature specified as:

$$\varepsilon_t \big| \Omega_{t-1} \sim D(0, h_t)$$

$$h_t = \alpha_0 + \sum_{i=1}^{p} \alpha_i \varepsilon_{t-i}^2 + \sum_{j=1}^{q} \beta_j h_{t-j}. \qquad (3.46)$$

In a simple *GARCH(1,1)* model, the *ARCH* term $\alpha \varepsilon_{t-1}^2$ reflects the impact of "news" or "surprises" from previous periods that affects the volatility of a specific variable under research: a significant and positive α less than one depicts the extent of the shocks' effect on volatility, which is not destabilizing.[34] The *GARCH* term βh_{t-1}, on the other hand, measures the impact of the forecast variance from previous periods on the current conditional variance, or volatility. A significant coefficient β (close to one) thus means a high degree of persistence in volatility. The sum of both coefficients also tells us about the speed of convergence of the forecast of the conditional volatility to a steady state: the closer to one its value is, the slower the convergence.

3.7.4 DETECTING CONDITIONAL HETEROSKEDASTICITY

So far we have discussed the properties, definitions, and estimation of *ARCH* and *GARCH* models. In this and the following two sections, we will present procedures and formal tests helping us to decide if the residuals e_t from the estimated *ARMA* regression are generated with an *ARCH* or *GARCH* process. The presence of conditional heteroskedasticity, if ignored, can lead to serious misspecification of the estimated model. Typically, estimated *ARMA* models that do not control for conditional heteroskedasticity will be overparameterized. Therefore, procedures and tests detecting the presence of *ARCH* and *GARCH* processes are very important. Unfortunately, a general test of a white noise null against a *GARCH(p,q)* alternative is not available, nor is a test of a *GARCH(p,q)* null against a *GARCH(p + r_1, q + r_2)* alternative.

Nevertheless, a sufficient amount of tools applicable to detect *ARCH* and *GARCH* processes in the *ARMA* residuals exists. First, we will introduce an analogue to the *Box-Jenkins methodology* (see Box and Jenkins, 1976), which relies on an investigation of the *ACF* and *PACF* (autocorrelation and partial autocor-

---

34   When α is greater than one then shocks materializing in the past are destabilizing.

relation functions) of the squared residuals e_t^2 and on the application of the *Ljung-Box Q-test*. Second, we will present a formal *LM* test proposed by Engle (1982), which tests the null of constant conditional variance against the alternative of an *ARCH(p)* process. Third, we will mention a formal *LM* test suggested by Bollerslev (1986), which tests the null of the *ARCH(p)* process against a *GARCH(p,q)*, $q > 0$ alternative. Finally, we will introduce the *BDS* test devised by Brock, Dechert, and Scheinkman (1987) that was further developed by Brock, Dechert, Scheinkman, and LeBaron (1996), and the test from Kočenda (2001b). Both procedures test the null hypothesis of independently and identically distributed (i.i.d.) data against an unspecified alternative. They can be used to decide if the estimated *GARCH(p,q)* model is the correct data generating process.

1. The analogue to the Box-Jenkins methodology

In the previous section we saw that equation (3.44) of a *GARCH(p,q)* process (and thus also of any *ARCH(p)* process) can be rewritten as equation (3.45). According to equation (3.45) the squared *GARCH(p,q)* disturbances ε_t^2 follow an *ARMA(m,q)* process, where $m = \max(q,p)$:

$$\varepsilon_t^2 = \alpha_0 + \sum_{i=1}^{m}(\alpha_i + \beta_i)\varepsilon_{t-i}^2 + \omega_t - \sum_{i=1}^{q}\beta_i\omega_{t-i}.$$

Since the true errors ε_t are not available, we analyze the *GARCH(p,q)* behavior of the residuals e_t from an estimated *ARMA* model of a time series y_t. To do so we can use an analogue to the Box-Jenkins methodology: instead of checking the series of residuals e_t we concentrate on the squared residuals e_t^2. If a *GARCH(p,q)* process is present, then the sample *ACF* and *PACF* of the squared residuals e_t^2 should indicate an *ARMA(m,q)* model in the same fashion as described in section 3.1.6. Therefore, in an ideal case, based on the inspection of the sample *ACF* and *PACF* we could decide the correct orders m and q of the *ARMA(m,q)* process, and thus also the correct orders p and q of the *GARCH(p,q)* process.

However, identification based on a visual inspection of sample *ACF* and *PACF* can be problematic and often very ambiguous. A more formal way to test for the presence of *GARCH* is the *Ljung-Box Q-test* already described in section 3.1.3. The application of this test is again analogous to the Box-Jenkins methodology framework. However, this time we apply the test on the squared residuals e_t^2 from an *ARMA* model of a time series y_t. The i-th sample autocorrelation of e_t^2 can be written as

$$\hat{\rho}_i = \frac{\sum_{t=i+1}^{T}(e_t^2 - \hat{\sigma}^2)(e_{t-i}^2 - \hat{\sigma}^2)}{\sum_{t=1}^{T}(e_t^2 - \hat{\sigma}^2)^2}, \text{ where } \hat{\sigma}^2 = \frac{1}{T}\sum_{t=1}^{T}e_t^2.$$

The *Ljung-Box Q-statistics* is then defined as

$$Q = T(T+2) \sum_{i=1}^{k} \frac{\hat{\rho}_i^2}{T-i}.$$

Under the null hypothesis of the first k autocorrelations of e_t^2 being jointly equal to zero, the null hypothesis is specified as

$$H_0 : \rho_i = 0, \text{ for } i = 1,2,...,k,$$

which is equivalent to no *ARCH* or *GARCH* errors, and the Ljung-Box Q-statistics has a χ_k^2 distribution. If the Ljung-Box Q-statistics exceeds the appropriate χ_k^2 critical value, then we reject the null in favor of the alternative hypothesis of at least one of the first autocorrelations being non-zero,

$$H_A : \rho_i \neq 0, \text{ for at least one i.}$$

Obviously, the alternative is equivalent to the presence of *ARCH* or *GARCH*. In practice the test is performed for values of k ranging from 1 to $T/4$.

2. *The LM test for the presence of an ARCH(p) process*
The *LM* test proposed by Engle (1982) can be performed in the following way. We obtain the squared residuals e_t^2 from the most appropriate *ARMA* model of a time series y_t and run *OLS* to estimate the equation

$$e_t^2 = \alpha_0 + \alpha_1 e_{t-1}^2 + \alpha_2 e_{t-2}^2 + \cdots + \alpha_p e_{t-p}^2 + \mu_t,$$

where μ_t denotes the regression error. Under the null hypothesis of no *ARCH(p)* errors, which is equivalent to

$$H_0 : \alpha_i = 0, \text{ for } i = 1,2,...,p,$$

the test statistics given by the TR^2 of this regression will be distributed as χ_p^2, where p is an arbitrarily set number of lags in the preceding regression of squared residuals. If the test statistics exceeds the appropriate χ_p^2 critical value, then we reject the null in favor of the alternative hypothesis of the presence of an *ARCH* process. Formally, the alternative can be written as

$$H_A : \alpha_i \neq 0, \text{ for at least one i.}$$

Rejecting the null means that instead of the *ARMA* model of the time series y_t we should consider a *ARMA − ARCH(p)* model.

3. The LM test for the presence of a GARCH(p,q) process

Together with the *GARCH* models Bollerslev (1986) proposed an *LM* test that enables a test for the presence of a *GARCH* process in the residuals. It tests the null hypothesis of an *ARCH(p)* process against the alternative of a *GARCH(p,q)* process. To perform the test we need to estimate the most appropriate *ARMA* – *ARCH(p)* model of a time series y_t and save the squared residuals e_t^2 and the estimates of the conditional variance h_t. Then we run *OLS* to estimate the equation

$$\frac{e_t^2}{h_t} - 1 = \alpha_0 + \alpha_1 e_{t-1}^2 + \alpha_2 e_{t-2}^2 + \cdots + \alpha_p e_{t-p}^2 + \mu_t,$$

where μ_t denotes the regression error. Under the null hypothesis of *ARCH(p)* errors the test statistics given by the TR^2 of this regression will be distributed as χ_p^2. If the test statistics exceeds the appropriate χ_p^2 critical value, then we reject the null in favor of the alternative hypothesis of the presence of a *GARCH(p,q)* process with $q > 0$. Rejecting the null means that instead of the *ARMA* – *ARCH(p)* model of the time series y_t we should consider an *ARMA* – *GARCH(p,q)*, $q > 0$, model.

There exist cases when we are unable to make decisions based on the above techniques. High-frequency data that are used in applied research frequently originate from financial markets and their structures are complicated in that they contain non-linear patterns. The complexity of those patterns is often such that it cannot be distinguished from randomness by conventional methods. Then more potent techniques have to be used. These will be introduced in the following two sections.

3.7.5 THE BDS TEST

Chaotic systems of low dimensionality can generate seemingly random numbers that may give an impression of white noise, thereby hiding their true nature. Under presumed randomness, a non-linear pattern can hide without being detected. Exchange rates, stock market returns and other macroeconomic variables of generally high frequency, for example, may originate from low-dimensional chaos. Such features are illustrated in Figure 3.3 below. On the left we see the series of entirely random numbers while the right side shows data with non-linear dependencies (*GARCH* structure). With a naked eye both plots look alike, though.

The detection of non-linear hidden patterns in such a time series provides important information that helps to analyze the behavior of a time series and improves forecasting ability over short time periods. A test that enables revealing hidden patterns that should not occur in truly randomly distributed

Figure 3.3: Random time series vs. non-linear patterns.

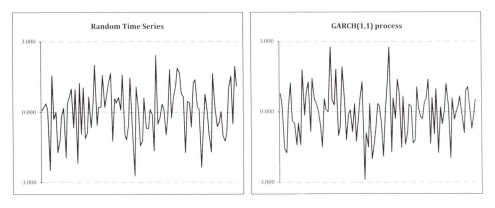

i.i.d. data was proposed by Brock, Dechert, and Scheinkman (1987) and further developed by Brock, Dechert, Scheinkman, and LeBaron (1996). Currently, the so-called *BDS* test is a well-known standard procedure. It is widely used due to its ability to deal with stochastic time series, which makes its application in modern macroeconomics and financial economics extremely appealing. The *BDS* test was not originally designed to test for the presence of *GARCH* processes. However, it proved to be very helpful in deciding if a chosen *GARCH* model is the correct one. The *BDS* test is a non-parametric test of the null hypothesis that the data are i.i.d. The alternative is unspecified; however, the test has power against both deterministic and stochastic systems. As mentioned above, it is able to reveal hidden patterns that should not occur in truly randomly distributed i.i.d. data. Therefore, when testing model residuals for being i.i.d., the *BDS* test can also be used as a test for correct model specification.

Let us define the standardized residuals u_t of an *ARMA – GARCH* model as

$$u_t = \frac{e_t}{\sqrt{h_t}}.$$

If the estimated model is the correct one, it follows from the definition of an *ARMA – GARCH* model given by equations (3.43) that u_t should be i.i.d. normal disturbances. Therefore, we can apply the *BDS* test on u_t in order to decide if our model choice was right. Rejecting the null means that the standardized residuals u_t are not i.i.d., and thus the estimated *ARMA – GARCH* model is not the true data generating process.

The analysis of chaotic systems often starts with computing a correlation dimension because of the ease of computation and the availability of sampling theory. The *BDS* test is also based on this technique. The method is based on the correlation integral described by Grassberger and Procaccia (1983) and is unique in its ability to detect non-linearities independent of linear dependencies in the data. To perform the *BDS* test on a time series $\{x_t\}_{t=1}^T$ (in the above-mentioned particular case the unspecified series x_t coincides with a series of standardized residuals u_t) we must compute the correlation integral at embedding dimension m denoted as $C_{m,T}(\varepsilon)$ and given by the expression

$$C_{m,T}(\varepsilon) = 2 \sum_{t=1}^{T_{m-1}} \sum_{s=t+1}^{T_m} I_\varepsilon(x_t^m, x_s^m) / (T_m(T_m - 1)),$$

where $x_t^m = (x_t, x_{t+1}, \ldots, x_{t+m-1})$ are the so-called *m*-histories, $T_m = T - m + 1$ with T being the sample size, and $I_\varepsilon(x_t^m, x_s^m)$ is an indicator function of the event

$$\left\| x_t^m - x_s^m \right\| = \max_{i=0,1,\ldots,m-1} \left| x_{t+i} - x_{s+i} \right| < \varepsilon.$$

Thus, the correlation integral measures the fraction of pairs that lie within the tolerance distance ε for the particular embedding dimension m.[35]
   The *BDS* statistics is then defined as

$$BDS_{m,T}(\varepsilon) = T^{1/2} \left[C_{m,T}(\varepsilon) - C_{1,T}(\varepsilon)^m \right] / \sigma_{m,T}(\varepsilon),$$

where $\sigma_{m,T}(\varepsilon)$ is the standard sample deviation of the statistics' numerator that varies with dimension m. The authors of the test show that $\sigma_{m,T}(\varepsilon)$ can be consistently estimated with $V_{m,T}(\varepsilon)$ given by the following expression:

$$V_{m,T}(\varepsilon) = 4 \left[\begin{array}{c} m(m-2)C(\varepsilon)^{2m-2}(K(\varepsilon) - C(\varepsilon)^2) + K(\varepsilon)^m - C(\varepsilon)^{2m} \\ +2\sum_{i=1}^{m-1} \left(C(\varepsilon)^{2i} \left(K(\varepsilon)^{m-i} - C(\varepsilon)^{2m-2i} \right) - mC(\varepsilon)^{2m-2}(K(\varepsilon) - C(\varepsilon)^2) \right) \end{array} \right]^{1/2},$$

where the constants $C(\varepsilon)$ and $K(\varepsilon)$ are

$$C(\varepsilon) = \frac{1}{T^2} \sum_{t=1}^{T} \sum_{s=1}^{T} I_\varepsilon(x_t, x_s), \text{ and}$$

$$K(\varepsilon) = \frac{1}{T^2} \sum_{t=1}^{T} \sum_{s=1}^{T} \sum_{r=1}^{T} I_\varepsilon(x_t, x_s) I_\varepsilon(x_r, x_s),$$

with $I_\varepsilon(x_t, x_s)$ being an indicator function of the event $|x_t - x_s| < \varepsilon$.

---

35   Note that in this test ε does not stand for error and has nothing to do with error. We use the same notation as in the original paper for the sake of consistency.

Under the null hypothesis that x_t are i.i.d., the computed $BDS_{m,T}(\varepsilon)$ statistics have an asymptotically (as $T \to \infty$) standard normal distribution, that is $BDS_{m,T}(\varepsilon) \sim N(0,1)$ as sample size increases substantially. Nevertheless, with finite samples we should use simulated distributions. Brock, Hsieh, and LeBaron (1991) used Monte Carlo simulations (see Appendix A for a description of the procedure) to tabulate the quantiles of the BDS statistics distribution for different values of the proximity parameter ε, embedding dimension m, and sample size T.[36] Their distribution quantiles are simulated particularly for standardized residuals u_t of any $GARCH$-type model. This, of course, limits their use. However, a $GARCH(1,1)$ is the most common conditional heteroskedasticity model to be estimated in practice. The simulated quantiles of the finite sample BDS statistics distribution can be found in the appendix to Brock, Hsieh, and LeBaron (1991). Note that unlike most tests presented throughout this text the BDS test is a two-sided test. We reject the H_0 at the $S\%$ significance level either if the BDS statistics is greater than the appropriate $(100 - S/2)\%$ distribution quantile, or if it is lower than the appropriate $S/2\%$ quantile. The software to run the test can be downloaded as freeware in different formats from the following web addresses:

http://ideas.repec.org/c/boc/bocode/t891501.html,
http://people.brandeis.edu/~blebaron/soft.html.

Some of the software also contains a built-in richer set of critical values than those reported by Brock, Hsieh, and LeBaron (1991).

The $BDS_{m,T}(\varepsilon)$ statistics depends on two arbitrary parameters m and ε. Clearly, the test results can also depend on these two parameters. In practice the test is typically performed for values of m ranging from 2 to 10 and for values of ε equal to a fraction of σ, where σ denotes the sample standard deviation of x_t, that is,

$$\sigma = \sqrt{\frac{1}{T}\sum_{t=1}^{T}(x_t - \bar{x})}, \text{ with } \bar{x} = \frac{1}{T}\sum_{t=1}^{T}x_t .$$

It remains to be noted that a relatively large share of empirical studies uses values of ε equal to σ and $\sigma/2$.[37]

The dependence on the two arbitrary *ex ante* chosen parameters is a disadvantage of the BDS test. It can make the test results ambiguous. It can happen

---

36   BDS critical values vary with the error distribution and the number of observations. Although the BDS statistics converges to a standard normal distribution under H_0, the convergence is very slow and does not occur for "small" samples of, say, 1000 observations or less.

37   The BDS test has been extensively used in the empirical literature. Table 1 in Kočenda and Briatka (2005) contains a list of some empirical studies that over a quarter of a century have employed the BDS test, including the variety of tolerance distances ε.

that for some values of m and ε the null hypothesis is rejected and for some not. This problem was partly solved by Kočenda (2001b) who proposed an alternative testing method that eliminates the arbitrariness in the choice of the proximity parameter ε, leaving unresolved only the question regarding the choice of the embedding dimension m.

3.7.6 AN ALTERNATIVE TO THE *BDS* TEST: INTEGRATION ACROSS THE CORRELATION INTEGRAL

While the *BDS* statistics is easy to compute, it suffers from an obvious drawback: the values of two parameters – the proximity parameter ε (also referred to as the tolerance distance or metric bound) and the embedding dimension m – must be determined *ex ante*.[38] Further, the *BDS* statistics, when used for testing, has often been evaluated for only few values of the proximity parameter ε. This was brought about, in part, by the Monte Carlo studies of Hsieh and LeBaron (1993) who tested the asymptotic normality of the statistics for three values of the parameter, and tabulated the corresponding critical values.

The alternative test of Kočenda (2001b) suggests considering an *OLS*-estimate of the correlation dimension (defined presently) over a range of ε-values, and is thus closer in spirit to the original correlation dimension than the *BDS* test (for full details see the original paper).[39] The test rests upon the concept of the correlation integral developed by Grassberger and Procaccia (1983). Formally, let $\{x_t\}$ be a scalar time series of size T generated randomly according to a density function f. First, form m-dimensional vectors, called m-histories, $x_t^m = (x_t, x_{t+1}, ..., x_{t+m-1})$. Then, the sample correlation integral (or correlation sum) at embedding dimension m is computed as

$$C_{m,T}(\varepsilon) = 2\sum_{t=1}^{T_{m-1}} \sum_{s=t+1}^{T_m} I_\varepsilon(x_t^m, x_s^m) / (T_m(T_m - 1)),\qquad(3.47)$$

where $T_m = T - m + 1$ and $I_\varepsilon(x_t^m, x_s^m)$ is the indicator of the event $\left\| x_t^m - x_s^m \right\| = \max_{i=0,1...,m-1} \left| x_{t+i} - x_{s+i} \right| < \varepsilon$. Further, the correlation integral at embedding dimension m is defined as

$$C_m(\varepsilon) = \lim_{T \to \infty} C_{m,T}(\varepsilon).\qquad(3.48)$$

---

38 Some guidance can be found in Dechert (1994), Brock et al. (1996), and Hsieh and LeBaron (1993). Again, note that in this text ε does not stand for error and has nothing to do with error.

39 It is worthwhile to note that originally an important reason to develop the *BDS* test was that point estimates of the correlation dimension were very unstable across values of ε.

Thus, the sample correlation integral measures the fraction of pairs that lie within the tolerance distance ε for the particular embedding dimension m. If, in the limit of large T and small ε, the correlation integral scales as ε^D, then the exponent D defines the correlation dimension as

$$D = \lim_{\varepsilon \to 0} \lim_{T \to \infty} \frac{\ln C_{m,T}(\varepsilon)}{\ln \varepsilon}. \tag{3.49}$$

The alternative statistics uses a number of tolerance distances chosen from a specific range for each particular embedding dimension by calculating the slope of the log of the correlation integral versus the log of the proximity parameter over a broad range of values of the proximity parameter. The graphical expression of the above idea is captured by Figure 3.4.

Figure 3.4 Slopes of coefficients β.

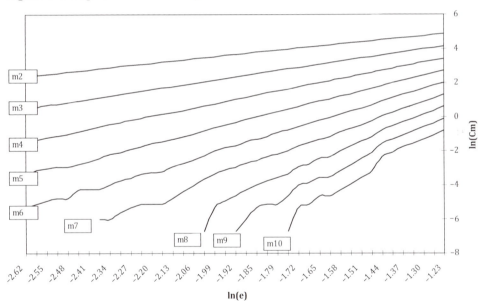

The estimates of the correlation dimension, or slope coefficients β_m, can be estimated as

$$\beta_m = \frac{\sum_\varepsilon \left(\ln \varepsilon - \overline{\ln \varepsilon}\right) \cdot \left(\ln C_{m,T}(\varepsilon) - \overline{\ln C_{m,T}(\varepsilon)}\right)}{\sum_\varepsilon \left(\ln \varepsilon - \overline{\ln \varepsilon}\right)^2}, \tag{3.50}$$

which equals calculating the slope coefficient β_m from the least squares regression

$$\ln C_{m,T}(\varepsilon_i) = \alpha_m + \beta_m \ln \varepsilon_i + u_i \,;\; i = 1,...,n \,, \tag{3.51}$$

where $\ln \varepsilon$ is the logarithm of the proximity parameter (the tolerance distance), $\ln C_{m,T}(\varepsilon)$ is the logarithm of the sample correlation integral (the correlation sum), m is the embedding dimension, and the variables with a bar denote the mean of their counterparts without a bar.[40]

Since a range of different tolerance distances ε is used the slope coefficients β_m do not depend on an arbitrary choice of ε. When computing the slope coefficient estimates of β_m, a cut-off point was set to eliminate the erratic portion of the trajectories at the highest embedding dimensions, m (7–10); see Figure 3.4. The use of a cut-off point effectively guarantees that the curve constructed from successive correlation dimensions over a given ε-range contains only a linear part and the erratic part is left out. Further, this approach means that the proximity parameters ε (used when particular estimates of the β_m coefficients are calculated) are in the range where the "scaling property" holds, e.g. $C_m(\varepsilon) \to \varepsilon^\alpha$ for some α; thus proximity parameters ε are in the "scaling region" (see Theiler and Lookman, 1993 and Diks, 2004 for details). Such a cut-off point does not affect the analysis for lower embedding dimensions m, but considerably reduces the increasing variance as the embedding dimension m grows larger and the tolerance distance ε becomes smaller ($\varepsilon \to 0$). The cut-off point represents the number of matches that maximizes the power of the test or, implicitly, minimizes error of the second kind.[41]

As for the choice of the embedding dimension m, a range of empirically endorsed dimensions m is used, which gives enough variety to capture a more complex dimensional structure without eliminating unexplored opportunities. One theoretical feature of the slope coefficients β_m is that under the null hypothesis that the data are i.i.d., these slopes should equal the respective embedding dimension m at which the statistics is calculated (i.e. $\beta_m = m$).[42] However, in reality slope coefficient estimates are smaller than the respective embedding dimension m, i.e. $\beta_m \leq m$.[43]

---

40 As β_m is, in fact, an OLS estimate of the slope coefficient, by econometric tradition it should be labeled as $\hat{\beta}_m$. For the sake of notational simplicity, we decide to omit the hat.

41 By simulation it was found that such a number lies in the interval between 40 to 50. To be on the safe side, the value of the correlation integral was constrained to 50. The "cut-off" value for $C_m(\varepsilon)$ must be chosen before slope coefficient estimates are computed. $C_m(\varepsilon) = 50$ resulted from simulations that were compared with various trajectories resulting from the analysis conducted on different time series.

42 See Hsieh (1991) for details.

43 For details see Kočenda (2001b).

Kočenda (2001b) performed a Monte Carlo study with 10,000 replications of the distribution of the β_m statistics under the null hypothesis of i.i.d. data.[44] Critical values were tabulated for data lengths of 500, 1000, and 2500 observations allowing for nine embedding dimensions: m (2–10). The range of the proximity parameter ε, for which the critical values were generated, extends over the specific interval of $n = 41$ proximity parameters ε ranging over the interval $(0.25\sigma, 1.00\sigma)$ in proportionally equal increments, with σ being the standard deviation of a sample.

The above original interval is chosen sensibly to allow for hidden patterns corresponding to very narrow tolerance distances. However, a single ε-range prevents observing whether and how sensitive the tabulated critical values are to a choice of a different ε-range. Further, the originally chosen ε-range does not need to be an optimal range; e.g. the range that, when used, maximizes the power of the test. The issue of the ε-range choice is complicated by the fact that we cannot theoretically derive a correct range of proximity parameters. This is due to the fact that the behavior of the β_m statistics within an ε-range is closely related to the composition of the analyzed data. Therefore, it is possible that one ε-range is more appropriate for some kinds of data and a different ε-range for others.

Kočenda and Briatka (2005) improved on the range selection and hence the operational ability of the procedure. They improved the choice of the range of the proximity parameter ε over which the correlation integral is calculated, tabulated new sets of critical values for various lengths of data, and provided a sensitivity check of the robustness of critical values with respect to the choice of the range of proximity parameters. A series of power tests was performed, resulting in a suggestion for the range that maximizes the power of the test. Unless assumptions of a particular research project dictate otherwise, the interval $(0.60\sigma, 1.90\sigma)$ for the ε-range choice should be used as a template option. Quantiles for the slope coefficient estimates β_m at different dimensional levels are given in Table 7 in Appendix B to allow hypothesis testing at levels of 1%, 2%, 5%, and 10% for time series of 500, 1000, and 2500 observations for the above optimal ε-range $(0.60\sigma, 1.90\sigma)$. Let L_α and U_α be lower and upper bounds of the $(100 - \alpha)$ percentage confidence interval. If $\left[x < L_\alpha \cup x > U_\alpha \right]$, then the null hypothesis of i.i.d. can be rejected at the α percent confidence level.[45] The

---

44 A compound random number generator based on Collings (1987) and constructed from 17 generators described by Fishman and Moore (1982) was employed to generate i.i.d. data.

45 Briatka (2006) builds on the test of Kočenda (2001b) and via Monte Carlo studies shows that non-normality of the data leads to an over-rejection of the null hypothesis. The reason is twofold: first, the data are not i.i.d., and second, the data are non-normal. It is suggested to employ bootstrapped critical values for a time series with a skewness coefficient greater than 0.5 in absolute value and the coefficient of kurtosis greater than 4. It is shown that by using the bootstrap and the optimal interval suggested by Kočenda and Briatka (2005), the power of the test increases significantly for data that do not look normally distributed although they still may be i.i.d.

software to run the test can be downloaded as freeware from http://home. cerge-ei.cz/kocenda/software.htm.

3.7.7 IDENTIFICATION AND ESTIMATION OF A *GARCH* MODEL

So far we have presented the basic theory and tools used in the estimation of *ARCH* and *GARCH* models. In this section, we will summarize the ideas present- ed above into an algorithm that should lead us through the estimation of *ARCH* and *GARCH* models. When we intend to estimate an *ARMA – GARCH* model of a time series $\{y_t\}_{t=1}^{T}$, then we should proceed in the following steps:

1. *ARMA estimation*
First, we estimate the most appropriate *ARMA(P,Q)* model of the time series $\{y_t\}_{t=1}^{T}$ using the *Box-Jenkins methodology* described in section 3.1. The mean equation can be specified simply as a general ARMA structure or may also contain other variables. Such inclusion should be based on a sound theory, though. Frequently, dummies are included in the mean equation specification. Such dummies are to capture, for example, a day-of-the-week or holiday effect, features empirically shown to exist on financial markets. In this specification, a dummy variable should be included for each business day and coded 1 at this day and zero otherwise. Further, the number of banking holidays or number of days when a market is closed should be included to capture a holiday effect; in this case Saturday or Sunday do not count as candidates for dummies since on these days the trading or services are suspended on a regular basis and markets *do* expect this. For more detail on such applications see the empirical examples given at the end of the section.

2. *GARCH detection*
Second, we test the squared residuals e_t^2 of the *ARMA(P,Q)* model for the pres- ence of conditional heteroskedasticity. We can apply the *Ljung-Box Q-test* (see Ljung and Box, 1978) or the *LM* test proposed by Engle (1982), both described in the previous section. Both of these tests must be applied on the squared residuals e_t^2. Rejecting the null hypothesis of the *Ljung-Box Q-test* means that the errors follow an *ARCH* or *GARCH* process. Rejecting the null hypothesis of the *LM* test proposed by Engle means formally that the errors follow an *ARCH* process only. Nevertheless, the test has power also against *GARCH* alternatives. Eventually, we can also test the residuals e_t (not squared!) using the *BDS* or Kočenda tests. Rejecting the null hypothesis here means that the residuals e_t are not i.i.d. which indicates a model misspecification that can be, among oth- ers, caused by the presence of conditional heteroskedasticity. To detect con- ditional heteroskedasticity in a less formal way we can also use pure visual

inspection of the sample *ACF* and *PACF* of the squared residuals e_t^2. If these indicate an *ARMA* model, then we should consider the presence of conditional heteroskedasticity. Nevertheless, the formal test results should be preferred.

3. GARCH identification

Third, we identify the orders of the *GARCH(p,q)* process. This step is the most problematic and in most cases is done in accordance with steps 4 and 5 explained below. Theoretically, we could use visual inspection of the sample *ACF* and *PACF* of the squared residuals e_t^2 here. If these indicate an *ARMA(m,q)* model, then the residuals should follow a *GARCH(p,q)* process with $m = \max(q,p)$. In most cases however, the identification with the sample *ACF* and *PACF* will not be so straightforward. Therefore, we must experiment with different orders p and q of the *GARCH* process, estimate the whole *ARMA(P,Q) – GARCH(p,q)* model, and then check the significance of the estimated coefficients and diagnose the standardized residuals u_t as described later in step 5. The information criteria and values of the Durbin-Watson statistics are also helpful to determine the best model specification. In practice such selection is not so cumbersome as it looks. Fortunately, in most cases the relevant *GARCH* processes will be of low orders.

4. ARMA – GARCH estimation

Once we have detected the presence of conditional heteroskedasticity and chosen the orders p an q of the *GARCH* process, we estimate the whole *ARMA(P,Q) – GARCH(p,q)* model using *MLE*. There are various likelihood specifications that are used for estimation and their choice is subject to the research goal and preferences. One of the specifications is that suggested by Bollerslev (1986) to estimate the model by using a log-likelihood function of the form

$$\ln L_t = -0.5(\ln(2\pi\sigma_t^2) + \sum_{t=t_0}^{T} \varepsilon_t^2 / \sigma_t^2)$$. Optimization methods applied on the *MLE*

estimation differ as well. Most software packages contain routines that enable a convenient estimation of *ARCH*-type models. The two most frequently used optimization methods are due to Bernd, Hall, Hall, and Hausman (1974) and Marquardt (1963).[46]

As a further step we must check the significance of the estimated coefficients and also the magnitude of the *GARCH(p,q)* coefficients that must satisfy the restrictions described in section 3.7.3. If some coefficients appear to be insignificant or if the *GARCH(p,q)* coefficients violate the restrictions, we should consider a different *ARMA(P,Q) – GARCH(p,q)*. Note that the inclusion of a *GARCH(p,q)* process in the model can also make some of the original *ARMA(P,Q)* coefficients

---

46   The former method (BHHH) allows for finer steps during the optimization process, e.g. an increased
      number of sub-iterations within each of the sequence of iterations the optimization process consists of.

insignificant. In fact, it is the presence of conditional heteroskedasticity we did not control for that could have led to misspecification (in most cases overpa-rameterization) of the original simple $ARMA(P,Q)$ model.

In order to avoid the risk of overestimating volatility we should not impose the i.i.d. normal distribution condition on the errors as is the case in many earli-er studies. Rather, we should allow for the generalized error distribution (GED) of Nelson (1991). The reason is that a conditional volatility series derived from the data is very likely to follow a leptokurtic data distribution (as reflected by an actual GED parameter considerably lower than 2, which is the value in the case of a normal distribution). Leptokurtosis of a high-frequency data volatility implies that it tends to concentrate around the mean during tranquil market periods, while the shocks to volatility are very large during turbulent times.

5. *Diagnostics of standardized residuals*

When we have passed successfully through the previous four steps and esti-mated an $ARMA(P,Q) - GARCH(p,q)$ model, we must diagnose the standardized residuals u_t, defined as $u_t = e_t / \sqrt{h_t}$; e_t is a series of residuals from the mean equation and h_t is the estimated conditional variance. If the estimated model is the correct one, then standardized residuals u_t should no longer be condition-ally heteroskedastic and, even more strictly, they should be i.i.d.. To diagnose the standardized residuals u_t, we can use the tools described in the previous sections. Namely, we can apply the Ljung-Box test against simple or higher or-der serial correlation or more strict tests such as the *BDS* and Kočenda tests. Rejecting the null hypothesis of those tests indicates that u_t are not i.i.d. In such a case we should go back to steps 3 and 4 and consider a different $ARMA(P,Q) - GARCH(p,q)$ model. We can consider changes in both the orders P and Q of the $ARMA(P,Q)$ process and the orders p and q of the $GARCH(p,q)$ process. Particu-larly, if we have estimated just an $ARMA - ARCH(p)$ model, then we can perform the *LM* test proposed by Bollerslev (1986). Rejecting the null hypothesis of this test means that we should consider an $ARMA - GARCH(p,q), q > 0$ model instead of the simpler $ARMA - ARCH(p)$ model.

The following examples taken from the empirical literature illustrate applica-tions of the *ARCH*-type models on various financial data. Kočenda (1996) ana-lyzed the volatility of exchange rates (Czech koruna under a currency basket peg arrangement) by employing a $GARCH(1,1)$ model on the exchange rate daily returns (r_t). An autoregressive process was chosen as a proxy to model an underlying process in the data. The *AIC* was used to determine the appro-priate number of lags. An $AR(10)$ structure was found to be an efficient way to filter the data so that the model yielded residuals free of autocorrelation and seasonality. To capture plausible changes of the distribution in different days during a business week, appropriate day-of-the-week dummy variables were

employed in mean and variance equations. The specification of the model resulted in the mean equation

$$r_t = a_0 + \sum_{i=1}^{10} a_i r_{t-i} + \gamma_1 d_{MO,t} + \gamma_2 d_{TU,t} + \gamma_3 d_{WE,t} + \gamma_4 d_{TH,t} + \gamma_5 d_{HO,t} + \varepsilon_t \, ,$$

where $\varepsilon_t | \Omega_{t-1} \sim D(0, h_t)$, and the variance equation

$$h_t = \omega + \alpha \varepsilon_{t-1}^2 + \beta h_{t-1} + \phi_1 d_{MO,t} + \phi_2 d_{TU,t} + \phi_3 d_{WE,t} + \phi_4 d_{TH,t} + \phi_5 d_{HO,t} \, ,$$

where $d_{MO,t}$, $d_{TU,t}$, $d_{WE,t}$, and $d_{TH,t}$ are dummy variables for Monday, Tuesday,
Wednesday, and Thursday, respectively, and $d_{MO,t}$ is the number of holidays
(specifically excluding weekends) between successive business days. The estimation of the model is performed by using a log-likelihood function of the
form $L = (-0.5 \ln h_t - 0.5\ \varepsilon_t^2 / h_t)$. The maximum likelihood estimates are obtained by using the numerical optimization algorithm described by Berndt et
al. (1974). The overall fit of the model is assessed by diagnostic tests on standardized residuals u_t constructed in the usual way. Diagnostic tests show that
the GARCH(1,1) model is capable of accounting for most of the non-linearity in
the particular exchange rate. Further, it was shown that under a well-managed
currency basket peg regime, exchange rate volatility mimics behavior that is
usually found under the floating exchange rate regime.

As stated earlier, GARCH-type models are a very useful tool in analyzing stock
market behavior. As the stock markets in the European emerging markets have
developed relatively recently the literature targeted on their analysis is less widespread. One of the examples is Vošvrda and Žikeš (2004), who analyze the time-
series and distributional properties of Central European stock market returns.
The behavior of the volatility of index returns over time is studied using the
GARCH-t model over the period 1996–2002 and alternatively also with threshold
ARCH and GARCH-in-mean specifications (see section 3.7.8 where these models
are described); the Student's t-distribution is employed to better account for excess kurtosis in stock returns. The BDS test is employed to assess the ability of
the estimated GARCH-t model to capture all non-linearities in stock returns (see
section 3.7.5 for the BDS test). The empirical findings reveal that the Czech and
Hungarian stock market indices are predictable from the time series of historical
prices, whereas the Polish stock index is not; none of the indices follow a random
walk, though. The returns on all three indices are conditionally heteroskedastic
and non-normal. The findings are also important in that they show a violation of
crucial assumptions for rational option pricing at these markets.[47]

---

47   Žikeš and Bubák (2006a) employ a periodic autoregressive GARCH model on the same set of markets
     to study seasonality and non-trading effects. For other applications of the ARCH/GARCH-type model on
     Czech and Estonian data see Hsing (2004, 2005).

Another example of using the standard *GARCH* framework on stock markets data from transition and post-transition countries include Rockinger and Urga (2001), who present an extension of the Bekaert and Harvey (1997) model, allowing for latent factors, time varying parameters and a general *GARCH* structure for the residuals. Using this framework they test if an emerging stock market becomes more efficient and more integrated with other already-established markets over time. When applying this model on the data from the Czech, Polish, Hungarian, and Russian stock markets, results show that these markets have a rather heterogeneous pattern with regard to seasonalities and exhibit significant asymmetric *GARCH* effects where bad news generates greater volatility. In a similar spirit are the findings of Hayo and Kutan (2005) who use a standard *GARCH*(1,1) framework to analyze the impact of news, oil prices and international financial market developments on daily returns on Russian bond and stock markets.

A different application of the *GARCH* framework is provided in Geršl (2005) and Geršl and Holub (2006), which analyzed the effectiveness of foreign-exchange interventions by the Czech National Bank in 2001–2002. Exchange rate volatility is derived via a *GARCH* model in which both mean and volatility equations include volumes of foreign-exchange interventions. The results indicate that the interventions by the central bank had only a minor and short term effect on the exchange rate and to some extent contributed to increased conditional and implied volatility. Another example of how the basic *GARCH* model can be augmented by parameters of interest is provided in Hanousek and Kočenda (2011b), which studies the impact of the four classes of Eurozone and U.S. macroeconomic announcements on stock prices in Central European stock markets; they also jointly model the volatility of the returns accounting for intra-day movements as well as day-of-the-week effects. It is shown that the announcements are not immediately absorbed by the market as they are not reflected instantaneously in prices; this is evidence of market inefficiency. Announcements originating in the Eurozone exhibit more effects than U.S. news. In terms of specific news, the EU current account, consumer confidence, and the purchasing managers index (PMI) affect all three markets while U.S. prices are the only other news of similar caliber. Finally, Égert and Kočenda (2014) analyze the impact of macroeconomic news and central bank communication on the exchange rates in Central Europe and show that currencies react to macroeconomic news during both pre-crisis (2004–2007) and crisis (2008–2009) periods in an intuitive manner that corresponds to exchange rate-related theories.

3.7.8 EXTENSIONS OF *ARCH* -TYPE MODELS

The great popularity and extensive application of *ARCH* and *GARCH* models gave rise to a large number of extensions and modifications. The sheer volume of these extensions allows discussing but a few of them. The majority of the advances in *ARCH* extensions occurred in the late 1980s and early 1990s, and these extensions as well as their applications are covered in surveys by Bollerslev, Chou, and Kroner (1992), Bera and Higgins (1993), Bollerslev, Engle, and Nelson (1994), and Boller-slev (2001). Some of these extensions will be listed very briefly in this section.

1. *Integrated GARCH (IGARCH)* and *Cointegrated GARCH (CIGARCH)*
Research on high-frequency financial and monetary data frequently concerns the presence of an approximate unit root in the estimated autoregressive poly-nomial for the conditional variance. To account for such a feature in modeling risk and uncertainty, the *IGARCH* model was presented by Engle and Bollerslev (1986). The specification allows for the presence of unit roots in the condition-al variance equation. Therefore, in an *IGARCH* model shocks to conditional vari-ance are highly persistent, which means that current information remains im-portant for forecasts in all future horizons. In the case of a simple *IGARCH*(1,1) the conditional variance h_t can be written as

$$h_t = E_{t-1}[\varepsilon_t^2] = \alpha_1 \varepsilon_{t-1}^2 + (1-\alpha_1)h_{t-1}.$$

Recall that in the case of a *GARCH*(1,1) model the conditional variance h_t is

$$h_t = E_{t-1}[\varepsilon_t^2] = \alpha_0 + \alpha_1 \varepsilon_{t-i}^2 + \beta_1 h_{t-i}.$$

Thus, an *IGARCH*(1,1) model is equivalent to a *GARCH*(1,1) model with $\alpha_0 = 0$ and $\alpha_1 + \beta_1 = 1$. It is the condition $\alpha_1 + \beta_1 = 1$ that allows for the shocks to have a permanent effect on conditional variance.

The idea of the *IGARCH* model can be extended to the multivariate frame-work. In chapter 4 we will deal with multivariate techniques in more detail, but for now we will very briefly introduce the idea of cointegration (see section 4.3 for details). If two nonstationary time series share a common long-run equilib-rium relationship, then their linear combination becomes a stationary series. In this spirit many time series may exhibit a persistence in variance, as captured by *IGARCH*, but some of them are likely to share the same long-run component. Under the occurrence of the common long-term component the variables are defined to be co-persistent in variance. The linear combination of such co-persistence can be interpreted as a long-run relationship and in this sense it is parallel to the linear combination in mean that characterizes cointegrated vari-ables. Following this line of reasoning Bollerslev and Engle (1993) proposed the cointegrated *GARCH* model (*CIGARCH*). This approach has strong implications for financial analysis since on financial markets the volatilities of many vari-ables move together. This feature is important, for example, for the pricing of portfolios, since these are combinations of assets, or for exchange rate analysis.

2. Exponential GARCH (EGARCH)

EGARCH models were proposed by Nelson (1990, 1991) and Pagan and Schwert (1990). The motivation was to develop a model in which the conditional variance h_t responds asymmetrically to positive and negative innovations. This property might be particularly useful for asset price applications. It was empirically observed that changes in stock return volatility are negatively correlated with the returns themselves. This means that the volatility tends to rise when returns are lower than expected, and to fall when returns are higher than expected. In order to model such an asymmetric reaction the conditional variance of a simple EGARCH(1,1) model is assumed to follow the equation

$$\ln h_t = \alpha_0 + \beta_1 \ln h_{t-1} + \alpha_1 (\theta u_{t-1} + (|u_{t-1}| - (2/\pi)^{1\,2})), \text{ where } u_t = \frac{e_t}{\sqrt{h_t}}.$$

Syriopoulos (2006) adopted the EGARCH model to investigate the dynamic linkages and effects of time-varying volatilities for major emerging Central European and developed stock markets (Germany and the USA). His results from the estimation of an asymmetric EGARCH model indicate varying but persistent volatility effects for the CE markets. The results, combined with those obtained from the error correction vector autoregressive model (see section 4.3), have strong implications for the effectiveness and limits of international portfolio diversification. Further, Yalcin and Yucel (2006) used an EGARCH-type model to detect limited day-of-the-week effects on stock market volatility and returns across twenty emerging markets.

3. GJR and Threshold GARCH models

From a similar perspective as the EGARCH model but in a different manner, the GRJ (Glosten, Jagannathan, and Runkle, 1993) and threshold (Zakoian, 1994) GARCH models also deals with the asymmetric issue. A standard GARCH specification implies a symmetric impact of innovations on volatility. Whether innovation ε_{t-1}^2 is positive or negative makes no difference on the expected variance in the ensuing period. Only the size of the innovation matters – simply speaking, good news and bad news have the same effect. The issue of asymmetry is addressed in both models where the conditional variance equation is modified to account for asymmetries in the conditional variance.

In addition to the standard ARCH and GARCH terms, the simple GRJ-GARCH (1,1) model includes a dummy term S_t that takes a value of 1 if $\varepsilon_{t-1} < 0$ (negative shock) and a value of 0 if $\varepsilon_{t-1} > 0$ (positive shock) in the variance equation

$$h_t = \alpha_0 + \alpha_1 \varepsilon_{t-1}^2 + \beta_1 h_{t-1} + \lambda \varepsilon_{t-1}^2 S_{t-1}.$$

The *GRJ-GARCH* model is also known as the *Leverage effect GARCH* model (*GARCH – L*) introduced by Glosten, Jagannathan, and Runkle (1993). The asymmetric term $\lambda \varepsilon_{t-1}^2 S_{t-1}$ measures and accounts for the effect of the difference between good and bad news. The value of the statistically significant leverage coefficient λ indicates the magnitude of the leverage effect, and the sign its direction. A positive value of coefficient λ indicates an increase – and a negative coefficient a decrease – in the subsequent volatility of a given time series. The *GRJ-GARCH* specification of volatility with leverage effect was applied to exchange rates in the transition context by Kočenda (1998) and Orlowski (2003). In the case of the exchange rate, the leverage effect represents the fact that a decrease in the price of a foreign currency in terms of a domestic currency, or a domestic currency's appreciation, would tend to increase the subsequent volatility of the domestic currency more than would a depreciation of equal magnitude.

Threshold *GARCH* (*TGARCH*) model of Zakoian (1994) also distinguishes negative and positive parts of the errors (or noise) as the *GRJ-GARCH* but it differs from other class of GARCH models in that it specifies conditional standard deviation rather than conditional variance. Hence, the *T-GARCH* process is written in a general form as:

$$\varepsilon_t = \sigma_t Z_t \text{ and } \sigma_t = \alpha_0 + \sum_{i=1}^p \alpha_i^+ \varepsilon_{t-i}^+ - \alpha_i^- \varepsilon_{t-i}^- + \sum_{j=1}^q \beta_j \sigma_{t-j},$$

where ε_t, is real valued discrete-time process, $\varepsilon_{t-1} = (\varepsilon_{t-1}, \varepsilon_{t-2}, ...)$ is the information set (σ-field) of all information through time t, Z_t is an i.i.d. (0,1) process independent of the ε_{t-1} for all t, $\varepsilon_t^+ = \max(\varepsilon_t, 0)$ and $\varepsilon_t^- = \min(\varepsilon_t, 0)$ are the positive and negative parts of errors ε_t, and $(\alpha_i^+)_{i=1,p}$, $(\alpha_i^-)_{i=1,p}$, and $(\beta_j)_{j=1,q}$ are real scalar sequences. Due to its set-up the conditional standard deviation of the *TGARCH*, defined above, is driven by linear combinations of past positive and negative components of the error process as well as past conditional standard deviations.

4. ARCH/GARCH in mean (ARCH – M, GARCH – M)

In the *ARCH – M* model proposed by Engle, Lilien, and Robbins (1987) the mean of a time series is allowed to depend on its own conditional variance. The motivation rests again in the domain of finance, particularly in attempts to model asset returns. According to the theory of optimal portfolio choice the mean of a risky asset return should depend on its variance. A simple *AR(1) – ARCH(1) – M* model can be written as

$$y_t = a_0 + a_1 y_{t-1} + \delta h_t + \varepsilon_t,$$

$$h_t = E_{t-1}[\varepsilon_t^2] = \alpha_0 + \alpha_1 \varepsilon_{t-i}^2.$$

An *ARMA – GARCH* generalization of this simple model is also possible.

A variation of this extension is a *GARCH in mean* model (*GARCH-M*) which also allows for the path dependence of the variance on the mean equation. Kočenda and Valachy (2006) combined *GARCH-M* with a threshold component and adopted the *TGARCH-M-GED* specification to analyze exchange rate volatility under different exchange rate arrangements. The volatility issue is approached in the spirit of the excess volatility debate, i.e. whether and to what extent the volatility of exchange rates exceeds the volatility of underlying fundamentals (interest rates in this case).[48] The model takes the following form:

$$\Delta s_t = a_0 + \sum_{i=1}^{k} a_i \Delta s_{t-i} + b \ln \sigma_t^2 + \lambda \cdot SD_t + \varepsilon_t; \ \varepsilon_t \sim N(0, \sigma_t^2)$$

with

$$\sigma_t^2 = \omega + \sum_{i=1}^{p} \alpha_i \varepsilon_{t-i}^2 + \sum_{j=1}^{q} \beta_j \sigma_{t-j}^2 + \xi d_{t-1} \varepsilon_{t-1}^2 + \delta_1 (i_t - i_t^*)^2 + \delta_2 (\Delta(i_t - i_t^*))^2,$$

where Δs_t is the difference of the log of the exchange rate between time t and $t-1$ (exchange rate change over two consecutive trading days), and k is the number of lags chosen by the Schwarz-Bayesian lag selection criterion, as is the number of lags p and q; the log of the conditional variance in the mean equation ($\ln \sigma_t^2$) allows for an exponential rather than quadratic effect of observed volatility. The leverage effect dummy variable (*TARCH* term) d_{t-1} is equal to 1 if $\varepsilon_{t-1} < 0$ (negative shock or good news) and 0 otherwise (positive shock or bad news); $(i_t - i_t^*)$ and $(\Delta(i_t - i_t^*))$ are the annualized interest rate differential and the change in interest rate differential, respectively. The shock dummy (SD_t) in the mean equation accounts for a few infrequent outliers of currencies' appreciation and depreciation movements that are associated with specific events (e.g. the resignation of a minister) rather than with regular market developments. The overall findings are that volatility path dependence has a limited effect on exchange rate developments and the introduction of floating regimes tends to increase exchange rate volatility. The markedly lower volatility during a tight regime and higher overall volatility under the flexible regime are illustrated in Figure 3.5. Further, an asymmetric news effect tends to decrease volatility under the float. Interest differential impacts exchange rate volatility under either regime, while an interest differential intertemporal effect is not found.

---

48   In a similar manner, Poghosyan, Kočenda, and Zemčík (2008) include foreign-exchange risk factors (central bank interventions and total volume of deposits) in the conditional variance equation to test the impact of these factors on the volatility and risk premium of the Armenia *dram*. Further, Hanousek, Kočenda, and Kutan (2009) include single versus multiple macroeconomic news into a mean equation to study the impact on stock prices and also include a conditional variance in the mean equation to analyze the stock returns from the path-dependency perspective.

Figure 3.5: Conditional volatility of an exchange rate under tight and flexible exchange rate regimes.

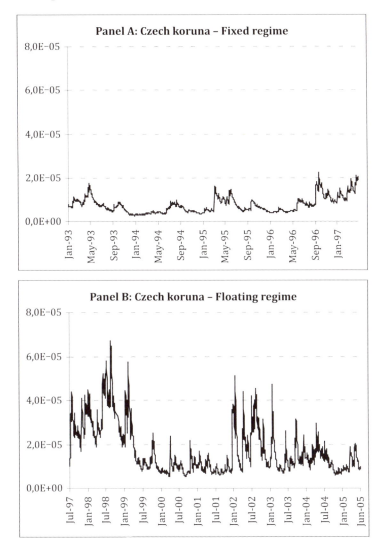

5. *Switching regime ARCH (SWARCH)*

Autoregressive conditional heteroskedasticity models often attribute a lot of persistence to the volatility of financial variables and yet give relatively poor forecasts. A reasonable argument for these deficiencies is the potential existence of structural changes in *ARCH* processes. It is speculated that extremely large shocks (e.g. a stock exchange crash) arise from quite different causes and have different consequences for the subsequent volatility than do small shocks (e.g. the release of a quarterly report on a company's profits that are significantly below market expectations). Hamilton and Susmel (1994) designed a switching regime *ARCH* (*SWARCH*) model to account for such phenomena.[49] They suggest modeling the residuals ε_t from the mean equation ($y_t = \alpha + \phi y_{t-1} + \varepsilon_t$) as

$$\varepsilon_t = \sqrt{g_{s_t}} \times \tilde{\varepsilon}_t,$$

where g_s is a regime specific constant, and $\tilde{\varepsilon}_t$ is assumed to follow a standard leverage *ARCH* process (*ARCH-L(q)*) of

$$\tilde{\varepsilon}_t = h_t \cdot v_t,$$

with v_t a zero mean and unit variance i.i.d. sequence. Conditional variance h_t is specified as

$$h_t = a_0 + a_1 \tilde{\varepsilon}_{t-1}^2 + a_2 \tilde{\varepsilon}_{t-2}^2 + \cdots + a_q \tilde{\varepsilon}_{t-q}^2 + \xi d_{t-1} \tilde{\varepsilon}_{t-1}^2,$$

where d_{t-1} = 1 if $\tilde{\varepsilon}_{t-1} \leq 0$ and d_{t-1} = 0 if $\tilde{\varepsilon}_{t-1} > 0$. To account for different regimes of volatility (low, high, etc.) the underlying *ARCH-L(q)* variable $\tilde{\varepsilon}_t$ is then multiplied by the constant $\sqrt{g_1}$ when the process is in the regime represented by s_t = 1, multiplied by $\sqrt{g_2}$ when the process is in the regime represented by s_t = 2, etc. The factor for the first state g_1 is normalized at unity with $g_j \geq 1$ for j = 2, 3,..., K. The purpose is to model changes in regimes as changes in the magnitude of the process. Conditional on knowing the current and past regimes, the variance implied for the residuals u_t is specified as

$$E(\varepsilon_t^2 | s_t, s_{t-1}, ..., s_{t-q}, \varepsilon_{t-1}, \varepsilon_{t-2}, ..., \varepsilon_{t-q})$$

$$= g_{s_t} \{a_0 + a_1 (\varepsilon_{t-1}^2 / g_{s_{t-1}}) + a_2 (\varepsilon_{t-2}^2 / g_{s_{t-2}}) + \cdots + a_q (\varepsilon_{t-q}^2 / g_{s_{t-q}}) + \xi d_{t-1} (\varepsilon_{t-1}^2 / g_{s_{t-1}})\}$$

$$\equiv \sigma_t^2 (s_t, s_{t-1}, ..., s_{t-q}),$$

whereas in the previous case d_{t-1} = 1 if $\varepsilon_{t-1} \leq 0$ and d_{t-1} = 0 if $\varepsilon_{t-1} > 0$. If the leverage effect is absent (ξ = 0) then the residuals ε_t follow a K-state, q-t-order Markov-switching *ARCH* process that is denoted as $\varepsilon_t \sim$ *SWARCH(K, q)*. If the leverage effect is present ($\xi \neq 0$) then the residuals ε_t follow a K-state, q-t-order Markov-switching leverage *ARCH* process that is denoted as $\varepsilon_t \sim$ *SWARCH-L(K, q)*.

Hamilton and Susmel (1994) applied their specification to U.S. weekly stock returns, allowing the parameters of an autoregressive conditional het-

---

49   The Markov switching-regime *ARCH* model was independently introduced by Cai (1994).

eroskedasticity process to come from one of several different regimes, with transitions between regimes governed by an unobserved Markov chain. They estimate models with two to four regimes in which the latent innovations come from Gaussian and Student t distributions.

6. Component GARCH (CGARCH) model

The *CGARCH* model was introduced by Engle and Lee (1999) and it distinguishes between short-term and long-term conditional volatility. The model contains a long-term volatility component (q_t) while the short-term volatility component $(\sigma_t^2 - q_t)$ captures the transitory effect from a variance innovation. A mean equation is specified in the standard manner and the short-term conditional variance model is specified as

$$\sigma_t^2 - q_t = \overline{\omega} + \alpha \cdot (\varepsilon_{t-1}^2 - \overline{\omega}) + \beta \cdot (\sigma_{t-1}^2 - \overline{\omega}).$$

The time-varying long-term volatility converges to ω with ρ as in

$$q_t = \omega + \rho \cdot (q_{t-1} - \omega) + \delta \cdot (\varepsilon_{t-1}^2 - \sigma_{t-1}^2).$$

CGARCH makes it possible to model separately for example the effect of interventions on exchange rate volatility in the short and long run or the long run volatility of currency bond futures, etc. Using high-frequency intra-day data Égert and Kočenda (2007) applied the *CGARCH* model to analyze spillovers affecting returns and volatility among various European stock markets. A limited number of short-term relationships between the stock markets was found but in general spillover effects were found to be stronger in the direction from volatility to volatility than from return to return series.

3.7.9 MULTIVARIATE (G)ARCH MODELS

Aside from the above-mentioned modifications of *ARCH* and *GARCH* models many others exist that are beyond the scope of this text. One branch that extends *ARCH* models cover its multivariate extensions. Bauwens, Laurent, and Rombouts (2006) survey the most important developments in multivariate *ARCH*-type modeling, review the model specifications and inference methods, and identify the likely directions of future research. In this section we outline only the essence of multivariate *ARCH*-type models.

The simplest extension of the univariate *ARCH*-type model is a bivariate *GARCH* model proposed by Engle and Kroner (1995). Besides mean and variance equations, the specification contains also a conditional covariance equation that enables better assessment of the interaction between variables. Contrary to univariate models, a bivariate specification introduces dependence between two series, and allows observing their co-movements, which may help to better understand the developments of the two series.[50]

Rapid developments in *ARCH* modeling brought a number of general multivariate *GARCH* models that, when compared with other methods, provide more efficient tools for analyzing comovements and volatility spillovers predominantly among financial assets.[51] Still, the first class of multivariate *GARCH* models implied substantial computing requirements as they contain a high number of unknown parameters that increases exponentially with the number of variables used. However, a multivariate *GARCH* can be substituted by various extensions of a univariate *GARCH*. One solution to circumvent the problem of computational complexity is the Dynamic Conditional Correlation *GARCH* model of Engle and Sheppard (2001) and Engle (2002), which represents a non-linear combination of a univariate *GARCH*.

For ease of exposition the bivariate version of the Dynamic Conditional Correlation *GARCH* (*DCC-GARCH*) models is described below. This technique enables an analysis of pairwise dynamic correlations for two variables, say stock market returns r_1 and r_2. The estimation of the *DCC-GARCH* model consists of two stages. In the first stage, a univariate *GARCH* model is estimated for the individual time series. In the second stage, the standardized residuals obtained from the first stage are used to derive the conditional correlation estimator.

Following Engle (2002), the *DCC-GARCH* model for the bivariate vector of returns $r_t \equiv [r_{1t}, r_{2t}]'$ is specified as follows:

$$r_t \,|\, \Omega_{t-1} \sim N(0, D_t R_t D_t) \tag{3.52}$$

$$D_t^2 = diag\{\omega_1 \omega_2\} + diag\{\kappa_1 \kappa_2\} \odot r_{t-1} r_{t-1}' + diag\{\lambda_1 \lambda_2\} \odot D_{t-1}^2 \tag{3.53}$$

$$\varepsilon_t = D_t^{-1} r_t \tag{3.54}$$

50 Babetskaia-Kukharchuk, Babetskii, and Podpiera (2008) employed a bivariate version of the Baba-Engle-Kraft-Kroner GARCH (BEKK-GARCH) model proposed by Engle and Kroner (1995) over the period 1994–2005 and found convergence in exchange rate volatilities between Visegrad Four currencies and the Euro. The degree of synchronization is in line with the composition of currency baskets and the share of the Euro as a trade invoicing currency in those economies.

51 The use of multivariate ARCH specifications to model the conditional mean and volatility of stock prices is still not as widespread as is the use of conventional univariate models. The methodology is usually used in two strands of financial modeling. One is the modeling of the behavior of stock prices, related financial instruments or stock indices in order to exploit the effect of conditional variance and covariance. Ledoit, Santa-Clara, and Wolf (2003), Bystrom (2004), Hutson and Kearney (2005), McKenzie and Kim (2007), and Kearney and Muckley (2008), and Baruník, Kočenda, and Vácha (2015) are examples of such applications. Testing the validity of the CAPM model is another line of research where Engle and Rodrigues (1989) and Clare et al. (1998) can serve as examples in which the CAPM model with time-varying covariances is rejected.

$$Q_t = S(1 - \alpha - \beta) + \alpha(\varepsilon_{t-1}\varepsilon'_{t-1}) + \beta Q_{t-1} \qquad (3.55)$$

$$R_t = diag\{Q_t\}^{-1} Q_t diag\{Q_t\}^{-1}, \qquad (3.56)$$

where equation (3.54) represents the standardized errors, S is the uncondi-tional correlation matrix of the errors, $\odot$ denotes the Hadamard product of two matrices of the same size (element-by-element multiplication), and R_t is a time-varying correlation matrix. The parameters of the *DCC-GARCH* model can be obtained by maximum likelihood estimation.

The following conditions reflect what type of model should be used, e.g. ei-ther mean reverting or integrated. If $\alpha + \beta < 1$ then equation (3.55) is mean re-verting, which implies a mean reverting *DCC-GARCH*. Subsequently, if $\alpha + \beta = 1$ then equation (3.55) collapses to equation (3.55′):

$$Q_t = (1 - \varphi)(\varepsilon_{t-1}\varepsilon'_{t-1}) + \varphi Q_{t-1}, \qquad (3.55')$$

which implies the integrated *DCC-GARCH* model. A standard Likelihood Ratio test ($LR = 2(\log L_{\alpha+\beta=1} - \log L_{\alpha+\beta<1})$; $LR \sim \chi^2$) can be used to discriminate be-tween (3.55) and (3.55′).

In practice, the preferred (*G*)*ARCH*-type model is estimated for the series of interest (returns in the above case) as described in sections 3.7.7. and 3.7.8. As an alternative approach, a bivariate Vector Autoregression (*VAR*) model for the series of interest can be estimated and the residuals of the *VAR* model are used as inputs for the univariate *GARCH* models. Then, the pairwise specifications of the *DCC-GARCH* model are estimated with the choice between the integrated and mean reverting *DCC* models being made based on the log likelihood ratio test. The obtained conditional correlation estimates provide precise informa-tion on comovements between variables under research.[52]

Quite an illustrative application of the *DCC-GARCH* modeling strategy can be found in Crespo-Cuaresma and Wojcik (2006), who aim to verify the mon-etary independence hypothesis that has been the main framework for consid-ering monetary policy under different exchange rate regimes. Under floating exchange rate regimes, countries are free to choose the optimal levels of infla-tion and interest rates. Under fixed exchange rate regimes, countries are forced to import monetary policy from abroad. However, it has been speculated that the hypothesis does not hold for emerging markets. With the help of the *DCC-GARCH* model the degree of time-varying correlation in interest rate shocks with Germany and the U.S. under different exchange rate regimes is estimated for the Czech Republic, Hungary and Poland. Cross-country comparisons pro-

---

52   Dijk et al. (2011) extend the DCC model by allowing for structural breaks in unconditional correlations among five European currencies.

vide evidence that countries with more flexible exchange rate regimes tend to display higher degrees of monetary independence. However, the correlation dynamics of an individual country over time provides mixed results. Although the dynamic behavior of the correlations in interest rate shocks in the Czech Republic appear to be consistent with the theory, no evidence is found to support the validity of the monetary hypothesis in Hungary and Poland.

A further application of the *DCC-GARCH* approach is illustrated in Égert and Kočenda (2011) on the same set of countries but for a different topic. Intra-day dynamic correlations are estimated within the group of the Czech, Hungarian, and Polish stock markets and between these markets and the developed EU stock markets. Very little intra-day comovements are found between the emerging and developed EU stock markets as well as among the emerging EU markets themselves, though. On the contrary, very sizable comovements were found among the mature EU stock markets. Different geographical coverage is adopted in Horváth and Petrovski (2013), who analyze daily stock market comovements between mature EU stock markets and Central European markets (the Czech Republic, Hungary, and Poland), and include less-researched South-Eastern European markets (Croatia, Macedonia, and Serbia). It is found that the degree of daily comovements with mature EU stock markets is quite high for Central European markets. However, the correlations of the South-Eastern European stock markets with mature EU markets are virtually zero; the Croatian market is an exception but its comovement degree is still below the levels typical for Central Europe.

The *DCC-GARCH* model introduced above does not account for the asymmetric effects present in the volatility on markets and comovements among them; this is analogical to the difference between a simple *GARCH* model and specifications allowing for asymmetries (see Section 3.7.8). Cappiello et al. (2006) introduced the asymmetric *DCC* (*ADCC*) specification to account for asymmetries in the conditional variances and in the conditional correlations.

The *ADCC-GARCH* model specification begins like the *DCC-GARCH* specification above. However, the dynamic correlation structure in the bivariate *ADCC* model is specified as:

$$Q_t = \left(1 - \sum_{m=1}^{M}\theta_m - \sum_{n=1}^{N}\varphi_n\right)\overline{Q} - \sum_{k=1}^{K}\tau_k\overline{N} + \sum_{m=1}^{M}\theta_m\left(\varepsilon_{t-m}\varepsilon_{t-m}'\right) + \sum_{k=1}^{K}\tau_k\left(n_{t-k}n_{t-k}'\right) + \sum_{n=1}^{N}\varphi_t Q_{t-n},$$

where ε_t are standardized returns as in (3.54). $\overline{Q} = \mathrm{E}\left[\varepsilon_t\varepsilon_t'\right]$ is the unconditional correlation of the standardized returns; its expectation is estimated using the sample analogue $T^{-1}\sum_{t=1}^{T}\varepsilon_t\varepsilon_t'$. Further, $n_t = I_{[\varepsilon_t<0]}\odot\varepsilon_t$ with $I_{[\varepsilon_t<0]}$ $k\times 1$ is an indicator function, which takes on a value of 1 when $\varepsilon_t<0$ and 0 otherwise.

$\overline{N} = \mathrm{E}\left[n_t n_t'\right]$ can be estimated using the sample analogue $T^{-1}\sum_{t=1}^{T} n_t n_t'$. Unlike in the univariate processes, the asymmetric term can be applicable when both indicators are equal to 1. This means that two returns are negative in the presence of joint negative news. The asymmetric effect implies that correlations will be lower after joint positive news and higher after joint negative news. The following restrictions are imposed to ensure that the correlation matrix Q_t is positive definite:

1. $\sum_{m=1}^{M} \theta_m + \eta \sum_{k=1}^{K} \tau_t + \sum_{n=1}^{N} \varphi_n < 1$

2. $\theta_m \geq 0$ for $m = 1,2,...,M$

3. $\tau_k \geq 0$ for $k = 1,2,...,K$

4. $\varphi_n \geq 0$ for $n = 1,2,...,N$,

where η = maximum eigenvalue $\left[\overline{Q}^{-\frac{1}{2}} \overline{N} \overline{Q}^{-\frac{1}{2}}\right]$ can be estimated based on the data sample.

Maximum likelihood estimation, with an assumption of conditional multivariate normality, is used to estimate the $ADCC\text{-}GARCH$ model. The conditional distribution is often misspecified, however, there exists a consistent and asymptotically normal quasi-maximum likelihood estimator (Engle and Sheppard, 2001). The joint log-likelihood function is specified as:

$$QL_1(\phi \mid r_t) = -\frac{1}{2}\sum_{t=1}^{T}\left(k\log(2\pi) + 2\log(|D_t|) + \log(|R_t|) + \varepsilon_t' R_t^{-1} \varepsilon_t\right)$$

$$L(\theta) = -\frac{1}{2}\sum_{t=1}^{T}\left(k\log(2\pi) + \log(|H_t|) + r_t' H_t^{-1} r_t\right)$$

$$= -\frac{1}{2}\sum_{t=1}^{T}\left(k\log(2\pi) + \log(|D_t R_t D_t|) + r_t' D_t^{-1} R_t^{-1} D_t^{-1} r_t\right) \ .$$

$$= -\frac{1}{2}\sum_{t=1}^{T}\left(k\log(2\pi) + 2\log(|D_t|) + \log(|R_t|) + \varepsilon_t' R_t^{-1} \varepsilon_t\right)$$

The joint log-likelihood function above can be divided into volatility and correlation parts. For this purpose, the parameters are divided into two groups. The first group corresponds to the parameters of the univariate $GARCH$ model: $\phi = (\phi_1, \phi_2,...,\phi_k)$, where $\phi_i = (\omega_i, \alpha_{i1},...,\alpha_{iP_i}, \gamma_{i1},...,\gamma_{io_i}, \beta_{i1},...,\beta_{iQ_i})$. The second group corresponds to the parameters of the dynamic correlations: $\psi = (\theta_1,...,\theta_m, \tau_1,...,\tau_k, \varphi_1,...,\varphi_n)$.

During the estimation, the first step is to replace the time-varying correlation matrix R_t with an identity matrix I_k of dimension k. Hence, the first stage quasi-likelihood function is specified as:

$$QL_1(\phi|r_t) = -\frac{1}{2}\sum_{t=1}^{T}\left(k\log(2\pi) + 2\log(|D_t|) + \underbrace{\log(|I_t|)}_{=0} + r_t'D_t^{-1}I_kD_t^{-1}r_t\right)$$

$$= -\frac{1}{2}\sum_{t=1}^{T}\left(k\log(2\pi) + 2\log(|D_t|) + r_t'D_t^{-2}r_t\right)$$

$$= -\frac{1}{2}\sum_{t=1}^{T}\left(k\log(2\pi) + \sum_{i=1}^{k}\left(\log(\sigma_{it}^2) + \frac{r_{it}^2}{\sigma_{it}^2}\right)\right)$$

$$= -\frac{1}{2}\sum_{i=1}^{k}\sum_{t=1}^{T}\left(\log(2\pi) + \log(\sigma_{it}^2) + \frac{r_{it}^2}{\sigma_{it}^2}\right).$$

The quasi-likelihood function of the first stage is the sum of the individual *GARCH* likelihood functions. Hence, maximizing the joint likelihood function is equivalent to maximizing each univariate *GARCH* likelihood function individually.

In the second stage, the quasi-likelihood function is estimated conditioned on the first stage parameters as:

$$QL_2(\psi|\hat{\phi},r_t) = -\frac{1}{2}\sum_{t=1}^{T}\left(k\log(2\pi) + 2\log(|D_t|) + \log(|R_t|) + r_t'D_t^{-1}R_tD_t^{-1}r_t\right)$$

$$= -\frac{1}{2}\sum_{t=1}^{T}\left(k\log(2\pi) + 2\log(|D_t|) + \log(|R_t|) + \epsilon_t'D_t^{-1}R_tD_t^{-1}\epsilon_t\right).$$

Given the fact that quasi-likelihood function is estimated conditioned on the first stage parameters, and the constant term is excluded because its first derivative with respect to the correlation parameters is zero, the second step quasi-likelihood function can be specified as:

$$QL_2^*(\psi|\hat{\phi},r_t) = -\frac{1}{2}\sum_{t=1}^{T}\left(\log(|R_t|) + \epsilon_t'R_t\epsilon_t\right).$$

Finally, the parameters from the second stage are obtained by maximizing the quasi-likelihood function QL_2^* as $\hat{\psi} = \arg\max_{\psi}QL_2^*$. The full estimation is not simple but the necessary codes are readily available.[53]

53   The codes to estimate the *ADCC-GARCH* are available at http://www.kevinsheppard.com/wiki/MFE _Toolbox.

One of the recent applications of the *ADCC-GARCH* model is presented by Gjika and Horváth (2013), who examine stock market comovements among three Central European markets (the Czech Republic, Poland, and Hungary) and comovements between these markets and the aggregate Euro area market. Their results show that asymmetric volatility is common in the stock markets under research. However, in terms of conditional correlations, asymmetric effects are found only between the Hungarian and Polish stock exchanges. Hence, asymmetries in the correlations are not as widespread as in conditional variances.

3.7.10 STRUCTURAL BREAKS IN VOLATILITY

In sections 3.5 and 3.6 we focused on structural changes in the mean equation. In this section we present methodologies that are specifically designed to detect structural breaks in the variance or volatility of a given time series. The quest for determining changes in the volatility of diverse macroeconomic series has shown that significant changes – mostly decreases – in the volatility of a large number of macroeconomic fundamentals has taken place in industrialized countries, chiefly over the past quarter century, because considerable reforms have influenced the institutional framework, markets, and the functioning of monetary and fiscal policies.[54] Very little empirical research of this issue has been conducted with respect to emerging markets of Central and Eastern Europe.

The two procedures introduced here are the Iterated Cumulative Sums of Squares (*ICSS*) algorithm developed by Inclán and Tiao (1994) and a Bayesian procedure for estimating breakpoints developed by Wang and Zivot (2000). Inclán and Tiao (1994) propose a cumulative sums of squares algorithm to estimate the number of changes in variance and the point in time of each variance shift. Let

$$C_k = \sum_{t=1}^{k} \varepsilon_t^2 , \; k = 1,...,n \tag{3.57}$$

be the cumulative sum of the squared observations from the start to the k-th point in time, where n is the number of observations and denotes a series of independent observations from a normal distribution with zero mean and with unconditional variance. From equation (3.57), Inclán and Tiao (1994) propose to use the statistics given by:

---

54 These developments have been documented, among others, by Sensier and van Dijk (2004) for the U.S.A., and by Mills and Wang (2003) and Blanchard and Simon (2001) for other developed countries.

$$IT = \sup_k \sqrt{n/2} |D_k|, \tag{3.58}$$

where $D_k = \frac{C_k}{C_n} - \frac{k}{n}$. Under the null hypothesis of constant unconditional variance, asymptotically D_k behaves as a Brownian bridge. The critical value of 1.36 is the 95th percentile of the asymptotic distribution of $\sup_k \sqrt{n/2} |D_k|$. Thus, upper and lower boundaries can be set at ± 1.36 in the D_k plot. Exceeding these boundaries marks a significant change in the variance of the series. If the series under study has multiple break points, the D_k function alone is not enough because of the masking effects. To avoid this problem, Inclán and Tiao (1994) design an algorithm that is based on a successive evaluation of D_k at different parts of the series, dividing consecutively after a possible change point is found.

Another procedure to detect structural breaks in volatility is based on a Bayesian procedure for estimating the existence of structural changes in level, trend and variance at the same time developed by Wang and Zivot (2000). They consider a segmented deterministically trending and heteroskedastic autoregressive model

$$y_t = a_t + b_t t + \sum_{i=1}^{p} \phi_i y_{t-i} + s_t u_t, \tag{3.59}$$

for $t = 1, 2,..., T$, where $u_t \mid \Omega_t \sim$ i.i.d. $N(0,1)$ and Ω_t denotes the information set at time t. They assume that the parameters a_t, b_t and s_t are subject to $m < T$ structural changes. m is initially known, with break dates $k_1, k_2,..., k_m$, $1 < k_1 < k_2 < ... < k_m \le T$, so that the observations can be separated into $m + 1$ regimes. Let $k = (k_1, k_2,..., k_m)$ denote the vector of break dates. For each regime i ($i = 1, 2,..., m + 1$), the parameters a_t, b_t and s_t are given by

$$a_t = \alpha_i, \ b_t = \beta_i, \ s_t = \sigma_i \ge 0$$

for $k_{i-1} \le t < k_i$ with $k_0 = 1$ and $k_{m+1} = T + 1$.

Let I_A denote an indicator variable such that I_A is equal to one if event A is true and zero otherwise. Then (3.59) can be re-written as

$$y_t = \sum_{i=1}^{m+1} I_{\{k_{i-1} \le t < k_i\}} (\alpha_i + \beta_i t) + \sum_{i=1}^{p} \phi_i y_{t-i} + s_t u_t,$$

or as

$$y_t = x_t' B + s_t u_t, \tag{3.60}$$

where

$$
X_t = \begin{bmatrix} I_{\{k_0 \le t < k_1\}} \\ \dots \\ I_{\{k_m \le t < k_{m+1}\}} \\ t \cdot I_{\{k_0 \le t < k_1\}} \\ \dots \\ t \cdot I_{\{k_m \le t < k_{m+1}\}} \\ y_{t-1} \\ \dots \\ y_{t-p} \end{bmatrix}
$$

and $B = (\alpha_1, ..., \alpha_{m+1}, \beta_1, ..., \beta_{m+1}, \phi_1, ..., \phi_p)'$. Let $\sigma = (\sigma_1, \sigma_2, ..., \sigma_{m+1})$ and define $\theta = (B', \sigma', k')'$ as the vector of the unknown parameters of equation (3.60), Y_0 as the vector of p initial values of y_t, and $Y = (y_1, ..., y_T)'$ as the vector of observed data. Given the normality of the errors u_t, the likelihood function of equation (3.60) takes the form

$$
L(\theta \mid \mathbf{Y}, \mathbf{Y}_0) = \left(\sum_{t=1}^{T} s_t \right)^{-1} \exp\{ -\frac{1}{2} \sum_{t=1}^{T} \frac{(y_t - x_t' B)^2}{s_{t^2}} \} \tag{3.61}
$$

$$
= |S|^{-1} \exp\{ -\frac{(Y - XB)' S^{-2} (Y - XB)}{2} \},
$$

where S is a diagonal matrix with $(s_1, ..., s_T)$ on the diagonal and X is a $T \times (2m + 2 + p)$ matrix with t-th row given by x_t'.

The estimation of the model is possible by using the Gibbs sampler. Wang and Zivot (2000) consider the determination of the number of structural breaks and the form of the breaks as a problem of model selection and compare the use of marginal likelihoods and Schwarz's *BIC* model selection criterion to se-lect the most appropriate model from the data.

An application of these methodologies can be found in Égert et al. (2006) who analyze the structural changes in the volatility of a monthly data series covering industrial production, prices, nominal exchange rates, the labor mar-ket and nominal wages in ten CEE countries. The results indicate that breaks in volatility occur across all investigated series and countries and series often ex-hibit multiple breaks. Most of the structural breaks found are clearly associated with landmark events at the macro level, such as the occurrence of currency, financial and banking crises or changes in the macroeconomic environment driven by the alteration of the macroeconomic policy framework or external conditions. The fact that most empirical studies dealing with prices, money demand, productivity, the labor market or exchange rates in the economies of Central and Eastern Europe do not take into account the presence of structural breaks in the variance of the series studied could be a reason for the bad performance of univariate and multivariate econometric time series models. Furthermore, ignoring structural breaks might also have important implications regarding the stability of the investigated relationships between variables with multiple breaks regarding the validity of the results and the ensuing recommendations for economic policy.

Further application can be found in Lyócsa et al. (2011b) who used improved version of the Inclán and Tiao (1994) test, that was suggested by Sansó et al. (2004), and analyzed volatility breaks in 25 different series of the CEE countries encompassing variables on economic output and activity, price, labor market and financial indicators. Numerous breaks were identified not at the beginning of the transformation period but, surprisingly, at later dates. This finding might be due to either intricacy of the economic transformation or simply to limitations of the testing procedure. Finally, Baumöhl et al. (2011) combined the *DCC-GARCH* model (section 3.7.9) and tests for structural breaks in volatility to present a methodology for validating the existence of shift contagion between stock markets (three Central and Eastern European (Czech Republic, Hungary, and Poland) and two developed stock markets (U.S. and Germany)). The use of endogenously detected changes in the volatility of stock market returns allowed defining relatively high- and low-volatility regimes for particular stock markets. Structural breaks in volatility had been identified by applying the Inclán and Tiao (1994) test and its modification by Sansó et al. (2004). By running a simple regression with dummy variables and time trend Baumöhl et al. (2011) verify whether endogenously detected volatility regimes are significantly associated with dynamic correlations. They show that when breaks are linked to a decrease in volatility, the correlations between the indices tend to decrease. Similarly, sudden increases in volatility are accompanied by an increase in correlations. Both types of results provide clear evidence of the presence of the shift contagion effect between stock markets.

4.
MULTIPLE TIME SERIES

So far we have investigated models of single time series variables, so-called *univariate time series models*. In the analysis we did not allow for any interaction with other time series, except for deterministic intercepts, trends, trend breaks, and eventually also deterministic seasonal variables.

The focus of economics lies partly in the study of interactions of different economic variables. Thus, in economic research it is very likely that we will face the question how to econometrically model and study interactions of multiple time series. To do this we need to apply the tools of *multiple time series analysis*. Multiple time series analysis is an extremely rich field of econometrics. In the following chapters we will introduce a set of selected methods and results that we consider to be essential. First, we will briefly define the concept of *vector autoregression* (*VAR*), which is the key modeling approach in multiple time series analysis. Then, we will focus on the issues of *Granger causality*, *cointegration*, and the *error correction model*.

Before turning to the *VAR* framework we briefly introduce *intervention and transfer function models* that lie on the border between univariate and multiple time series analysis. In these models univariate *ARMA* processes are augmented by exogenous right hand side variables. Using polynomial notation the augmented *ARMA* specification can in a general case be written as

$$A(L)y_t = a_0 + C(L)z_t + B(L)\varepsilon_t,$$

where $A(L)$ and $B(L)$ are the AR and MA polynomials of the lag operator L, and z_t is an exogenous variable uncorrelated with errors, thus satisfying the condition $cov(\varepsilon_{t-s}, z_t) = 0$ for all t and s. The exogeneity condition assures that current and past innovations in y_t have no effect on z_t. The polynomial $C(L)$ specifies how the changes in z_t affect the time evolution of y_t.

Intervention analysis was developed by Box and Tiao (1975) to measure the impact of a policy change on a dependent variable. This technique has since appeared in many diverse applications. In *intervention models* the exogenous variable z_t takes the form of a dummy variable that has the value of one from the time period when a specific intervention or measure was adopted, and value of zero for preceding periods. The model is estimated to see whether an adopted measure demonstrates any effect and if yes, then what is its magnitude, its pattern over time, etc.[55]

The setup is different in *transfer function models* where the exogenous variable z_t is allowed to be any continuous stochastic variable.[56] The polynomial $C(L)$ is called the transfer function. Here the question is: what is the effect of an independent time series on the variable under study? In other words, how is movement in an exogenous variable *transferred* into the development of a dependent variable. The coefficients on $C(L)$ associated with the exogenous variable z_t are called transfer function weights and depict the extent of the influence. The magnitude of the effect of a z_t shock on the sequence of dependent y_t can be shown with the help of the impulse response function that is given by $C(L)/[1 - A(L)]$. The crucial condition is the exogeneity of the variable z_t with respect to the dependent variable y_t. The exogeneity can be formally tested through the *Granger causality* technique introduced in section 4.2.

An application of the transfer function design in the context of a transforming economy is provided by David and Vašíček (2004). They introduced a New Keynesian multiple-equations small-open-economy macroeconomic model to capture links among model parameters to show how the system behaves when changes in the economy occur. In the spirit of transfer function analysis they applied the transfer function of the model to produce a new point of view on monetary stabilization in the context of the dynamic stability of the Czech economy and its influence on rational expectations under a regime of inflation targeting.

---

55 Krishnamurthi, Narayan and Raj (1989), in their application, improved on the way a control series can be incorporated in the *ARIMA* methodology to obtain more accurate estimates of the effect of the intervention.

56 The term *transfer function* comes from the field of chemical engineering.

4.1 *VAR* MODELS

The dominance of the *VAR* concept in multiple time series econometrics is mainly due to Sims (1980). Imagine that we face the problem of modeling two time series, y_{1t} and y_{2t}. We assume the two variables interact with each other but we do not know *ex ante* which of them is exogenous. Then the most appropriate approach is to treat the two variables symmetrically by formulating the following model:

$$y_{1t} = b_1 + \alpha_{12} y_{2t} + \sum_{i=1}^{p} \left(\gamma_{11}^{(i)} y_{1t-i} + \gamma_{12}^{(i)} y_{2t-i} \right) + u_{1t}, \tag{4.1}$$

$$y_{2t} = b_2 + \alpha_{21} y_{1t} + \sum_{i=1}^{p} \left(\gamma_{21}^{(i)} y_{1t-i} + \gamma_{22}^{(i)} y_{2t-i} \right) + u_{2t}, \tag{4.2}$$

where y_{1t} and y_{2t} are assumed to be stationary and u_{1t} and u_{2t} are assumed to be mutually uncorrelated white noise disturbances with variances σ_1^2 and σ_2^2. The model can be rewritten in matrix form as

$$A y_t = b + \sum_{i=1}^{p} \Gamma_i y_{t-i} + u_t, \tag{4.3}$$

where

$$y_t = \begin{bmatrix} y_{1t} \\ y_{2t} \end{bmatrix}, \; A = \begin{bmatrix} 1 & -\alpha_{12} \\ -\alpha_{21} & 1 \end{bmatrix}, \; b = \begin{bmatrix} b_1 \\ b_2 \end{bmatrix}, \; \Gamma_i = \begin{bmatrix} \gamma_{11}^{(i)} & \gamma_{12}^{(i)} \\ \gamma_{21}^{(i)} & \gamma_{22}^{(i)} \end{bmatrix}, \text{and } u_t = \begin{bmatrix} u_{1t} \\ u_{2t} \end{bmatrix}.$$

The model defined by equation (4.3) is called a *structural VAR* model. More precisely, it is a structural *p*-th-order *VAR* model of two variables. It can be easily extended to the case of *N* interrelated variables, which will only increase the size of the vectors from 2 × 1 to *N* × 1 and the size of matrices from 2 × 2 to *N* × *N*. The structural *VAR* defined by equation (4.3) cannot be estimated due to the endogeneity of dependent variables. Even if the error terms are mutually and serially uncorrelated, due to the structural specification y_{2t} is correlated with u_{1t}, and y_{1t} with u_{2t}. However, the structural *VAR* can be transformed to the *reduced form VAR* through premultiplying equation (4.3) by A^{-1} to obtain the identity matrix associated with y_t. The reduced form *VAR* can be written as

$$y_t = \mu + \sum_{i=1}^{p} \Pi_i y_{t-i} + \varepsilon_t, \tag{4.4}$$

where

$$\mu = A^{-1} b = \begin{bmatrix} \mu_1 \\ \mu_2 \end{bmatrix}, \; \Pi_i = A^{-1} \Gamma_i = \begin{bmatrix} \pi_{11}^{(i)} & \pi_{12}^{(i)} \\ \pi_{21}^{(i)} & \pi_{22}^{(i)} \end{bmatrix}, \text{and } \varepsilon_t = A^{-1} u_t = \begin{bmatrix} \varepsilon_{1t} \\ \varepsilon_{2t} \end{bmatrix}.$$

The reduced form p-th-order *VAR* defined by equation (4.4) can be estimated equation by equation using *OLS*. Only lagged values of y_{1t} and y_{2t} appear on the right hand side and those are uncorrelated with ε_{1t} and ε_{2t}. This is because ε_{1t} and ε_{2t}, being a linear combination of serially uncorrelated errors u_{1t} and u_{2t}, also remain serially uncorrelated. On the other hand, ε_{1t} and ε_{2t} become mutually correlated. The mutual correlation of error terms might suggest estimating the equations as *seemingly unrelated regressions* (*SUR*). However, this would bring no efficiency yield, because the right hand side variables are identical in both equations. If the original structural *VAR* consisted of N equations for N variables $y_{1t}, y_{2t}, ..., y_{Nt}$, then the reduced form *VAR* would be obtained analogically as in the two-variable case and would also consist of N equations for N variables $y_{1t}, y_{2t}, ..., y_{Nt}$.

4.1.1 STRUCTURAL FORM, REDUCED FORM, AND IDENTIFICATION

It is obvious that not all the coefficients of the structural form can be recovered from the reduced form coefficient estimates. In a general case of N equations and p lags the number of estimated parameters of the reduced form *VAR* is N intercepts, pN^2 elements of the matrices $\Pi^{(i)}$, and $N + (N^2 - N)/2$ variances and covariances of the error terms. The number of parameters of the structural form *VAR* is $N^2 - N$ elements of the matrix A, N intercepts, pN^2 elements of the matrices $\Gamma^{(i)}$, and N variances of the error terms. Clearly the number of estimated parameters with the reduced form *VAR* ($N + pN^2 + N + (N^2 - N)/2$) will be lower than the number of original parameters in the structural form *VAR* ($N^2 - N + N + pN^2 + N$). This is more clear after rearranging, which shows that ($N/2 + N^2/2$) < N^2 for all $N > 1$.

Thus the *identification problem* arises. In order to recover the parameters of the structural equations from the estimated parameters of the reduced form equations, we need to impose restrictions on some of the structural parameters. For example, with a two-variable first order *VAR* the structural form contains ten parameters, while the reduced form provides only nine parameter estimates. Thus, we need to impose *ex ante* at least one restriction on the structural parameters in order to recover them from the reduced form parameter estimates. If more then one restriction is imposed, then the system becomes *overidentified* and the restrictions imposed on the parameters of the structural form transform in a more or less complicated fashion into restrictions on the parameters of the reduced form as well. The *overidentifying restriction* can be tested in the process of the estimation of the reduced form *VAR*.

However, in the context of *VAR* models the issue of identification is not that crucial. When we slightly trivialize the arguments that led to the development and use of *VAR* models, we can say that *VAR* models stemmed from the criticism of estimating large economic models with the use of systems of structural equations. In order to estimate such systems of structural equations, many restrictions must be *ex ante* imposed and in many cases it is hard to find a sufficient number of restrictions that would make economic sense. Therefore, an estimation of the reduced form *VAR* model might be the right approach. Without the need to investigate the restrictions ensuring identification, the reduced form *VAR* model can be estimated and will still describe properly the dynamics of the system and will also provide unbiased forecasts. After all, in common econometric terminology that we will adopt from now on, the term "*VAR*" without modification stands for the reduced form *VAR* described by equation (4.4). Only if we need to refer to the structural model described by equation (4.3) do we use the term "structural *VAR*".

Naturally, the opposite criticism of *VAR* models exists as well. It claims that *VAR* models estimated without an attempt to identify the structural form have no economic meaning and are just statistical exercises. The truth lies probably somewhere in between. Extreme or incredible restrictions may lead to misspecified structural models on the one hand and the blind use of *VAR* models under any circumstances has no economic meaning on the other hand.

4.1.2 STABILITY AND STATIONARITY OF *VAR* MODELS

In sections 2.4 and 2.5 we presented the conditions for the stability and stationarity of a general univariate *ARMA(p,q)* model. Recall that in the case of an *AR(p)* model,

$$y_t = \mu + \sum_{i=1}^{p} a_i y_{t-i} + \varepsilon_t \ \text{ or } \ A(L)y_t = \mu + \varepsilon_t,$$

where $A(L) = 1 - \sum_{i=1}^{p} a_i L^i$, the necessary and sufficient conditions for the stability of the *AR(p)* equation and the stationarity of the generated time series required that all the roots of the characteristic equation $\alpha^p - a_1\alpha^{p-1} - a_2\alpha^{p-2} - \cdots - a_p = 0$ (solved with respect to α) lie within the unit circle. It means that all the roots must be less than one in absolute value. The conditions can be equivalently expressed in terms of the inverse characteristic equation $A(L) = 0$. All the roots of the inverse characteristic equation solved with respect to L must lie outside the unit circle, that is, must be in absolute value greater than one.

The necessary and sufficient conditions for the stability and stationarity of an *AR(p)* model can be generalized to the case of a *p*-th-order *VAR* model of N time series. For simplicity we will start with a first order *VAR* of N time series specified as

$$y_t = \mu + \Pi_1 y_{t-1} + \varepsilon_t \text{ or } A(L)y_t = \mu + \varepsilon_t, \qquad (4.5)$$

where $A(L) = I - \Pi_1 L$, and with I denoting the $N \times N$ identity matrix. The first order VAR is a multivariate generalization of a simple AR(1) model $y_t = \mu + a_1 y_{t-1} + \varepsilon_t$ or $A(L) y_t = \mu$, where $A(L) = 1 - a_1$. Here the characteristic and inverse characteristic equations are $\alpha - a_1 = 0$ and $1 - a_1 L = 0$, respectively. Thus, the necessary and sufficient condition for stability and stationarity is $|a_1| < 1$.

The necessary and sufficient condition for the stability and stationarity of a first order VAR can be defined in a similar way. The first order VAR defined by equation (4.5) is stable and the time series generated by the VAR are stationary, if and only if all the *eigenvalues* $\alpha_1, \alpha_2,..., \alpha_N$ of the matrix Π_1 lie within the unit circle, that is, are less than one in absolute value. Note that the eigenvalues $\alpha_1, \alpha_2,..., \alpha_N$ are the roots of the characteristic equation

$$\left| \alpha I - \Pi_1 \right| = 0, \qquad (4.6)$$

where $|M|$ indicates the determinant of a matrix M. Similar to the univariate case, the stability and stationarity conditions can be formulated in terms of the roots of the inverse characteristic equation, which in the multivariate case can be written as

$$\left| I - \Pi_1 L \right| = 0. \qquad (4.7)$$

With this formulation, all the roots are required to be greater than one in absolute value.

Note that with the simple AR(1) model

$$y_t = \mu + a_1 y_{t-1} + \varepsilon_t,$$

there was just one stability and stationarity condition:

$$\left| a_1 \right| < 1.$$

However, with the first order VAR model of N time series

$$y_t = \mu + \Pi_1 y_{t-1} + \varepsilon_t,$$

there are N stability and stationarity conditions:

$$\left| \alpha_i \right| < 1, \text{ for } i = 1, 2,..., N,$$

where $\alpha_1, \alpha_2,..., \alpha_N$ are the N eigenvalues of the matrix Π_1.

In the case of a general p-th-order *VAR* we can use the result obtained for the first order *VAR*, because any p-th-order *VAR*

$$y_t = \mu + \sum_{i=1}^{p} \Pi_i y_{t-i} + \varepsilon_t$$

can be expressed as a first order *VAR* using the so-called *companion form*

$$Y_t = A_0 + A_1 Y_{t-1} + E_t,$$

where Y_t, A_0, and E_t are $Np \times 1$ vectors – $Y_t = (y_t, y_{t-1}, ... y_{t-p})'$, $A_0 = (\mu, 0, 0, ..., 0)'$ and $E_t = (\varepsilon_t, 0, 0, ..., 0)'$ – and A_1 is a $Np \times Np$ matrix:

$$A_1 = \begin{bmatrix} \Pi_1 & \Pi_2 & \cdots & \Pi_{p-1} & \Pi_p \\ I & 0 & \cdots & 0 & 0 \\ 0 & I & \cdots & 0 & 0 \\ \cdot & \cdot & \cdots & \cdot & \cdot \\ 0 & & \cdots & I & 0 \end{bmatrix}.$$

Therefore, the necessary and sufficient conditions for the stability and stationarity of the p-th-order *VAR* require all the eigenvalues of the matrix A_1 to be less than one in absolute value. This means that all the roots of the characteristic equation

$$\left| \alpha I_{Np} - A_1 \right| = 0$$

must be less than one in absolute value. In terms of the inverse characteristic equation, all the roots of

$$\left| I_{Np} - A_1 L \right| = 0$$

must be greater than one in absolute value. Using the properties of the determinants the inverse characteristic equation can be rewritten as

$$\left| I - \Pi_1 L - \Pi_2 L^2 - \cdots - \Pi_p L^p \right| = 0.$$

Again we can see the analogy to the inverse characteristic equation of an univariate $AR(p)$ model, which can be written as

$$A(L) = 1 - a_1 L - a_2 L^2 - \cdots - a_p L^p = 0.$$

4.1.3 ESTIMATION OF A *VAR* MODEL

We have already mentioned that if we intend to model the behavior of *N* inter-related economic variables without knowledge of the exact structural model, that is, without *ex ante* knowledge of the restrictions that would make the structural model identifiable, we can still estimate a *VAR* model. A *VAR* model will describe the dynamic properties of the system and allow us to make unbiased forecasts. When estimating a *VAR* model we simply apply *OLS* to each of its equations separately.

In principle, we do not have to care about the restrictions that would identify the structural model, but still we have to choose the order of the *VAR*, that is, the number of lags *p* included. Typically, the number of lags *p* and also the number of regressors is the same in all *VAR* equations. That is, in each equation we employ all the lags up to the order *p*. Only if we have a very good reason to believe that some of the *VAR* coefficients should equal zero can we exclude the chosen lags for some of the variables or set different lag lengths in different equations. The resulting restricted system is then called a *near VAR*. Near *VAR* systems are estimated using *SUR* rather than *OLS*. From now on we will assume that we estimate a regular *p*-th-order *VAR* of *N* variables using *OLS* with each of the equations separately. To choose the order *p*, we can use one or a combination of the two methods described below.

1. Minimize the *Akaike (AIC)*, *Hannan-Quinn (HQIC)*, or *Schwarz Bayes (SBIC)* *information criteria* (see Akaike, 1978, Hannan and Quinn, 1979, or Schwarz, 1978). The multivariate generalizations of these information criteria are given by:

$$AIC = T \ln|\Sigma| + 2m,$$

$$HQIC = T \ln|\Sigma| + 2(\ln(\ln T))m,$$

$$SBC = T \ln|\Sigma| + (\ln T)m,$$

where $|\Sigma|$ is the determinant of the estimated variance-covariance matrix Σ of a model's residuals, T is the number of time observations in each of the *VAR* equations, and m is the total number of parameters estimated in all equations.

2. Use the cross-equation restriction *likelihood ratio test*. The *LR* test statistics is defined as

$$LR = T\left(\ln|\Sigma_R| - \ln|\Sigma_U|\right),$$

where $|\Sigma_R|$ is the determinant of the estimated variance-covariance matrix Σ_R of the restricted model of the order p_2 and $|\Sigma_U|$ is the determinant of the estimated variance-covariance matrix Σ_U of the unrestricted model of the order p_1, where $p_1 > p_2$. Under the null hypothesis of the order being p_2 rather than p_1 the *LR* statistics has a χ_n^2 distribution with degrees of freedom n equal to the number of restrictions in the whole system, which is $n = (p_1 - p_2)\, N^2$; N is the number of variables. The cross-equation restriction likelihood ratio test can be in principle used not only to determine the order of the model p but for any type of cross-equation restrictions. For example, we can test whether to include seasonal dummies in the *VAR*. Also we can use the test to decide if a variable y_N should be included in the *VAR*. To perform the test we estimate the $N - 1$ equations for the variables $y_1, y_2, \ldots, y_{N-1}$ in the unrestricted form, that is, with the lags of the variable y_N included, and also in the restricted form, that is, with the lags of y_N excluded. Then we compute the *LR* statistics, and compare it to the critical values of the χ_n^2 distribution. The number of restrictions n in this case equals $(N - 1)\, p$. This test is in fact a multivariate generalization of the *Granger causality test* that will be presented in section 4.2.

The last topic in this section is devoted to the issue of the stationarity of individual time series employed in a *VAR* model. From a statistical point of view, all time series should be stationary, e.g. $I(0)$ and free of any deterministic trend. If this is not the case, then the *VAR* should be estimated in first differences or with detrended variables. However, an opinion exists that in practical application a *VAR* model can be estimated also with variables that contain a unit root, that are $I(1)$ or contain a deterministic trend. The argument supporting this view claims that with differencing and detrending we lose important information. *VAR* models are, after all, designed to describe the dynamic properties of a system. The dynamic properties can be described also with $I(1)$ variables or with deterministically trending variables, where the deterministic trend can be well approximated with a random walk with drift. The answer to this dispute is not clear. We would suggest estimating *VAR* models with stationary $I(0)$ variables and to use a *VAR* in first differences if the variables are trending or contain a unit root. Only if we investigate the cointegration of the $I(1)$ variables (see section 4.3), then we should leave the variables in levels, because, as will be described in the following sections, a *VAR* in first differences would be a specification error in this case.

The *VAR* methodology has attracted considerable attention in analyzing developments during the transition process as well as ensuing emergence of European post-transition markets. The *VAR*-associated research has been done from various perspectives. Two recent applications merge transition issues with European integration. Moore and Pentecost (2006) use the structural *VAR* (*SVAR*) approach of Blanchard and Quah (1989) to analyze and compare the degree of labor market flexibility, measured as the responsiveness of real and nominal wages to permanent and temporary shocks, in eight EU member states. The analysis includes Poland, Hungary, Slovakia, and the Czech Republic to assess their suitability for euro-area membership. It is found that for Hungary and the Czech Republic real wages are more responsive to real (permanent) shocks than some current members of the Euro zone, such as Italy. On the other hand, in Poland and Slovakia, real wage flexibility seems to be extremely low, making higher unemployment more likely than in other EU countries. From this perspective, for these two countries early euro-area membership cannot be advised. Elbourne and de Haan (2006) use structural *VAR* to analyze monetary transmission for ten new EU member countries. They find no clear evidence of relations between financial structure and the impact of monetary policy shocks. In the current Economic and Monetary Union (EMU), differences in monetary transmission hamper the European Central Bank (ECB) in realizing its primary objective of price stability. It seems likely that the upcoming enlargement of the EMU will only make these problems more acute since those differences will probably increase.[57]

4.2 GRANGER CAUSALITY

The concept of *Granger causality* was introduced by Granger (1969). Even though his definition of the causality is formally complicated, the econometric application is very simple. It enables testing for causality between variables in the spirit of *VAR* models, without the need to define the exact structure of the causality chains. In this sense Granger causality represents just a statistical causality and the results of Granger causality tests do not tell us anything about the underlying structure or the investigated linkages (for a systematic account on causal relationships see Pearl, 2000). The link that would illustrate causality in an economic sense has to be established on the basis of a theoretical model that would predict specific causal relationships. These relationships are then formally tested.

Granger causality tests are very popular in economic research. Particularly, they are often used to test linkages and information flows between different markets. For example, the test can be used to study the relationships between returns on different stock markets, returns on spot and future markets, short and long interest rates, etc. To test the null hypothesis of x_t not Granger causing y_t we estimate the following unrestricted and restricted model specifications.

---

57 Other applications of the *VAR* framework on various economic issues in the European emerging markets are numerous. Some of them can be found in Festić (2006), Horská (2002), Hušek and Formánek (2005), and Stavrev (2006), to name just a few.

Unrestricted:
$$y_t = \alpha + \sum_{i=1}^{p} \gamma_i y_{t-i} + \sum_{i=1}^{p} \delta_i x_{t-i} + \varepsilon_t. \qquad (4.8)$$

Restricted:
$$y_t = \alpha + \sum_{i=1}^{p} \gamma_i y_{t-i} + \varepsilon_t. \qquad (4.9)$$

The intuition behind the test is straightforward. Under the null hypothesis of x_t not Granger causing y_t the lagged values of x_t are assumed to have no explanatory power on the current values of y_t. For that we test the null hypothesis $H_0: \delta_1 = \delta_2 = \dots = \delta_i = 0$ using a simple F-test. We compute the F-statistics

$$F = \frac{(SSR_R - SSR_U)/p}{SSR_U/(T-2p-1)},$$

where SSR_R and SSR_U stand for the sum of the squared residuals of the restricted and unrestricted regressions, respectively, p is the number of restrictions, in this case equal to the number of lags, and $(T - 2p - 1)$ is the number of degrees of freedom of the unrestricted regression, as T stands for the number of observations. Under the null hypothesis the F-statistics has an F-distribution with p and $(T - 2p - 1)$ degrees of freedom.

Before performing the test, similar to *VAR* models, we need to choose the appropriate lag length p. The common approach is to choose the lag length p that minimizes the information criteria of the unrestricted equation (4.8). We use the simple univariate versions of the *Akaike* (*AIC*), *Hannan-Quinn* (*HQIC*), or *Schwarz Bayes* (*SBIC*) *information criteria* that were introduced and referenced in section 3.1.5.

Note that for each pair of variables y_t and x_t, we can perform two Granger causality tests. We can test the null hypothesis of x_t not Granger causing y_t and the null hypothesis of y_t not Granger causing x_t. Typically, each of these tests is performed separately in a univariate framework and the lag length p is also determined separately, and therefore can differ with each of the tests. An alternative way would be to perform the tests in a *VAR* framework using the cross-equation restriction *likelihood ratio test* as described in the previous section. The lag length p would be then chosen, when estimating the unrestricted two equation *VAR* model and consequently, would be the same with both tests. However, the univariate approach clearly dominates in empirical literature.

After having performed the two Granger causality tests with the pair of variables y_t and x_t we can get three types of results. If no Granger causality relationship is detected, then the two variables do not interact with each other. If y_t Granger causes x_t and x_t also Granger causes y_t, then a feedback causality is present between the two variables. If one of the variables, say y_t, Granger causes x_t, but x_t does not Granger cause y_t, then y_t can be seen as weakly exogenous to x_t.

Similar to the variables employed in *VAR* models, it is important to real-ize that Granger causality tests applied to level variables make sense only if the two variables are stationary, that is $I(0)$.[58] If the series are nonstationary in levels but stationary in first differences, then Granger causality tests should be carried out in first differences. An additional problem that arises in this con-text is that ignoring long-run *cointegration* relationships among the variables (see the following sections) may lead to spurious causality. Thus, causality tests for $I(1)$ variables linked with a long-term *cointegration* relationship should be conducted in an *error correction model* framework as described in the follow-ing sections. Only if the two $I(1)$ variables are not connected via a *cointegrating vector*, a simple Granger causality test in first differences can be performed. A coherent testing strategy for determining causality between pairs of vari-ables is summarized in Figure 4.2 in the next section.

Application of the *VAR* framework in conjunction with Granger-causality is competently adopted by Dibooglu and Kutan (2001), who examine Brada's (1998) conjecture that real exchange rates in some economies should follow a path that mirrors the effect of real shocks and in others they should follow a path that reflects monetary shocks. To test this hypothesis, they apply a struc-tural *VAR* model and, assuming the long-run neutrality of nominal shocks, they decompose real exchange rate and price movements into those attributable to real and nominal shocks. Using monthly data from 1990 to 1999 for Hungary and Poland, they find that nominal shocks had a major influence in explaining real exchange rate movements in Poland, while real shocks had a larger influ-ence on real exchange rate movements in Hungary. Another example also em-ploys monetary data. Gilman and Nakov (2004) empirically test the dynamics of the endogenous growth monetary economy model on data from two (at that time) accession countries – Hungary and Poland. They estimate a *VAR* system with endogenously determined multiple structural breaks (see section 3.6.2 for details). Their results indicate Granger causality positively running from money to inflation and negatively from inflation to growth for both countries.

The methodology has also been widely used in analyzing capital markets. Hanousek and Filer (2000) employed a Granger causality technique to exam-ine whether secondary equity markets in the Czech Republic, Hungary, Poland and Slovakia exhibited the key characteristics of semi-strong efficiency, i.e. the ability to fully reflect newly-released public information in stock prices. They found substantial evidence of a relationship between lagged economic factors

58 Toda and Yamamoto (1995) proposed a procedure that allows causal inference to be conducted in level *VAR*s that may contain integrated processes but does not involve rigorous attention and strict reliance upon integration and cointegration properties of any or all variables in the system. Therefore, it is preferred to retain a conservative approach. For application of Toda and Yamamoto (1995) procedure in the context of cointegration between economic activity and stock markets in CEE, see Lyócsa et al. (2011a).

and equity returns in Poland and Hungary, thus detecting possibilities for profitable trading strategies. A different pattern was found for the Czech and Slovak markets, but based on other factors the two markets could hardly be considered as efficient during the period researched. Further, Stavárek (2005) analyzed causal relationships among stock prices and effective exchange rates in a mix of the U.S. and old and new EU countries. The results show much stronger causality in countries with developed capital and foreign-exchange markets (e.g. old EU countries and the U.S.). Causal links are also found to be running predominantly from stock prices to exchange rates.[59]

Further application to capital markets is provided by Baumöhl and Výrost (2010) who applied the concept of Granger causality to analyze relationships between stock market indices in the U.S., Europe, and Asia during 2000–2010 period. The main contribution of this work is not the estimation itself, but the extensions to account for the effects of nonsynchronous trading due to (i) the fact that during the same time period number of active trading days differs for each stock exchange, and (ii) the problem arising from stock exchanges operating in various time-zones. To deal with both issues the authors proposed (i) a matching process based on continuous returns, (ii) a modification of the functional form of the original Granger specification. When nonsynchronous trading was *not* accounted for the results showed significant Granger causality in the direction from the U.S. indices to other regions, but no significant causality could be identified in the opposite direction. However, when the modified model accounting for nonsynchronous trading effects was estimated, the bilateral causality links among all markets were found to be significant. The results demonstrate the importance of the choice of methodology with respect to the nature of the data in general, and need to account for nonsynchronous trading in particular.

An important feature of Granger causality tests often neglected in empirical research but emphasized already by Granger (1969) is their sensitivity to *data frequency* or in other words to the time intervals in which the data are collected. When looking at the construction of Granger causality tests, the sensitivity to data frequency is not surprising. The test of Granger causality investigates if lagged values of one variable have explanatory power over the current values of other variables. For example, when moving from quarterly to yearly data, what used to be information contained in the lagged values with quarterly data becomes information contained in current values with yearly data. The dependence on data frequency can be even more dramatic. For example, Černý and Koblas (2004) or Černý (2008) investigate the time structure

---

59   The versatility of the Granger causality technique is evidenced in its application on various economic topics researched during recent developments in Central and Eastern Europe. The applications can be found in Bekő (2003), Feridun (2006), Horská (2002), and Oplotnik (2003), among many others.

in which markets react to the information revealed in prices on other markets. They use high frequency intra-day data on indices from major world stock markets as well as from emerging Central and Eastern European stock markets and show that the results of Granger causality tests change significantly with data frequency shifts in a range of only several minutes.

Another study with high-frequency daily data in the Central European marketplace is Hanousek and Kočenda (1998) who analyzed the interactions between the interest rates of short and long maturities on the Czech interbank market, and compared results before and after the financial crisis in 1997. In this environment strong bilateral links from one maturity to another support the hypothesis of market integration, while unilateral links point at market segmentation and arbitrage opportunities. It was found that the relatively stable environment of the fixed exchange rate regime and semi-regulated interest rates provided a soft environment for the links among key interest rates to evolve; before the crisis the links among key interest rates were very weak. During the turbulent times of a financial crisis, the prevailing links among interest rates gained strength. The financial crisis caused some damage to the economy, but its occurrence also led to a reestablishment of links on the money market.

4.3 COINTEGRATION AND ERROR CORRECTION MODELS

A typical feature of economic time series is the presence of a unit root in levels and stationarity in first differences (see section 3.4). Such time series are said to be $I(1)$, or integrated of the order 1.[60] The behavior of $I(1)$ time series is substantially different from the behavior of time series that are stationary in levels, that is, integrated of the order 0 (denoted as $I(0)$).

To illustrate the differences imagine the simplest examples of $I(0)$ and $I(1)$ time series, a white noise

$$y_t = \varepsilon_t$$

and a random walk

$$y_t = y_{t-1} + \varepsilon_t = \left(y_{t-2} + \varepsilon_{t-1}\right) + \varepsilon_t = \left(\left(y_{t-3} + \varepsilon_{t-2}\right) + \varepsilon_{t-1}\right) + \varepsilon_t = \dots = \sum_{i=0}^{t} \varepsilon_i.$$

---

60 Recall that Nelson and Plosser (1982) found thirteen out of the fourteen investigated U.S. macroeconomic time series to be $I(1)$. These findings were later revisited by Perron (1989) who allowed for the presence of structural changes in his unit root test and found ten out of the fourteen time series to be broken trend stationary (see section 3.5.1). Thus, the $I(1)$ property of economic time series is probably not as dominant as Nelson and Plosser (1982) might suggest, but still, it is very common.

Note that the random walk time series can be expressed as the sum of all previous white noise disturbances ε_i and that differencing the random walk time series yields the white noise time series. In other words the random walk time series *integrates* all the previous white noise disturbances. As a result the two time series differ in many crucial aspects. For example, a white noise and generally any zero mean $I(0)$ time series y_t has a finite variance and autocorrelations ρ_k that decrease with large enough k so that their sum is finite. Hence, an innovation has only a temporary effect on y_t and the expected time between crossings of the value 0 is finite. Conversely, a random walk and generally any $I(1)$ time series with $y_0 = 0$ has a variance that goes to infinity with t, its theoretical autocorrelations ρ_k approach 1 as t goes to infinity for all k, an innovation has a permanent effect on y_t, and the expected time between crossings of the value 0 is infinite.

Having in mind the "wild" properties of $I(1)$ time series, it is not surprising that $I(1)$ is a dominant property. If x_t is $I(0)$ and y_t is $I(1)$, then any linear combination of x_t and y_t will be $I(1)$. Typically, any linear combination of $I(1)$ time series will be also $I(1)$. However, in some cases, particular linear combinations of $I(1)$ time series can be $I(0)$. If such a linear combination exists, then the time series are called *cointegrated*. This property is intuitively illustrated in Figure 4.1. Its left panel shows developments of two upward trending series that are thus obviously nonstationary, while the right panel shows their stationary linear combination that mean-reverts to a constant. Cointegration is a prominent property of $I(1)$ time series, because linear combinations of $I(0)$ time series will be always trivially $I(0)$.

The concept of cointegration was first introduced by Granger (1981) and Granger and Weiss (1983), while the classical reference is Engle and Granger (1987). The presence of cointegration among economic time series is interesting not only from a statistical point of view but also has important implications for the properties of the economy that generated a cointegrated time series. If two time series are cointegrated, then the time series of the deviations from the cointegrating linear combination is stationary. Therefore, the cointegrating linear combination defines a long run equilibrium relationship. The existence of this equilibrium must be due to some real economic forces. Naturally, most of the time the variables will be out of the equilibrium but will never drift too far away, as they will always be forced back towards it. Formally, this idea can be expressed with so-called *error correction models*. In error correction models, the direction and the magnitude of the current movement of a variable is a function of its past deviation from the long run equilibrium. The *Granger representation theorem* proved in Granger (1983) or Engle and Granger (1987) shows that cointegrated time series can always be represented by an error correction model and conversely that the existence of an error correction model implies cointegration. Thus, we can expect cointegration among variables

Figure 4.1: Example of two cointegrated time series.

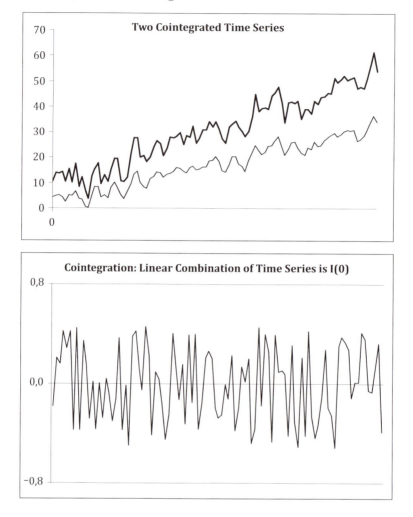

where intuition or economic theory suggests the presence of some forces that would push these variables towards an equilibrium. For example, Engle and Granger (1987) find in their examples the following pairs of variables to be cointegrated: consumption and income, short and long term interest rates, and nominal GDP and M2.

In the following sections we will first define cointegration and discuss some of its important aspects and then introduce the two most popular approaches to testing for cointegration: the *Engle-Granger methodology* (Engle and Granger, 1987) and the *Johansen methodology* (Johansen, 1988, 1991 and Johansen and Juselius, 1990).

4.3.1 DEFINITION OF COINTEGRATION

Lets start with a simple definition for two $I(1)$ variables. A pair of time series x_t and y_t that are both $I(1)$ and free of any deterministic components (having no drift or trend in mean) are said to be *cointegrated* of the order $(1,1)$, denoted by $CI(1,1)$, if there exist a non-trivial (non-zero) linear combination $z_t = \beta_1 x_t + \beta_2 y_t$ that is $I(0)$. The vector $\beta = (\beta_1, \beta_2)' \neq 0$ is called the *cointegrating vector*.

In reality, more complicated cases can occur than those described by this simple definition. Therefore, we will list below several important aspects of the issue of cointegration.

1. The definition can be generalized to the case of N variables and higher orders of integration than $I(1)$. Recall that a time series is said to be integrated of the order d, denoted $I(d)$, if it achieves stationarity after differencing d times. The N components of a vector $y_t = (y_{1t}, y_{2t}, ..., y_{Nt})'$ are said to be cointegrated of the of the order (d, b), denoted $CI(d,b)$, if each of the N components of y_t is $I(d)$, and if a non-trivial linear combination $z_t = \beta_1 y_{1t} + \beta_2 y_{2t} + \cdots + \beta_N y_{Nt} = \beta' y_t$ exists that is $I(d - b)$. The cointegrating vector β has $N \times 1$ dimensions, in this case, $\beta = (\beta_1, \beta_2, ..., \beta_N)' \neq 0$. The generalization to higher orders of integration does not have many applications in economics, because integration of an order higher than 1 is very rare with meaningful economic time series. Therefore, from now on by cointegration we will always mean the $I(1,1)$ case. On the other hand, the generalization to more than two variables has numerous applications in economics, because economic theory often suggests defining the equilibrium relationship with more than two variables.

2. With $N > 2$ variables there might be more than one cointegrating linear combination or in other words more than one equilibrium relationship. In general the number of linearly independent cointegrating relationships r can range between 0 and $N - 1$ ($0 \leq r \leq N - 1$). The number r is called the *cointegrating rank*. With $r > 1$ linearly independent equilibrium relationships there are r linearly independent cointegrating vectors $\beta^{(i)} = (\beta_1^{(i)}, \beta_2^{(i)}, ..., \beta_N^{(i)})'$, $i = 1,..., r$, and β becomes a $N \times r$ *cointegrating matrix*:

$$\beta = \left(\beta^{(1)}, \beta^{(2)}, ..., \beta^{(\ )} \right) = \begin{bmatrix} \beta_1^{(1)} & \beta_1^{(2)} & \cdots & \beta_1^{(\ )} \\ \beta_2^{(1)} & \beta_2^{(2)} & \cdots & \beta_2^{(\ )} \\ \cdot & \cdot & \cdot & \cdot \\ \cdot & \cdot & \cdot & \cdot \\ \cdot & \cdot & \cdot & \cdot \\ \beta^{(1)} & \beta_N^{(2)} & & \beta_N^{(\ )} \end{bmatrix}.$$

Note that the rank of the matrix β is by construction r.

3. The cointegrating vectors and consequently the equilibrium relationships are not uniquely identified. If there are r linearly independent cointegrating vectors, then any linear combination of these vectors is a cointegrating vector as well. Thus, the cointegrating vectors define an *equilibrium subspace* in the N dimensional space of the N cointegrated variables. The subspace is defined by the equilibrium equation $\beta'y_t = 0$ and its dimension is $N - r$. In the simplest case of two cointegrated variables x_t and y_t the subspace is a one-dimensional line defined by the equation $\beta_1 x_t + \beta_2 y_t = 0$.

4. Note that the cointegrating linear combination $z_t = \beta'y_t$ is a time series of the deviations from the long run equilibrium defined by the equation $\beta'y_t = 0$. Because z_t is $I(0)$, or in other words stationary, it tends to return to 0 in the long run; therefore, $\beta'y_t = 0$ can be interpreted as the long run equilibrium.

5. Cointegrated variables *share common stochastic trends*. To illustrate this statement imagine two $I(1)$ time series x_t and y_t decomposed into a stationary component and a random walk

$$x_t = s_{1t} + r_{1t},$$

$$y_t = s_{2t} + r_{2t},$$

where s_{1t} and s_{2t} are stationary $I(0)$ processes and r_{1t} and r_{2t} are random walks defined by the equations

$$r_{1t} = r_{1t-1} + \varepsilon_{1t},$$

$$r_{2t} = r_{2t-1} + \varepsilon_{2t}.$$

The random walks are obviously $I(1)$ and represent stochastic trends. Due to the dominance of the $I(1)$ property both time series x_t and y_t are $I(1)$ as well. For x_t and y_t to be cointegrated there must exist a linear combination $z_t = \beta_1 x_t + \beta_2 y_t$ that is $I(0)$. With such a linear combination the random walk components must cancel out, otherwise z_t could not be $I(0)$:

$$z_t = \beta_1 x_t + \beta_2 y_t = \beta_1 s_{1t} + \beta_2 s_{2t} + \beta_1 r_{1t} + \beta_2 r_{2t}.$$

The linear combination of two $I(0)$ variables $\beta_1 s_{1t} + \beta_2 s_{2t}$ is trivially $I(0)$. However, the linear combination of the two stochastic trends $\beta_1 r_{1t} + \beta_2 r_{2t}$ is in general always $I(1)$, unless $\beta_1 r_{1t} + \beta_2 r_{2t} = 0$. Thus, for z_t to be $I(0)$ it must hold that

$r_{1t} = -\beta_2/\beta_1 r_{2t}$. This means that the two stochastic trends must be generated by the same random walk processes and can differ only in a linear scaling factor $-\beta_2/\beta_1$.

6. The presented definition of cointegration requires the cointegrated time series to be free of any deterministic components. This is not a common feature of economic time series. With such a definition we would have to subtract all the deterministic components before we could proceed to the study of cointegration. In practice and particularly in the tests for cointegration, a different approach is used. The linear cointegrating combination is almost always allowed to be stationary up to a constant and optionally also up to a constant and a deterministic time trend. Thus, the $I(0)$ equilibrium relationship can be written as

$$z_t = \mu + \gamma t + \beta_1 y_{1t} + \beta_2 y_{2t} + \cdots + \beta_N y_{Nt} = \beta_0 + \beta' y_t, \text{ where } \beta_0 = \mu + \gamma t.$$

If there is more than one equilibrium relationship, then β is the cointegrating matrix consisting of the r cointegrating vectors and β_0 is a vector of r deterministic components for each of the equilibrium relationships. The inclusion of the constant or deterministic time trend in the cointegrating linear combination might also have other reasons than the presence of a constant or a deterministic trend in the cointegrated data. It might be the case that a constant or time trend is present not in the data but in the cointegrating combination itself, meaning that the equilibrium linear combination does not sum up to zero or is not constant over time. Unlike the Engle-Granger methodology, these cases are distinguished in the Johansen methodology of testing for cointegration (see section 4.3.4.).

   According to the *Granger representation theorem* cointegrated time series can always be represented by an *error correction model* and conversely, the existence of an error correction model implies cointegration. The simplest error correction model of two cointegrated variables x_t and y_t can be written as

$$\Delta x_t = \mu_1 + \alpha_1 z_{t-1} + \varepsilon_{1t}, \tag{4.10}$$

$$\Delta y_t = \mu_2 + \alpha_2 z_{t-1} + \varepsilon_{2t}, \tag{4.11}$$

where ε_1 and ε_2 are white noise disturbances that might be correlated and z_t is the equilibrium cointegrating linear combination $z_t = \beta_1 x_t + \beta_2 y_t$. Because the long run equilibrium is defined by the equation $\beta_1 x_t + \beta_2 y_t = 0$, z_t denotes the $I(0)$ deviations from this equilibrium and the meaning of equations (4.10) and (4.11) is that current changes of x_t and y_t are proportional to the previous deviation from the equilibrium z_{t-1}. For the model to be an error correction model at least one of the *adjustment coefficients* α_1 or α_2 must be non-zero and the sign of the adjustment coefficients α_1 and α_2 must be such that the deviations from the equilibrium are being corrected and not magnified. Note that due to the presence of cointegration, all elements of equations (4.10) and (4.11) are $I(0)$.

In general cases the simplest specification of the error correction model described by equations (4.10) and (4.11) might not suffice to assure that ε_1 and ε_2 are white noise disturbances, free of any autocorrelations. Therefore, the error correction model equations should be augmented with lags of Δx_t and Δy_t (similar to when we proceeded from the simple to the augmented Dickey-Fuller test in section 3.4.2):

$$\Delta x_t = \mu_1 + \alpha_1 z_{t-1} + \sum_{i=1}^{p} \left(\pi_{11}^{(i)} \Delta x_{t-i} + \pi_{12}^{(i)} \Delta y_{t-i} \right) + \varepsilon_{1t} , \qquad (4.12)$$

$$\Delta y_t = \mu_2 + \alpha_2 z_{t-1} + \sum_{i=1}^{p} \left(\pi_{21}^{(i)} \Delta x_{t-i} + \pi_{22}^{(i)} \Delta y_{t-i} \right) + \varepsilon_{2t} . \qquad (4.13)$$

The generalization to more than two cointegrated variables is straightforward. The error correction model for N cointegrated variables can be written in matrix form as

$$\Delta y_t = \mu + \alpha \beta' y_{t-1} + \sum_{i=1}^{p} \Pi_i \Delta y_{t-i} + \varepsilon_t , \qquad (4.14)$$

where $y_t = (y_{1t}, y_{2t}, ..., y_{Nt})'$ is the $N \times 1$ vector of the N cointegrated variables, $\varepsilon_t = (\varepsilon_{1t}, \varepsilon_{2t}, ...\varepsilon_{Nt})'$ is a $N \times 1$ vector of N possibly correlated white noise disturbances, $\mu = (\mu_1, \mu_2, ..., \mu_N)'$ is a $N \times 1$ vector of intercepts, Π_i are $N \times N$ matrixes of autoregressive coefficients, $\beta = (\beta^{(1)}, \beta^{(2)}, ..., \beta^{(r)})$ is the $N \times r$ cointegrating matrix consisting of the r cointegrating vectors, and α is a $N \times r$ matrix of the r adjustment coefficients for each of the N variables. Equation (4.14) can be rewritten as

$$\Delta y_t = \mu + \Pi y_{t-1} + \sum_{i=1}^{p} \Pi_i \Delta y_{t-i} + \varepsilon_t , \qquad (4.15)$$

where the $\Pi = \alpha \beta'$ is a $N \times N$ matrix that is by construction not of the full rank N but of the rank $r \le N - 1$. Thus the rank of the matrix equals the cointegrating rank r.

Equation (4.15) resembles a *VAR* model in first differences, except for the term Πy_{t-1}, which is in levels. In fact, the term Πy_{t-1} makes it a *VAR* in levels rather than first differences, because any *VAR* model in levels can be rewritten in the form of equation (4.15) using the *ADF* factorization described in section 3.4.2 (though for the univariate case only). The only difference from a *VAR* model in levels lies in the reduced rank of matrix Π that makes equation (4.15) an error correction representation of the N cointegrated variables $y_{1t}, y_{2t}, ..., y_{Nt}$. A *VAR* in first differences would miss important information about cointegration. Thus, with cointegrated variables the error correction model is the only correctly specified multivariate model to be estimated. This brings us back to the issue of causality discussed in the section 4.2 devoted to Granger causality. Causality tests of $I(1)$ variables linked with a cointegration relationship should be conducted in the error correction model framework, rather than with the use of simple Granger causality tests applied on first differences. A coherent testing strategy is summarized in Figure 4.2. When following this strategy, a researcher is able to avoid possible traps due to incorrect approaches or misspecification of the chosen model.

Figure 4.2: Testing strategy for determining causality between pairs of variables.

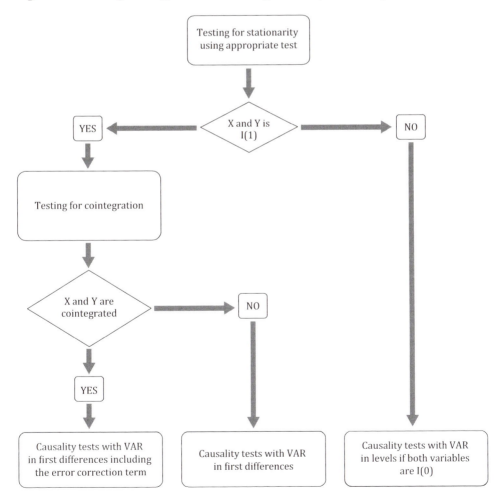

The vector of intercepts μ included in the error correction model means that there are either constants in the cointegrating relationships or linear trends in the data, or both. (Note that with Δy_t on the left hand side of equation (4.15) the intercept μ transforms into a trend in y_t.) When this is not the case, then the vector of intercepts should be excluded. If there are either linear trends in the cointegrating relationships or even quadratic trends in the data or both, then the error correction model should be specified with a vector of constants and linear trends as well.

In the following sections we will present the *Engle-Granger methodology* and briefly outline the *Johansen methodology* of testing for cointegration. While the Engle-Granger methodology is based on the *ADF* test applied to the time series of deviations from the equilibrium, the Johansen methodology departs from the error correction representation and focuses on the rank of matrix Π in equation (4.15).

4.3.2 THE ENGLE-GRANGER METHODOLOGY

Even though the issue of cointegration is very complex, the testing methodology proposed by Engle and Granger (1987) is surprisingly simple and straightforward. Unfortunately, the simplicity is not at zero cost. The test proposed by Engle and Granger (1987) is able to detect only a fraction of the whole phenomena of cointegration. It can distinguish if two or more variables are cointegrated and it enables the estimation of a simple form of the error correction model. The limitation becomes serious particularly in the case of more than two cointegrated variables, where the Engle-Granger methodology does not help to decide what is the cointegrating rank. Unlike the Johansen methodology (section 4.3.4), it can only test for the presence of cointegration but not for the number of cointegrating relationships among the variables.

We will present the Engle-Granger methodology for the simplest case of two cointegrated variables x_t and y_t, which is also its most common application. In the end of this section we will briefly discuss its generalization to more than two variables. The methodology can be divided into four steps:

1. Before we proceed with the test of cointegration, we have to pretest x_t and y_t for the order of integration. The two variables should be $I(1)$. To determine the order of integration of the two time series we can apply the unit root tests described in section 3.4. The tests must be applied both on the levels and first differences of x_t and y_t. Generally we can choose any of the unit root tests but the most common choice would be the *ADF* test (see section 3.4.2), or combined with the *KPSS* test (see section 3.4.4). For x_t and y_t to be $I(1)$ the two time series must appear nonstationary in levels and stationary in first differences.

Recall that the unit root tests can be performed in different types that enable testing for level or trend stationarity. A level stationary time series is stationary up to a level, while a trend stationary time series is stationary up to a level and a deterministic linear time trend.

The proper choice of the unit root test type is important. With the wrong choice we can make, for example, the following mistake. Imagine that both x_t and y_t can be decomposed into a deterministic component, consisting of a constant and linear time trend, and a stochastic stationary component. With the application of unit root tests that do not allow for the deterministic time trend, we will find the two time series to be nonstationary in levels and stationary in first differences, that is, $I(1)$. There will always be a linear combination of the two time series that will cancel out the deterministic time trends and will appear as $I(0)$. Therefore, we would conclude that the two time series are cointegrated, even though it would be a trivial result in this case. Thus, when we say that x_t and y_t should be both $I(1)$, we mean that the stochastic (non-deterministic) components of the time series should be $I(1)$. The unit root test types investigating this feature should be selected accordingly. If the time series appear to be trending, then we should test the levels for trend stationarity and the first differences for level stationarity (a linear time trend will cancel out in first differences.). If the two time series appear to be free of deterministic time trends, then we can test only for level stationarity with both the levels and first differences.

2. We use simple *OLS* to estimate the long run equilibrium relationship by estimating the equation

$$y_t = \mu + \beta x_t + \varepsilon_t \text{ or} \tag{4.16}$$

$$y_t = \mu + \gamma t + \beta x_t + \varepsilon_t. \tag{4.17}$$

With equation (4.16) we allow only for the presence of a constant, while with equation (4.17) we allow for the presence of a constant and a linear time trend. As was mentioned in the previous section, the presence of the constant or the linear time trend can in general be due either to a constant or linear time trend present in the data generating process of x_t and y_t, or in the cointegrating relationship itself. The Engle-Granger methodology does not distinguish between these cases. In fact, it does not even take into account the possibility that the linear time trend could be present in the cointegrating relationship. Thus, the linear time trend in equation (4.17) controls only for possible linear time trends in the two time series. This gives us an easy hint which of the two equations to choose. If the two time series appear to be trending, then we should estimate equation (4.17), otherwise we estimate equation (4.16). Engle and Granger do not provide any guidance for which of the variables x_t or y_t should be chosen as dependent in regressions (4.16) and (4.17). Therefore, we can try both alternatives. The results of the tests presented in the following steps should be the same with any of the alternatives. Unfortunately, in reality the two variables can sometimes appear as cointegrated in one case and as not cointegrated in the other, which is clearly an undesired ambiguous result. In other words, the Engle-Granger methodology sometimes appears inconsistent. Another objection can be risen against regressions (4.16) and (4.17). There is no control for the possible endogeneity of x_t and no correction for the serial correlation of the residuals. The issue of endogeneity and serial correlation is treated in extensions to the methodology that are discussed in section 4.3.3.

In spite of these objections, if the two variables are cointegrated with the normalized cointegrating vector $(1, -\beta)$, we can expect OLS to find a consistent estimate of β. If x_t and y_t are cointegrated, then only the residuals from the cointegrating linear combination are stationary and have finite variance, while the residuals from all other combinations contain a unit root and have infinite variances. Thus, when minimizing the least squares, we should clearly select the cointegrating linear combination. Engle and Granger even show that if x_t and y_t are cointegrated, then the OLS estimate of β from regression (4.16) or (4.17) converges to the true value of β with T^{-1} and not only $T^{-1/2}$ as usual OLS estimates do (T denotes the sample size).[61]

3. We apply the ADF test on the residual time series e_t from regression (4.16) or (4.17) in order to decide if the residuals are stationary or not. The null hypothesis claims that the residuals contain a unit root, while the alternative is that the residuals are stationary. In the context of the cointegration test the hypothesis can be restated as follows. H_0: x_t and y_t are not cointegrated; H_A: x_t and y_t are cointegrated. As e_t are regression residuals, we allow neither for an intercept nor for a trend with the ADF test. That is, we estimate the equation:

$$\Delta e_t = \gamma e_{t-1} + \sum_{i=1}^{K} \rho_i \Delta e_{t-i} + \varepsilon_t,$$

and proceed as described in section 3.4.2 on the ADF test. The only difference from a standard ADF test is that we have to use different critical values than those tabulated by Dickey and Fuller. With e_t being a series of regression residuals the critical values are even "stricter" than those used with standard ADF tests. By "stricter" we mean lower, that is, less likely to allow the rejection of H_0. The most commonly used critical values were computed with Monte Carlo simulations by MacKinnon (1991); critical values are built into most statistical

---

61   Such estimates are sometimes called superconsistent.

software packages. The critical values differ depending on the number of variables tested for cointegration. Different critical values should also be chosen for tests with residuals from regression (4.16) – no trend; and from regression (4.17) – with trend. Finally, the critical values also depend on the number of observations T. However, here the sensitivity is not that dramatic and the same critical values can with caution be used also with samples of different sizes than those simulated by MacKinnon (1991).

4. Last, if the *ADF* test indicates cointegration (stationarity of the residuals e_t), we should estimate the error correction model

$$\Delta x_t = \mu_1 + \alpha_1 z_{t-1} + \sum_{i=1}^{p} \left(\pi_{11}^{(i)} \Delta x_{t-i} + \pi_{12}^{(i)} \Delta y_{t-i} \right) + \varepsilon_{1t} \,,$$

$$\Delta y_t = \mu_2 + \alpha_2 z_{t-1} + \sum_{i=1}^{p} \left(\pi_{21}^{(i)} \Delta x_{t-i} + \pi_{22}^{(i)} \Delta y_{t-i} \right) + \varepsilon_{2t} \,,$$

where z_t denotes the deviation from the equilibrium. As we do not know the true value of this deviation, Engle and Granger suggest to replace it with the residuals e_t from the equilibrium equation (4.16) or (4.17). That is, the error correction model becomes

$$\Delta x_t = \mu_1 + \alpha_1 e_{t-1} + \sum_{i=1}^{p} \left(\pi_{11}^{(i)} \Delta x_{t-i} + \pi_{12}^{(i)} \Delta y_{t-i} \right) + \varepsilon_{1t} \,, \tag{4.18}$$

$$\Delta y_t = \mu_2 + \alpha_2 e_{t-1} + \sum_{i=1}^{p} \left(\pi_{21}^{(i)} \Delta x_{t-i} + \pi_{22}^{(i)} \Delta y_{t-i} \right) + \varepsilon_{2t} \,. \tag{4.19}$$

For x_t and y_t to be cointegrated, at least one of the coefficients α_1 or α_2 should be significantly different from zero and should have the proper sign, implying that the deviation e_{t-1} is being corrected and not magnified. To estimate equations (4.18) and (4.19) we can proceed similarly as with the estimation of *VAR* models (see section 4.1.3). The error correction equations (4.18) and (4.19) can be estimated separately using *OLS* or jointly as *SUR*. The *SUR* approach brings efficiency yields only if a different set of regressors is included in the two equations. This means that different lag lengths must be chosen in the two equations. In fact, the lag length can differ also for the first differences of x_t and y_t within each of the equations. To choose the proper lag length we can use the information criteria similarly as with the estimation of *VAR* models. We can use either the multivariate versions of the criteria or decide the lag length for each equation separately with the univariate versions of the criteria. Eventually, we can also apply the cross-equation restriction *likelihood ratio test* as described in section 4.1.3. If the lag lengths are chosen correctly, then the residuals from equations (4.18) and (4.19) should be free of any serial correlation. However, they can still be contemporaneously mutually correlated.

So far we have presented the Engle-Granger methodology only for the case of two potentially cointegrated variables. The application of the methodology to $N > 2$ potentially cointegrated variables $y_1, y_2, ..., y_N$ is the same. The only difference is that the estimated equilibrium equations (4.16) and (4.17) become

$$y_{1t} = \mu + \sum_{i=2}^{N} \beta_i y_{it} + \varepsilon_t \,, \tag{4.20}$$

$$y_{1t} = \mu + \gamma t + \sum_{i=2}^{N} \beta_i y_{it} + \varepsilon_t \,. \tag{4.21}$$

It should be noted that with more than two variables the shortcomings of the Engle-Granger methodology become more obvious. With no guidance on which of the variables should be chosen as dependent in regression (4.20) or (4.21), there are N alternative ways in which the equilibrium equation can be estimated. The danger that we will get ambiguous results (in some cases suggesting cointegration and in some not) is therefore much higher than in the two-variable case. Moreover, always the residuals e_t from just one of the N alternative estimates of the equilibrium relationship can be included in the error correction model:

$$\Delta y_{1t} = \mu_1 + \alpha_1 e_{t-1} + \sum_{i=1}^{p} \left(\pi_{11}^{(i)} \Delta y_{1t-i} + \pi_{12}^{(i)} + \cdots + \pi_{1N}^{(i)} \Delta y_{Nt-i} \right) + \varepsilon_{1t}$$

$$\Delta y_{2t} = \mu_2 + \alpha_2 e_{t-1} + \sum_{i=1}^{p} \left(\pi_{21}^{(i)} \Delta y_{1t-i} + \pi_{22}^{(i)} + \cdots + \pi_{2N}^{(i)} \Delta y_{Nt-i} \right) + \varepsilon_{2t}$$

$$\cdot$$
$$\cdot$$
$$\cdot$$

$$\Delta y_{Nt} = \mu_N + \alpha_N e_{t-1} + \sum_{i=1}^{p} \left(\pi_{N1}^{(i)} \Delta y_{1t-i} + \pi_{N2}^{(i)} + \cdots + \pi_{NN}^{(i)} \Delta y_{Nt-i} \right) + \varepsilon_{Nt}$$

As a result, the error correction model can be also estimated in N different ways. Additionally, the error correction model is incomplete if more than one cointegrating relationship exists among the N variables. The error correction model is incomplete in the sense that it contains a deviation from only one of the equilibrium relationships that just happened to be estimated with equation

(4.20) or (4.21). It does not help in this case that the residuals can be generated in N alternative ways.

There are numerous applications of the cointegration and vector error correction model in the literature and understandably the techniques were used to study transition and integration phenomena in Central Europe.[62] An illustrative application with strong policy implications is Orlowski (2004), who examines the feasibility of adopting money growth rules as indicator variables of monetary policies for the countries converging to the euro. The analytical framework assumes an inflation target as the ultimate policy goal. The converging countries – Poland, Hungary, and the Czech Republic – act as "takers" of the inflation target, which is the eurozone's inflation forecast. The feasibility of adopting money growth rules depends on stable relationships between money and target variables, which are low inflation and a stable exchange rate. Long-run interactions between these variables are examined by employing the Johansen cointegration test (see section 4.3.4), along with short-run effects assessed with a vector error correction procedure. Empirical findings show that the nexus between money, inflation, and exchange rates is yet to be established in Poland, Hungary, and the Czech Republic. However, there are some encouraging signs from the VEC tests that at least short-run changes in M2 money have some bearing on inflation. Although it is not plausible to determine sensible money growth targets on the basis of the long-run cointegration relationships between these variables, policy-makers may consider giving more attention to the actual and projected money growth trends. This is because the above-mentioned transition-related processes are believed to be almost completed; therefore, the link between money and monetary policy target variables can be expected to become stronger in the future, during the period of active convergence to the euro.

The methodology has been applied also on issues related to capital markets. Podpiera (2001) considers the interaction among equity markets in the Czech Republic and those in developed countries as well as links with cross-listed securities traded in the Czech Republic whose global depository receipts (GDRs) are listed in London. The models used include Granger causality, cointegration, and error-correction models. The results demonstrate that the Czech market is indeed affected by the development of major international equity indices. This, however, explains little of the domestic market variability, so other factors related to stock market development need to be explicated. The prices of cross-

---

62 Examples of less traditional topics that employ cointegration and the ECM framework are the following two. Bulíř (2005) used a *univariate ECM* framework to study the stability of exchange rates in the Visegrad Four countries and showed a link between exchange rate stability and the liberalization of financial markets. Based on cointegration analysis and a vector error correction mechanism and using macroeconomic data, Feridun (2006) validated the German dominance hypothesis in the context of the Eastern enlargement of the EU in 2004.

listed securities on the domestic and London markets are cointegrated and an error-correction mechanism exists that corrects random deviations from parity. As this error-correction mechanism appears to be rather symmetric, and as the Granger causality tests suggest different causality patterns for individual stocks, neither of the two markets emerges as the dominant one. A variety of interactions exist between the local and London GDR markets.

From a different angle Syriopoulos (2006) investigates the dynamic linkages and effects of time-varying volatilities for major emerging Central European (CE) and developed stock markets (Germany and the USA). He estimates an error correction *VAR* and detects the presence of one cointegration vector indicating market comovements towards a stationary long-run equilibrium. His results from the estimation of an asymmetric *EGARCH* model indicate varying but persistent volatility effects for the CE markets. As an implication of his findings he concludes that international portfolio diversification can be less effective across cointegrated markets because risk cannot be reduced substantially and return can exhibit a volatile reaction to domestic and international shocks.

4.3.3 EXTENSIONS TO THE ENGLE-GRANGER METHODOLOGY

In the following sections we will outline selected techniques that can help to alleviate some of the shortcomings of the Engle-Granger methodology. The Engle-Granger residual-based cointegration test asserts that variables $y_1, y_2, ..., y_N$ form a long-term relationship if the residuals obtained from equation (4.20) or (4.21) are stationary. As already mentioned, the standard Granger-Engle specification (4.20) or (4.21) does not account for the potential endogeneity of the right-hand side variables. This shortcoming can be alleviated with several alternative cointegration methods.

The dynamic ordinary least squares method (*DOLS*) introduced by Stock and Watson (1993) accounts for the endogeneity of the regressors and serial correlation in the residuals by incorporating lags and leads of the regressors in first differences. The testing model is specified as

$$y_{1t} = \mu + \sum_{i=2}^{N} \beta_i y_{it} + \sum_{i=2}^{N} \sum_{j=-p_1}^{p_2} \delta_{ij} \Delta y_{it-j} + \varepsilon_t \, , \qquad (4.22)$$

where p_1 and p_2 denote leads and lags, respectively. The length of leads and lags can be determined on the basis of the information criteria. The presence of cointegration is assessed upon the stationarity of the residuals obtained from the long-term relationship (4.22), in a way similar to the Engle-Granger approach.

Another approach is a method that allows a mixture of $I(0)$ and $I(1)$ variables. The autoregressive distributed lag ($ARDL$) approach proposed by Pesaran, Shin and Smith (2001) departs from the error correction model, whose form under the $ARDL$ specification is given by

$$\Delta y_{1t} = \mu + \alpha \left(y_{1t-1} + \sum_{i=2}^{N} \beta_i y_{it-1} \right) + \sum_{j=1}^{p_1} \pi_1^{(j)} \Delta y_{1t-j} +$$

$$+ \sum_{j=1}^{p_2} \left(\pi_2^{(j)} \Delta y_{2t-j} + \pi_3^{(j)} \Delta y_{3t-j} + \cdots + \pi_N^{(j)} \Delta y_{Nt-j} \right) + \varepsilon_t \ . \qquad (4.23)$$

Here, the dependent variable in first differences is regressed on the lagged values of the dependent and independent variables in levels and first differences. To detect the presence of cointegrating relationships, Pesaran, Shin and Smith (2001) employ the so-called "bounds testing approach". Using conventional F-tests, the null of H_0: $\alpha = \beta_2 = \beta_3 = ... = \beta_N = 0$ is tested against the alternative hypothesis of H_A: $\alpha \neq 0$, $\beta_2 \neq 0$, $\beta_3 \neq 0$,..., $\beta_N \neq 0$. Pesaran, Shin and Smith (2001) tabulate two sets of critical values, one for the case when all variables are $I(1)$, i.e. upper bound critical values, and another for when all variables are $I(0)$, i.e. lower bound critical values. If the test statistics is higher than the upper bound critical value, the null of no cointegration is rejected in favor of the presence of cointegration. On the other hand, a F-statistics lower than the lower bound critical value implies the absence of cointegration. In the event that the calculated F-statistics lies between the two critical values, there is no clear indication of the absence or existence of a cointegrating relationship, though. An alternative to the single equation methods presented above is the Johansen cointegration technique briefly introduced in the next section.

A combination of the cointegration techniques introduced earlier, $DOLS$ and $ARDL$, is employed by Babetskii and Égert (2005) who study the development of the Czech national currency during 1993–2004 in the framework of the behavioral equilibrium exchange rate (BEER). It is found that an increase in productivity and a decrease in net foreign assets in the Czech economy lead to real exchange rate appreciation. The finding is complemented with an analysis of periods of over- and undervaluation. The authors conclude that the Czech BEER is of fine quality.

An application of the ARDL approach is adopted by Kočenda et al. (2013) to analyze the short- and long-term effects of exchange rate adjustment with respect to economic growth. An econometric exercise conducted for 60 countries in total provides evidence that exchange rate adjustments stimulate growth in the short term, but put a drag on the long-term growth performance. A crisis-related policy implication of Kočenda et al. (2013) is that exchange rate depreciation as a crisis solution strategy can be expected to provide short-term relief, but long-term pain.

One final note is that in section 5 we introduce unit root tests in panel data. This additional dimension helps to mitigate the chronic problem of unit root tests, which is their low power against the alternative hypothesis of stationarity. A similar strand of research can be traced with cointegration tests that, after all, are also based on unit root tests. Generalizing the standard Engle Granger methodology, Phillips and Ouliaris (1990) or Pedroni (1999 and 2004) proposed cointegration tests in panel data with a null hypothesis of no cointegration. Alternatively, McCoskey and Kao (1998) or Westerlund (2005 and 2007) developed panel data cointegration tests with a null hypothesis of cointegration.

4.3.4 THE JOHANSEN METHODOLOGY

The methodology proposed by Johansen (1988, 1991) investigates the issue of cointegration in its full complexity. Unlike the Engle-Granger methodology, it enables testing for the number of cointegrating vectors (the *cointegrating rank*) among *N* variables. We will only briefly outline the basic idea of the Johansen methodology that was further developed in Johansen and Juselius (1990, 1992). An elaborate description is available for example in Patterson (2000).

Johansen's approach departs from the *error correction model* specification described by equation (4.15). It relies on the relationship between the cointegrating rank, the rank of the matrix $\Pi = \alpha\beta'$ in (4.15), and the number of the non-zero eigenvalues of the matrix. Johansen formulates the following model of *N* variables $y_1, y_2,..., y_N$:

$$\Delta y_t = \Psi D_t + \Pi y_{t-1} + \sum_{i=1}^{p} \Pi_i \Delta y_{t-i} + \varepsilon_t, \qquad (4.24)$$

where $y_t = (y_{1t}, y_{2t},..., y_{Nt})'$ is a $N \times 1$ vector of *N* possibly cointegrated variables. Ψ is a $N \times d$ matrix of coefficients, while D_t is a $d \times 1$ vector of deterministic terms that might contain 1 to capture a constant, time trend *t*, or eventually also seasonal dummy variables or other intervention variables, if needed. Π and $\Pi_i, i = 1...p$ are $N \times N$ matrices of coefficients and $\varepsilon_t = (\varepsilon_{1t}, \varepsilon_{2t},..., \varepsilon_{Nt})$ is a $N \times 1$ vector of *N* normally distributed disturbances. The disturbances might be mutually correlated, but must be free of any serial correlation, which should be assured by a proper choice of the lag length *p*. Typically, *p* is chosen based on information criteria combined with a test for the absence of serial correlation in ε_t (e.g. the *LM* test).

Note that equation (4.24) represents an *ADF* factorization of a *VAR* in levels. Therefore, Johansen's test is sometimes interpreted as a generalization of the

ADF test. Similarly as with the *ADF* test, with Johansen's test we focus on the coefficient by y_{t-1}, on matrix Π. The rank of Π is of particular interest in this case. Matrix Π can be in the error correction spirit interpreted as $\Pi = \alpha\beta'$ with β being a $N \times r$ cointegrating matrix consisting of r cointegrating vectors and α being a $N \times r$ matrix of the adjustment coefficients. If there are r cointegrating vectors, then the rank of matrix Π is r, which is less than N (recall that the maximum number of cointegrating vectors is $N - 1$). Theoretically, the rank r of matrix Π can range from 0 to N meaning that equation (4.24) can cover the following cases:

1. $r = 0$ implies that Π is a zero matrix, all elements of y_t are $I(1)$, and (4.24) describes a *VAR* in first differences.
2. $0 < r < N$ implies that all elements of y_t are $I(1)$, r cointegrating vectors exist among y_t, and (4.24) describes an *error correction model*.
3. $r = N$ implies that all elements of y_t are $I(0)$ and (4.24) describes a *VAR* in levels.

Johansen proposes a *maximum likelihood estimator* of matrix Π and of its eigenvalues λ_i, $i = 1,..., N$. The rank of Π is in general equal to the number of its non-zero eigenvalues. Therefore, the test for the rank of Π can be interpreted as a test for the number of non-zero eigenvalues of Π. Based on the ordered sample of the estimated eigenvalues $\lambda_1 > \lambda_2 > \lambda_3 > ... > \lambda_N$, Johansen proposes two test statistics:

$$\lambda_{trace}(r) = -T \sum_{i=r+1}^{N} \ln(1-\lambda_i)$$
$$\lambda_{max}(r+1) = -T \ln(1-\lambda_{r+1}).$$

$\lambda_{trace}(r)$ is designed to test the hypothesis $H_0 : rank\ \Pi \leq r$ against the alternative $H_A : rank\ \Pi > r$, while $\lambda_{max}(r+1)$ is used to test the hypothesis $H_0 : rank\ \Pi \leq r$ against the alternative $H_A : rank\ \Pi = r+1$. A large value of $\lambda_{trace}(r)$ or $\lambda_{max}(r+1)$ leads to the rejection of H_0 in both cases. Using an appropriate sequence of tests with $\lambda_{trace}(r)$ and $\lambda_{max}(r+1)$ statistics and with different choices of r, the true rank of matrix Π can be estimated. Critical values for the $\lambda_{trace}(r)$ and $\lambda_{max}(r+1)$ statistics were computed with Monte Carlo simulations and are reported in Patterson (2000), for example. The critical values depend on $N - r$ and on the specification of the vector of deterministic terms Dt.

   The Johansen cointegration methodology is frequently used on various topics. One interesting application that is underlined by the assumption of a long-term relationship among variables is shown in Speight and McMillan (2001), who examine the time series properties of the monthly black-market dollar exchange rates in Bulgaria, former Czechoslovakia, former East Germany, Hungary, Poland, Romania, and former USSR using monthly data over the period 1955–1990. They find that all black market exchange rate series with the exception of the Deutschemark (expressed in logs) exhibit a unit root, and there is evidence of at least two cointegrating vectors linking the remaining rates. Weak exogeneity is rejected for the Bulgarian lev, Hungarian forint, and Romanian lei, but strong exogeneity cannot be rejected for the Czechoslovak koruna, Polish zloty, and Soviet ruble. This finding implies causality running from the latter group to the former group, which may be interpreted as reflecting channels of policy interdependence.[63]

The Johansen cointegration methodology has an evident advantage over the Engle-Granger methodology, since it can be used to estimate more than one cointegration relationship between two or more time series. Instead of depending on OLS estimation, the Johansen procedure depends on maximum likelihood estimation and uses sequential tests to determine the number of cointegrating vectors. Given the advantage of testing for multiple cointegration relationships, the Johansen procedure has found numerous application in the literature. The following example serves to illustrate the application of the methodology.

An important application of the Johansen cointegration test in finance is to test the Efficient Market Hypothesis (EMH) by examining the long-run relationship among the time series of prices of different assets. For example, if the prices in two markets are cointegrated, the long-run equilibrium relationship between those prices implies the possibility to forecast the price on one market based on the price on the other market. Since in an efficient market prices should not be predictable based on previous prices, the existence of a cointegration relationship suggests that markets are either not efficient or that market indices are driven by time-varying risk factors. However, the absence of a cointegration relationship is necessary but not sufficient condition for the EMH to hold. In one of the recent applications of the Johansen methodology, Fu and Pagani (2012) investigate the cointegration relationship among a group of international stock indices on five developed markets over the period 1974–1990. The results of the applied procedure provide evidence of a strong cointegration relationship, which suggests that there is a common trend among those stock indices and a long-run equilibrium relationship.

The methodology involves estimating an econometric model in which the link between five international stock indices is investigated. The cointegration test is formulated as the following VAR model:

$$\Delta y_t = \mu + \Pi y_{t-1} + \sum_{i=1}^{p} \Pi_i \Delta y_{t-i} + u_t.$$

63 Some additional applications of the Johansen methodology are Gerdtham and Löthgren (2002), Bekő (2003), Komárek and Melecký (2003), and Festić et al. (2011), among others.

In the above specification, $y_t = (y_{1t}, y_{2t}, y_{3t}, y_{4t}, y_{5t})$ is a 5 × 1 vector of potentially cointegrated variables, MSCI indices for five countries: the United States, Japan, the United Kingdom, Germany, and Canada.[64] The error u_t is assumed to be an i.i.d Gaussian process. All stock indices, in form of the natural logarithm, are I(1) processes. Thus, performing the Johansen test on the five I(1) variables means examining if there is a linear combination of these variables that is an I(0) process. In that sense, the Johansen test has an advantage over Engle and Granger's test procedure, which tests only for a pairwise cointegration relationship.

The long-run equilibrium and the short-run dynamics are examined. More precisely, the Johansen cointegration test is performed on quarterly data in a VAR specification with different lag lengths, eg. different values of p in the specification above. Testing for the presence of a cointegration relationship between series of the same order of integration involves the Johansen maximum likelihood test procedure. Specifically, the maximum likelihood estimator of matrix Π and its eigenvalues λ_i (i = 1,..., 5) is obtained. Since matrix Π can have rank r between 0 and 5, testing for the number of cointegrating relationships is equivalent to testing for the rank of Π, which also means testing for the number of nonzero eigenvalues. In order to determine the number of cointegration vectors, the trace statistics (λ_{trace}) is computed as

$$\lambda_{trace}(r) = -[T(\sum_{i=r+1}^{5} \ln(1 - \lambda_i))]$$

to test the null hypothesis of r cointegrating vectors against the alternative of more than r cointegrating vectors. The Johansen test starts with the null hypothesis of r = 0 (no cointegration). If the null hypothesis is rejected, then test proceeds by testing the hypothesis that r = 1 (one cointegrating relationship/vector). Since cointegration among n = 5 markets is analyzed the procedure continues until testing the hypothesis that r = 4, that is, $r = n - 1$.

Fu and Pagani (2012) report the results of the Johansen cointegration tests, with a lag specification p = 2 to analyze short-run cointegration and p = 8 to analyze long-run cointegration. The cointegration test results for a lag length of 8 reveal that the null hypothesis of no cointegretion is strongly rejected at the 1% significance level. Moreover, the hypotheses of a cointegration rank of up to three are all strongly rejected, which implies that the cointegration rank is four among the five stock indices. In VAR with a lag length of 2, the no-cointegration null hypothesis is rejected at the 5% significance level. These results indicate that there is little evidence of cointegration in short lag models but strong evidence in long lag models. The findings imply the existence of the

---

64   Morgan Stanley Capital International originally created the MSCI Index.

long run cointegration relationship between five international stock indices. This are grounds to reject the market efficiency hypothesis among these five markets.

5.

PANEL DATA AND UNIT ROOT TESTS

Combinations of the time series and cross-section dimensions allows assembling panels of data. In time series analysis panel data are used for various purposes, albeit less frequently than conventional time series. A relatively new segment of literature dealing with issues of economic convergence is closely related to methods known as panel unit root tests.

The growing body of empirical literature on economic growth has prompted research testing growth convergence among various countries. The issue of the appropriate technique has evolved over time. Early methods for testing for convergence in key economic variables were developed by Baumol (1986), Barro (1991), and Barro and Sala-i-Martin (1991, 1992). These, among others, pioneered the conventional approach that examined cross-sectional relationships between the per capita growth rate over time and its initial level, the so called catch-up effect; this has become known as β convergence. The later research of Bernard and Durlauf (1996) showed that this conventional approach is too simple and is valid only under very strong assumptions. Another strand of convergence technique has become known as σ convergence. It was introduced by Friedman (1992) and Quah (1993) who tested whether the variance between poor and rich countries is diminishing.[65]

---

65 In this respect we need both beta and sigma convergence for true convergence to occur. Further, there is a difference between absolute and stochastic convergence. Absolute convergence examines whether the units, say countries, are getting to some common point or a steady state, while stochastic convergence checks whether they are already in a steady state and have temporary deviations around that point.

A qualitatively new approach in convergence testing has begun with the panel data unit root tests advanced by Quah (1992, 1994), Levin and Lin (1992), Levin, Lin, and Chu (2002), and Choi (2001). These important contributions have their limits, though. The former method does not accommodate heterogeneity across groups, namely individual specific effects and different patterns of serial correlation in residuals. The latter techniques provide a more general testing framework by allowing for individual fixed effects and time trends.

The general model for N series and T time periods that encompasses all panel unit root tests is:

$$\Delta y_{1t} = \mu_1 + \gamma_1 y_{1t-1} + \sum_{j=1}^{K_1} \rho_{1j} \Delta y_{1t-j} + \varepsilon_{1t}, \quad t = 1,...,T$$

$$\cdot$$
$$\cdot$$
$$\cdot$$

$$\Delta y_{Nt} = \mu_N + \gamma_N y_{Nt-1} + \sum_{j=1}^{K_N} \rho_{Nj} \Delta y_{Nt-j} + \varepsilon_{Nt}, \quad t = 1,...,T .$$

From this framework various techniques introduced in this section originate.

5.1 LEVIN, LIN, AND CHU PANEL UNIT-ROOT TEST WITH A NULL OF UNIT ROOT AND LIMITED COEFFICIENTS HETEROGENEITY

Levin, Lin, and Chu (2002) introduced a panel unit root test where the degree of persistence in individual regression error, the intercept and trend coefficients are allowed to vary freely across individual units in a panel.[66] Several specifications are suggested for specific types of the model and these include fixed effects, individual-specific time trends, as well as common time effects. The generalized structure of the test can be specified as

$$\Delta y_{it} = \mu_i + \beta_i t + \theta_t + \gamma y_{it-1} + \varepsilon_{it}, \quad i = 1,...,N ; \quad t = 1,...,T .$$

The test is usually run in one of the simpler forms that contain fewer parameters since its power decreases with the number of parameters.

An example of the test which allows for varying (heterogeneous) intercepts as well as serially and contemporaneously correlated residuals is written in the form of the *ADF* test as

---

66   An earlier and more extensive version is Levin and Lin (1992).

$$\Delta y_{it} = \mu_i + \gamma y_{it-1} + \sum_{j=1}^{K_i} \rho_{ij} \Delta y_{it-j} + \varepsilon_{it} , \tag{5.1}$$

or alternatively in the context of a group of individual units as

$$\Delta(y_{it} - \bar{y}_t) = \mu_i + \gamma(y_{it-1} - \bar{y}_{t-1}) + \sum_{j=1}^{K_i} \rho_{ij} \Delta(y_{it-j} - \bar{y}_{t-j}) + \varepsilon_{it} , \tag{5.2}$$

where y_{it} is a variable of interest, $\bar{y}_t$ is its group average, $(y_{it} - \bar{y}_t)$ is the variable disparity from the mean performance (or alternatively from a defined benchmark) of $i = 1,..., N$ entities (countries, regions, industries, etc.) at time t. The null hypothesis in this specification is that all time series assembled in a panel contain a unit root and the alternative hypothesis is that all series are stationary. The number of lagged differences K in equations (5.1) and (5.2) is determined using the parametric method proposed by Campbell and Perron (1991) and Ng and Perron (1995) as outlined in section 3.4.2.

Regression (5.1) is estimated by regressing Δy_{it} and then y_{it-1} on the remaining variables in (5.1), which provides residuals $\hat{e}_{i,t}$ and $\hat{v}_{i,t-1}$, respectively. Estimating the regression of $\hat{e}_{i,t}$ on $\hat{v}_{it-1}$, $\hat{e}_{it} = \gamma \hat{v}_{it-1} + \varepsilon_{it}$ then yields the estimate of $\hat{\gamma}$.

In the case of *i.i.d.* disturbances, the unit root t-statistics converges asymptotically to the standard normal distribution as both time and cross-section dimensions of the panel approach infinity. Due to the presence of a unit root, the convergence rate is faster as $T \to \infty$ than as $N \to \infty$. In the cases of individual-specific fixed effects or serial correlation in the disturbances, the unit root t-statistics diverges, but in each case a straightforward transformation of the t-statistics does converge to $N(0,1)$.

Levin, Lin, and Chu (2002) present Monte Carlo results on the finite-sample properties of the unit root t-statistics for a wide range of panel dimensions likely to be encountered in applied research. However, in the case of a small sample size those values do not account for contemporaneous correlation in the residuals that can have a dramatic effect on those critical values. In light of this, it is essential to compute critical values using the Monte Carlo simulation. The exact finite sample critical values for each panel under investigation are computed in the following way. One randomly generates artificial panel data under the null hypothesis of a unit root. Each artificial data set has the same cross-section and time-series dimensions as the actual data, and contemporaneous residual correlation matching that of the sample estimates. Then this artificial data set is analyzed using the same unit root test procedure, including lag order selection, as applied to the real data. Finally, after repeating these steps for several thousand artificial data sets (at least 5000 replications is recommended), the test statistics values are sorted to determine the 1, 5, and 10 percent critical values that allow the verification of the statistical significance of the convergence coefficient.

With respect to convergence, to detect its β version, the statistically significant coefficient γ is to be smaller than one. Once estimated, coefficient γ provides an indication of the speed of convergence. From the construction of the test it follows that as the value of the statistically significant coefficient γ approaches unity the rate of convergence decreases. In order to make the speed of convergence much more readily interpretable it is useful to compute the so-called "half-life". The half-life of the convergence process is the number of time periods that it takes for the gap to be cut in half. The half-life is derived and used in Ben-David (1993, 1996) and is given by $\ln(0.5)/\ln \gamma$.

The procedure of Levin, Lin, and Chu (2002) has been widely employed in empirical work related to issues of cointegration and convergence. Its potential can be best exploited when analyzing groups of entities that share common features potent enough to affect the path of convergence. An example can be a common monetary, industrial or trade policy among a group of countries. A common exchange rate policy with a strong commitment to a currency basket peg with rigid fluctuation band is an underlying principle in Kočenda and Papell (1997) who examined whether there exists convincing evidence of inflation convergence within the European Union and whether the Exchange Rate Mechanism (ERM) helped to accelerate the convergence. The analysis is done over two time periods: from the late-1950s to the mid-1990s with 1979 (the inception of the ERM) as a midpoint. The results are supportive of inflation convergence among the EU countries in general. However, the countries that continuously participated in the narrow ERM bands show a dramatically higher convergence rate during the period following the establishment of the mechanism than the rest of the countries.

Another example can be drawn from Kočenda (2001a) who analyzed the performance of the Central and Eastern European transition economies in terms of their convergence in selected macroeconomic fundamentals (nominal and real industrial output, producer and consumer prices, a money aggregate (M1), and nominal and real interest rate spreads) over the period 1991 to 1998. The analysis is carried out within distinctive groups of countries to reflect different institutional and geographical aspects of transition. The specific degree of convergence differs for particular variables as well as groups of countries. Figure 5.1 illustrates the process of convergence in a graphical form; in this particular example a decline in inflation rate measured by the change in producer prices is accompanied by a diminishing difference from the average inflation rate over time. In the case of the convergence among the CEE countries, two important factors are shared by groups of countries. First, international trade within the Central European Free Trade Area (CEFTA) serves as a natural means of coordinating economic development. Second, in the 1990s the prospect of accession to the EU serves as an institutional means of coordination in order to satisfy a set of pre-accession criteria.

Other example of the application of the Levin, Lin, and Chu (2002) test is shown in the next section 5.2 to provide a contrast with other technique described therein.

Figure 5.1: Producer prices growth rate: CEFTA Group.

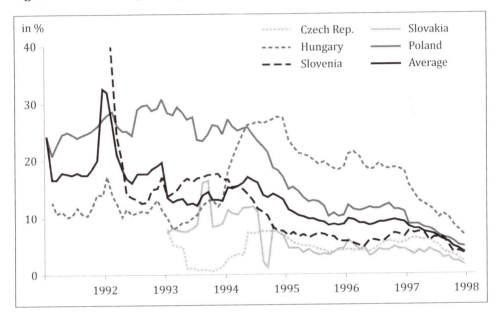

5.2. IM, PESARAN, AND SHIN UNIT-ROOT TEST WITH A NULL OF UNIT ROOT AND HETEROGENEOUS COEFFICIENTS

The method of Levin, Lin, and Chu (2002) assumes that the convergence co-efficient (hence, the convergence rate) is equal for all entities within a tested group. In a growth convergence context such an assumption requires all countries within a specified group to share a common rate of adjustment towards a steady state. While such a concept has a rich potential to test for the convergence of a cross-section of entities that share joint specifics, it is limiting when the aim is to explore individual convergence rates within a particular group.

Im, Pesaran, and Shin (2003) introduce a method that is based on averaging individual unit root test statistics for panels, which allows for heterogeneous convergence rates. They propose a test based on the average of the augmented version of the Dickey and Fuller (1979) test statistics computed for each group in the panel and they refer to it as the t-bar test. The test allows for serial correlation in residuals and the heterogeneity of the dynamics and error variances across groups.

The adapted specification is formally written as

$$\Delta(y_{it} - \bar{y}_t) = \gamma_i(y_{it-1} - \bar{y}_{t-1}) + \sum_{j=1}^{K} \rho_{ij}\Delta(y_{it-j} - \bar{y}_{t-j}) + Z'_{it}\eta_i + \varepsilon_{it} , \qquad (5.3)$$

where y_{it} is a variable of interest, $\bar{y}_t$ is its group average, $(y_{it} - \bar{y}_t)$ is the variable disparity from the mean performance (or alternatively from a defined benchmark) of $i = 1,..., N$ entities (countries, regions, industries, etc.) at time t. Z_{it} contains an optional modification depending on the desired purpose of specification: it may be zero, be one (with same η for all i), represent the fixed effects, or represent the fixed effects as well as the time trend. The above specification allows for heterogeneity in coefficient γ by testing the unit root null hypothesis H_0: $\gamma_i = 0$ for all i against the alternative H_A: $\gamma_i < 0$ for at least one i. This formulation of the null hypothesis and its alternative allows coefficients to vary across variables of entities within a panel. The limiting distribution for the IPS test t-statistics is given as

$$\sqrt{N}\frac{\left(\bar{t}_{ADF} - \mu_{ADF}\right)}{\sqrt{\sigma^2_{ADF}}} \to N(0,1),$$

where the moments μ_{ADF} and σ^2_{ADF} are obtained from Monte Carlo simulations and $\bar{t}_{ADF}$ is the average estimated ADF t-statistics from the sample. The simulations show that the power of the tests should increase by order of $\sqrt{N}$ when compared with univariate models. An important assumption of the IPS technique is the i.i.d. error structure. When this assumption is violated and residuals are contemporaneously correlated, Maddala and Wu (1999) and Strauss and Yigit (2003) show that this technique will suffer from significant size distortions, which do not disappear by simple demeaning. For this reason size adjustments of the critical values for this test may be required. The procedure is suitable to measure individual speed of convergence in specific variables for each individual country, sector or other particular subject.[67]

The joint application of several techniques to achieve a research goal is not only common but often also quite insightful. In the next example the concurrent use of the tests described in sections 5.1 and 5.2 is presented.

---

67 Kutan and Yigit (2004) extended Kočenda (2001a) by applying the test on convergence of the selected transition countries during the period 1993–2001.

Panel data sets with a large cross-sectional dimension and a long time horizon have been used to examine the long-run purchasing power parity (PPP) theory. The PPP theory suggests that there is a long-run equilibrium relationship between the aggregate levels of the prices of two countries when expressed in common currency units. A necessary condition for the PPP theory to hold is that in an econometric sense real exchange rates are stationary. Hence, testing for the long-run PPP theory implies testing for the unit root in real exchange rates. The first studies on PPP employed univariate Augmented Dickey-Fuller tests and failed to find evidence supporting the PPP theory. The offered explanation for the failure to find evidence of the PPP is the low power of univariate tests in small samples. To address the issue of the low power of univariate tests, panel data unit root tests have been proposed as an alternative. These tests are more powerful than those based on individual time series unit roots tests since they exploit information from cross-sectional dimensions to infer stationarity versus non-stationarity.

The two frequently used tests by Levin, Lin, and Chu (2002), and by Im, Peseran, and Shin (2003), henceforth LLC test and IPS test, respectively, represent efficient tools to investigate the above issue. Alba and Papell (2007) examine long-run PPP by employing these two tests. Their findings suggests that PPP holds for European and Latin America countries, while it fails to hold for African and Asian countries. Furthermore, they find that PPP holds in countries with higher openness to trade, lower inflation and similar growth rates to the United States.

As mentioned above, testing for long-run PPP means testing for the stationarity of the real exchange rate. The real exchange rate can be defined as:

$$q = e + p^* - p,$$

where all the variables are in logs such that q is the real exchange rate, e is the nominal US dollar exchange rate, p is the domestic consumer price index (CPI), and p^* is the CPI in the United States. The two panel unit root tests, LLC and IPS, are conducted by estimating the following regression:

$$\Delta q_{it} = \mu_i + \gamma_i q_{it-1} + \sum_{j=1}^{K_i} \rho_{ij} \Delta q_{it-j} + \varepsilon_{it},$$

where i is the country index, μ_i represents the heterogeneous intercept, and lag lengths k_i and coefficients ρ_{ij} are heterogeneous across countries, with the latter to allow for serially and contemporaneously correlated residuals. The difference between the LLC test and IPS test is that the LLC test places a restriction on γ_i in that the autoregressive coefficients for unit roots are in particular assumed to equal across countries ($\gamma_i = \gamma_j = \gamma$). This restriction means that the LLC test is applicable for homogeneous panels. The null hypothesis is that all the real exchange rates contain unit roots against the alternative that all the real exchange rates are stationary. If γ is negative and significantly different from zero, the null hypothesis of the non-stationarity of all real exchange rates is rejected in favor of the alternative. Unlike the LLC test, the IPS test allows for heterogeneous panels and γ_i are allowed to vary across countries. The null hypothesis is that all real exchange rates contain unit roots, but the alternative is that at least one of the real exchange rates is stationary.

Alba and Papell (2007) report the results of two tests for a panel of 84 countries with the United States dollar as a common denominator. For these as well as further tests sample-specific critical values for each panel are calculated using Monte Carlo simulation (see Appendix A). The LLC test suggests that the null hypothesis of a unit root in a panel of the real exchange rates of all 84 countries cannot be rejected at the 10% significance level. Since the alternative hypothesis is that all the real exchange rates are stationary, non-rejection can be interpreted as evidence that all the exchange rates are stationary, but that does not imply that all of the series contain unit roots. Further, the IPS test suggests that the null hypothesis that all the exchange rates contain unit roots can be rejected in favor of the alternative that at least one exchange rate is stationary at the 1% significance level. Based on the combination of the results from both tests, one cannot conclude that all of the exchange rates contain unit roots or that all of them are stationary. This implies an ambiguous conclusion that PPP neither holds nor does not hold for all countries. Since a clear conclusion about PPP cannot be drawn, Alba and Papell (2007) transform their data into panels organized according to geographic and country-specific characteristics (trade openness, distance from the U.S., inflation development, and per capita real GDP growth). The results of the LLC test performed on newly formed and smaller panels provide evidence that PPP holds for Europe and Latin America, but no evidence of PPP for African and Asian countries, even for high-income Asian countries. Further they show that the evidence of PPP is stronger for countries that are more open to trade, are closer to the United States, have lower inflation, and have a per capita real GDP growth rate similar to that of the United States. Taken as a whole, the findings emphasize the relevance of country characteristics in explaining the adherence to and deviations from long-run PPP.

5.3 HADRI UNIT-ROOT TESTS WITH A NULL OF STATIONARITY

It is known that panel tests with a null of unit roots might not be very powerful against relevant alternatives. Hadri (1999, 2000) proposed a test that has a null of stationarity rather than that of the unit root. This is an approach similar in spirit to that of Kwiatkowski et al. (1992), see section 3.4.4. It is a residual-

based Lagrange multiplier (*LM*) test for a null that the individual observed series are stationary around a deterministic level or around a deterministic trend
against the alternative of a unit root in panel data. The tests that are asymptotically similar under the null hypothesis belong to the locally best invariant (*LBI*)
test statistics. The test assumes that panel data tested for trend stationarity can
be decomposed in the sum of a deterministic trend $\beta_i t$, a random walk r_{it}, and
a stationary error ε_{it}:

$$y_{it} = r_{it} + \varepsilon_{it} \ \text{or} \ y_{it} = r_{it} + \beta_i t + \varepsilon_{it} ,$$

$$r_{it} = r_{it-1} + u_{it} .$$

The null of stationarity is expressed as H_0: $\sigma_{u1} = \sigma_{u2} = \ldots = 0$ and is tested against
the alternative that $\sigma_{ui} > 0$ for some i. The hypothesis is assessed by the normalized one-sided *LM* statistics:

$$LM_j = \frac{1}{N} \sum_{i=1}^{N} \left(\frac{\frac{1}{T^2} \sum_{t=1}^{T} S_{it}}{\sigma_{S_i}^2} \right), \tag{5.4}$$

where S_{it} is the partial sum of residuals, $S_{it} = \sum_{k=1}^{t} \varepsilon_{ik}$, and $j = \mu, \tau$ for mean and
trend stationarity. The asymptotic distributions of the statistics are derived un-
der the null and are shown to be normally distributed. Thus, asymptotically the
statistics has a normal distribution

$$\frac{\sqrt{N} \left(LM_j - \mu_j \right)}{\sigma_j} , \tag{5.5}$$

where μ_j and σ_j are the asymptotic mean and standard deviation of the *LM* statistics. Finite sample sizes and powers are considered in a Monte Carlo experiment. The empirical sizes of the tests are close to the true size even in small
samples but the simulations show the good size and power of the test especially when *T* is above 50. Monte Carlo simulations are recommended to derive
critical values specific to the cross-correlation structure of the finite samples
used in empirical research when the time dimension of a panel is not large
enough. The testing procedure is easy to apply, including, to panel data models
with fixed effects, individual deterministic trends and heterogeneous errors
across cross-sections. The test can also be applied to the more general case of
serially correlated disturbance terms.

Holes and Otero (2010) employ an AR-based bootstrap approach to Hadri
(2000) to test for the stationarity of EU current account deficits. They produce

only mixed evidence of current account stationarity for individual countries. However, they find evidence of stationarity when considering panels comprising both EU and non-EU members. The results are interpreted as support of the current account deficits of the EU countries being sustainable in the long run with some caveats related to detailed findings.

Hadri and Larsson (2005) expand the tests of Hadri (2000) for the null hypothesis of stationarity against the alternative of a unit root in panel data to the case where the time dimension of the panel is finite. This improves the finite sample properties of the tests for micro and macro panels. More importantly, the derivation of the tests for finite T as opposed to a joint asymptotic where N and $T \to \infty$ avoids the imposition of the rate condition $N/T \to 0$ and hence makes the test valid for any (T, N) combination. The asymptotic distributions of the tests are derived under the null and are shown to be normally distributed.[68] Finite sample size and power are considered in a Monte Carlo experiment. The proposed tests have empirical sizes that are very close to the nominal 5 percent level. The Monte Carlo results clearly show that the power of the test statistics increases substantially with N, T and the number of unit root processes under the alternative. The results indicate that the assumption that T is asymptotic rather than fixed leads to tests that are substantially oversized particularly for relatively short panels with large N.

5.4 BREUER, MCNOWN, AND WALLACE TEST FOR CONVERGENCE

Breuer, McNown, and Wallace (2002) introduce an alternative test procedure that exploits the power of panel data analysis without imposing uniformity across the panel under either the null or alternative hypotheses. The test is based on seemingly unrelated regressions, with no across-panel restrictions imposed under either hypothesis. The procedure also handles heterogeneous serial correlation across panel members.

In their *SURADF* method, Breuer, McNown, and Wallace (2002) start with a simple specification and test N null and alternative hypotheses individually:

$$H_0^1 : \gamma_1 = 0 \ \ vs. \ \ H_A^1 : \gamma_1 < 0$$

.

.

.

$$H_0^N : \gamma_N = 0 \ \ vs. \ \ H_A^N : \gamma_N < 0 .$$

---

68   The moments for T fixed are derived analytically using Ghazal's (1994) lemma 1.

They make use of the cross correlation among the members of the panel, which interestingly constitutes a disadvantage for the other panel unit root methodologies and necessitates a correction of the critical values via Monte Carlo simulations. In fact, the higher the cross correlation (which causes more problems in the panel unit root tests), the more power one gains over the single equation methods. The flexible nature of this panel estimation not only increases the power relative to single equation methods, but it also allows for varying orders of autocorrelation among the panel units. Beside these features the test allows deriving conclusions on the stationarity (or convergence) of individual series in the panel. The necessity to generate panel-specific critical values for each sample due to the uniqueness of correlation matrices in differing panels is a limitation that has to be taken into account. However, when drawing Monte Carlo simulations for a variety of scenarios, Breuer, McNown, and Wallace (2002) show significant power improvements over single equation methods, especially when the correlation among the panel members is high.

An application of this methodology can be illustrated with the work of Kutan and Yigit (2005) who use it to investigate the convergence of the new EU members to EU standards in terms of convergence in annual growth rates in monthly output (industrial production), price (PPI and CPI), and nominal interest rate spreads. They find strong evidence of real stochastic convergence across all new members, indicating that all adjust to euro area output shocks. However, the degree of nominal convergence is quite idiosyncratic.

5.5 VOGELSANG TEST FOR β-CONVERGENCE

The enlargement of the EU has motivated researchers and policymakers to revisit the issue of the "catching up" of the new entrants to the core EU members. Carlino and Mills's (1993) argument that both β-convergence and stochastic convergence are necessary for real convergence further motivated the literature on β-convergence. Cross-sectional tests, which were used to analyze β-convergence until recently, were criticized on the grounds of over-rejecting the null hypothesis of no convergence (Quah, 1996; Bernard and Durlauf, 1996).

A test by Vogelsang (1998, 1999) deals with the β-convergence issue by relying on time-series methodology. Correspondingly, a simple model of convergence towards a benchmark is specified as

$$y_t = \mu + \delta t + \varepsilon_t,$$ (5.6)

where y_t is the difference of the natural logarithm of a variable minus a benchmark (for example, some macroeconomic performance variable of a country under research minus some specific benchmark at time t). Further, μ is an intercept to capture the initial level of the deviation, t is a deterministic time trend, and ε_t is the residual term.[69] In such a set-up, β-convergence requires that for countries where μ is initially significantly negative, that is, for countries lagging behind in a particular performance, the trend coefficient δ should be positive and statistically significant.

Carlino and Mills (1993) developed this test with a very restricted form of serial correlation for the residual term, namely $AR(2)$. Vogelsang (1998) extended the analysis of this specification to ε_t with an unknown form of serial correlation by allowing a span of stationary and non-stationary serial correlation specifications for the error term ranging from order of zero, $I(0)$, to order of one, $I(1)$. Since the possibility of no convergence implies the non-stationarity of the error terms, one can draw a false inference on the trend coefficient when the errors are assumed to be stationary $AR(2)$.[70] Vogelsang (1998) corrects for this problem by developing a trend function hypothesis test with an undetermined degree of serial correlation.

To explain the methodology in the spirit of equation (5.6), consider two specifications

$$y_t = X_{yt}\beta + \varepsilon_t, \text{ and}$$

$$z_t = X_{zt}\beta + S_t, \tag{5.7}$$

where z_t is $\sum_{j=1}^{t} y_t$ and $S_t = \sum_{j=1}^{t} \varepsilon_t$, while X_{yt} and X_{zt} consist of $[1\ t]$ and $\left[t\ \sum_{j=1}^{t} j\right]$, respectively. For more than one coefficient restriction, the tests can be summarized as:[71]

$$T^{-1}W_T = \frac{T^{-1}\left(R\hat{\beta} - r\right)'\left[R\left(X_y'X_y\right)^{-1}R'\right]^{-1}\left(R\hat{\beta} - r\right)}{s_y^2}, \tag{5.8}$$

$$PS_T = \frac{T^{-1}\left(R\hat{\beta} - r\right)'\left[R\left(X_z'X_z\right)^{-1}R'\right]^{-1}\left(R\hat{\beta} - r\right)}{\left(s_z^2\exp\left(bJ_T(m)\right)\right)}, \tag{5.9}$$

---

69 A similar steady state representation of the neoclassical growth model and convergence can also be found in Lee, Pesaran, and Smith (1997).

70 When u_t is $I(1)$, the estimate of β obtained from the above regression is not related to the true trend, and information on β must be obtained from the estimate of the intercept in the autoregressive representation of y_t.

71 See Vogelsang (1998) for a deeper elaboration on the tests, and Tomljanovich and Vogelsang (2002) for their application to U.S. regional data.

$$PSW_T = \frac{T^{-1}\left(R\hat{\beta}-r\right)'\left[R\left(X_y'X_y\right)^{-1}R'\right]^{-1}\left(R\hat{\beta}-r\right)}{\left(100T^{-1}s_z^2\exp\left(bJ_T(m)\right)\right)}, \tag{5.10}$$

where J_T is the Park and Choi (1988) unit root test statistics obtained from the following regression

$$y_t = X_{yt}\beta + \sum_{i=2}^{m} c_i t^i + \varepsilon_t,$$

$$J_T(m) = \frac{(RSS_y - RSS_j)}{RSS_j}. \tag{5.11}$$

J_T is the Wald statistics that tests the joint hypothesis of $c_2 = c_3 = ... = c_m = 0$. In Monte Carlo simulations, Vogelsang (1998) finds the values of b and m for which the above tests would be comparable and valid for every type of serial correlation form, including unit roots.

Despite the great flexibility of these tests in deriving the mean and trend coefficient estimates in time series with varying stationarity properties, one needs to be careful in using this methodology in the analysis of countries that are not in a steady state, for example transition and post-transition economies or emerging markets. The reason stems from the volatile nature of these economies and the presence of structural shifts that are documented in the empirical literature.[72]

Vogelsang's (1999) extension of Vogelsang (1998) allows for structural breaks in the modification of the statistics by including the possibility of shifts in the trend function. Spanning the standard set of breaks introduced by Perron (1989), namely the mean, trend, and the mean and trend, Vogelsang (1999) derives asymptotic critical values using 10,000 replications in cases of both known and unknown break dates.[73] It is preferable not to impose a break date and favor the second approach that first endogenously determines a break date.[74] As a second step, using the estimated break date, normalized critical

---

[72] The problem of structural breaks during the transition process is given serious empirical consideration in Fidrmuc and Tichit (2009) who provide evidence of significant breaks for macroeconomic data. They argue that empirical analyses of transition economies must account for the possibility of structural changes, otherwise inferences are misleading. Literature dealing with structural breaks related to transition issues is limited, though (see for example Dibooglu and Kutan, 2001; Kočenda, 2005; and Hanousek and Kočenda, 2011).

[73] Interestingly, one of the supremum statistics he suggests performs better than some popular statistics in identifying shifts in slope.

[74] See section 3.6 for the procedures. Often in these tests, the break date is first estimated by using the optimal break tests of Andrews and Ploberger (1994) for a break date T_b belonging to Λ, where Λ is the trimmed sample (from both ends).

values are obtained using the altered versions of equation (5.7) as follows (only the y_t version is displayed):

$$y_t = \mu_1 DU_{1t} + \mu_2 DU_{2t} + \delta_1 DT_{1t} + \delta_2 DT_{2t} + \varepsilon_t, \qquad (5.12)$$

where $DU_{1t} = 1$ if $t \leq T_b$ (the break date) and zero otherwise, $DU_{2t} = 1$ if $t > T_b$ and zero otherwise, $DT_{1t} = t$ if $t \leq T_b$ and zero otherwise, and finally $DT_{2t} = t$ if $t > T_b$ and zero otherwise. It has to be noted that the Vogelsang (1999) methodology allows for only a single break. On other hand, realistically, due to data availability we quite frequently do not consider more than one break. If we do need to consider more than one break, it would call for adjusting the technique in the spirit of Bai and Perron (1998). To verify the ability of the procedure, in his analysis Vogelsang (1999) uses the aggregate data of Maddison (1991). Further, Tomljanovich and Vogelsang (2002) apply the method to study economic convergence on U.S. regional data. Finally, Sayginsoy and Vogelsang (2011) improve on the original methodology and design a family of OLS-based trend function structural change tests that are size robust to the presence of strong serial correlation or a unit root.

Kočenda, Kutan, and Yigit (2006) applied the method on issues of real and monetary convergence embedded in the process of European integration and the enlargement of the Economic and Monetary Union (EMU). Despite the observed widening of the gap between per-capita GDP levels in euros, the faster growth rate of the new members will help narrow this gap, leading to the "catching-up" of new members in the next few decades. Especially the stronger growth rates after the beginning of the accession talks (post-break) are indicative of the benefits of the prospect of membership or the membership itself, strengthening convergence to the Union. Results on inflation and interest rates indicate that the new EU members have achieved significant nominal convergence and are making steady progress towards real convergence. From the perspective of EMU membership the findings support common arguments that it is the fiscal part of the Maastricht criteria that matters most. This argument is further explored in Kočenda, Kutan, and Yigit (2008), which empirically examine the fiscal convergence of ten new European Union (EU) members using the Maastricht fiscal convergence criteria. They test for absolute beta and sigma convergence of the new members in comparison to the Maastricht benchmarks as well as the EU15 figures, allowing for structural breaks in fiscal performance. The results show poor fiscal performance in the European Union in general, suggesting that monetary unions do not necessarily encourage fiscal convergence for its members.

APPENDIX A –
MONTE CARLO SIMULATIONS

If some properties of a particular estimation method are not known or cannot be described analytically, then *Monte Carlo technique* can be used to simulate these properties. The most common application in econometrics is the *simulation of critical values* for a statistics that has unknown distribution or a distribution that cannot be expressed in a closed form. Many other applications exist as well. Monte Carlo simulations can be, for example, used to determine the power of a particular test, or to measure a simultaneous equations bias in the case when endogenous variables are treated as exogenous, or to determine the effect that heteroskedasticity of residuals can have on different types of tests, etc.

The central idea of Monte Carlo simulations is to create a representative (large enough) random sample from the investigated unknown distribution. To perform a Monte Carlo simulation we proceed in the following steps. First, we randomly generate the data with the desired properties using an appropriate data generating process. Second, we perform the regressions and compute the investigated test statistics or other parameters of interest and save them. Third, we go to the first step. The whole procedure is repeated N times. The larger N is, the more representative will be the sampled distribution collected from the saved values of the test statistics or other parameters of interest. At the current level of computer power, replication is extremely fast and one should perform at least 10,000 replications.

As an example we will describe how we could simulate critical values of the *t*-statistics used in the Dickey-Fuller *unit root test*. Recall, that in the simplest version of the Dickey-Fuller test we estimate the equation

$$y_t = a_1 y_{t-1} + \varepsilon_t \qquad \text{(A1)}$$

and test the hypothesis H_0: a_1 = 1 using the standard *t*-statistics of the estimated coefficient a_1

$$t = \frac{\widehat{a_1}}{Se(\widehat{a_1})} \qquad \text{(A2)}$$

Under the null hypothesis the series y_t is not stationary (contains a unit root) and the *OLS* estimate of a_1 is biased to be below one. Moreover, the limiting distribution of the a_1 estimate is not normal. Thus, the critical values for the distribution of the computed *t*-statistics do not equal those of a standard *t*-distribution and must be simulated using the Monte Carlo method.

The simulation can be conducted in the above outlined steps. First, we would generate a unit root containing time series y_t of a desired length T using the equation $y_t = y_{t-1} + \varepsilon_t$ and a series of randomly generated errors $\{\varepsilon_t\}_{t=1}^{T}$ drawn from the standard normal distribution $N(0,1)$.

For simplicity we would assume the initial value y_0 = 0 and compute recursively $y_1, y_2, ..., y_T$

$$y_1 = y_0 + \varepsilon_1$$
$$y_2 = y_1 + \varepsilon_2$$

.

.

.

$$y_T = y_{T-1} + \varepsilon_T$$

Second, using the generated time series $\{y_t\}_{t=1}^{T}$ we would run the regression (1) and compute the *t*-statistics defined by the equation (A2). Then we would repeat the first and second steps N times and order the set of N values of the *t*-statistics from the lowest to the highest. The relevant $p\%$ critical value would correspond to the p-th percentile of the sampled distribution.

Even though the procedure looks simple, it could be much more complicated in practice. For example, robustness checks must be performed in order to determine the sensitivity of the sampled distribution and of its critical values to the number of simulations N or to various properties of the randomly generated time series. In the case of the Dickey-Fuller test the simulated critical values depend only on the sample size T and on the type of the test. In the simplest version we performed the test without a trend or intercept included in the estimated equation (A1). Simulated critical values would be different for the versions of the test that allow for an intercept or intercept and trend n the estimated equation. On the other hand, Dickey and Fuller (1979) show analytically that the t-statistics' limiting distribution would be the same with the simple and augmented versions of the test. Knowing this, robustness check for sensitivity of the sampled distribution to serial correlation in regression residuals ε_t can be skipped. Thus, theoretical study of the simulated distribution's properties can be still very useful, even if it does not lead to the analytical computation of its critical values or to its closed form expression.

APPENDIX B –
STATISTICAL TABLES

Table 2: Dickey-Fuller critical values

Time span	Critical level			
Model A	**0.10**	**0.05**	**0.025**	**0.01**
T = 25	−1.6	−1.95	−2.26	−2.66
T = 50	−1.61	−1.95	−2.25	−2.62
T = 100	−1.61	−1.95	−2.24	−2.6
T = 250	−1.62	−1.95	−2.23	−2.58
T = 300	−1.62	−1.95	−2.23	−2.58
T = ∞	−1.62	−1.95	−2.23	−2.58
Model B	**0.10**	**0.05**	**0.025**	**0.01**
T = 25	−2.62	−3	−3.33	−3.75
T = 50	−2.6	−2.93	−3.22	−3.58
T = 100	−2.58	−2.89	−3.17	−3.51
T = 250	−2.57	−2.88	−3.14	−3.46
T = 300	−2.57	−2.87	−3.13	−3.44
T = ∞	−2.57	−2.86	−3.12	−3.43
Model C	**0.10**	**0.05**	**0.025**	**0.01**
T = 25	−3.24	−3.6	−3.95	−4.38
T = 50	−3.18	−3.5	−3.8	−4.15
T = 100	−3.15	−3.45	−3.73	−4.04
T = 250	−3.13	−3.43	−3.69	−3.99
T = 300	−3.13	−3.42	−3.68	−3.98
T = ∞	−3.12	−3.41	−3.66	−3.96

Source: Fuller, W. A. (1976). Introduction to statistical time series. New York: John Wiley&Sons. © John Wiley&Sons.

Table 3: KPSS test critical values for η_μ and η_τ

Critical level	Critical value	
	for η_μ	for η_τ
0.1	0.347	0.119
0.05	0.463	0.146
0.025	0.574	0.176
0.01	0.739	0.216

Source: Kwiatkowski, D., Phillips, P., Schmidt, P., Shin, Y. (1992). Testing the null hypothesis of stationarity against the alternative of a unit root. Journal of Econometrics, 54, 159–178. © Elsevier.

Table 4: Perron's critical values

Pre-break fraction λ	Critical level			
Model A	**0.1**	**0.05**	**0.025**	**0.01**
λ = 0.1	−3.40	−3.68	−3.93	−4.30
λ = 0.2	−3.47	−3.77	−4.08	−4.39
λ = 0.3	−3.46	−3.76	−4.03	−4.39
λ = 0.4	−3.44	−3.72	−4.01	−4.34
λ = 0.5	−3.46	−3.76	−4.01	−4.32
λ = 0.6	−3.47	−3.76	−4.09	−4.45
λ = 0.7	−3.51	−3.80	−4.07	−4.42
λ = 0.8	−3.46	−3.75	−3.99	−4.33
λ = 0.9	−3.38	−3.69	−3.97	−4.27
Model B	**0.1**	**0.05**	**0.025**	**0.01**
λ = 0.1	−3.36	−3.65	−3.94	−4.27
λ = 0.2	−3.49	−3.8	−4.08	−4.41
λ = 0.3	−3.58	−3.87	−4.17	−4.51
λ = 0.4	−3.66	−3.94	−4.20	−4.55
λ = 0.5	−3.68	−3.96	−4.26	−4.56
λ = 0.6	−3.66	−3.95	−4.20	−4.57
λ = 0.7	−3.57	−3.85	−4.13	−4.51
λ = 0.8	−3.50	−3.82	−4.07	−4.38
λ = 0.9	−3.35	−3.68	−3.96	−4.26
Model C	**0.1**	**0.05**	**0.025**	**0.01**
λ = 0.1	−3.45	−3.75	−4.01	−4.38
λ = 0.2	−3.66	−3.99	−4.32	−4.65
λ = 0.3	−3.87	−4.17	−4.46	−4.78
λ = 0.4	−3.95	−4.22	−4.48	−4.81
λ = 0.5	−3.96	−4.24	−4.53	−4.9
λ = 0.6	−3.95	−4.24	−4.49	−4.88
λ = 0.7	−3.86	−4.18	−4.44	−4.75
λ = 0.8	−3.69	−4.04	−4.31	−4.70
λ = 0.9	−3.46	−3.80	−4.10	−4.41

Source: Perron, P. (1989). The great crash, the oil price shock, and the unit root hypothesis. Econometrica, 57(6), 1361–1401. © The Econometric Society.

Table 5: Zivot and Andrews' critical values

	Critical level			
	0.1	**0.05**	**0.025**	**0.01**
Model A	−4.58	−4.80	−5.02	−5.34
Model B	−4.11	−4.42	−4.67	−4.93
Model C	−4.82	−5.08	−5.30	−5.57

Source: Zivot, E. and Andrews, D. (1992). Further evidence on the great crash, the oil price shock, and the unit root hypothesis. Journal of Business and Economic Statistics, 251–270. © American Statistical Association.

Table 6: Vogelsang's critical values

Stationary case. $\lambda^* = 0.01$									
Critical level	p = 0			p = 1			p = 2		
	MeanF	ExpF	SupF	MeanF	ExpF	SupF	MeanF	ExpF	SupF
0.1	2.00	1.59	9.24	3.49	2.76	13.62	4.74	3.70	16.06
0.05	2.66	2.20	10.85	4.42	3.52	15.44	5.65	4.41	17.89
0.025	3.34	2.80	12.46	5.36	4.18	17.26	6.69	5.22	19.57
0.01	4.21	3.63	14.49	6.64	5.24	19.90	8.14	6.24	21.65

Stationary case. $\lambda^* = 0.15$									
Critical level	p = 0			p = 1			p = 2		
	MeanF	ExpF	SupF	MeanF	ExpF	SupF	MeanF	ExpF	SupF
0.1	1.58	1.23	7.32	2.70	2.33	11.25	3.58	3.18	13.96
0.05	2.20	1.89	9.00	3.50	3.13	13.29	4.41	3.98	15.48
0.025	2.85	2.53	10.69	4.35	3.88	15.12	5.25	4.68	17.61
0.01	3.70	3.46	13.02	5.55	5.05	17.51	6.47	5.78	19.9

Unit root case. $\lambda^* = 0.01$									
Critical level	p = 0			p = 1			p = 2		
	MeanF	ExpF	SupF	MeanF	ExpF	SupF	MeanF	ExpF	SupF
0.1	3.32	4.02	16.14	7.14	6.98	22.6	10.18	9.58	28.11
0.05	3.91	4.84	18.20	8.22	8.18	25.27	11.74	11.09	31.35
0.025	4.53	5.68	20.23	9.29	9.27	27.76	13.17	12.50	34.45
0.01	5.35	6.69	22.64	10.54	10.56	30.44	14.80	14.42	38.43

Unit root case. $\lambda^* = 0.15$									
Critical level	p = 0			p = 1			p = 2		
	MeanF	ExpF	SupF	MeanF	ExpF	SupF	MeanF	ExpF	SupF
0.1	2.28	3.87	15.78	6.12	6.90	22.29	8.65	9.54	27.99
0.05	3.43	4.71	17.88	7.19	8.12	25.10	10.00	11.07	31.29
0.025	3.99	5.57	20.08	8.07	9.24	27.56	11.32	12.47	34.39
0.01	4.65	6.6	22.48	9.17	10.54	30.36	13.02	14.34	38.35

Source: Vogelsang, T. J. (1997). Wald-type tests for detecting breaks in the trend function of a dynamic time series. Econometric Theory, 13, 818–849. © Taylor&Francis.

Table 7: Quantiles of the slope coefficients β_m for ε-range (0.60σ – 1.90σ)

A. Quantiles of the slope coefficients βm for a sample size of 500 observations

Quantile	β_2	β_3	β_4	β_5	β_6	β_7	β_8	β_9	β_{10}
0.50%	1.544	2.305	3.056	3.785	4.505	5.197	5.771	6.254	6.71
1.00%	1.552	2.319	3.075	3.821	4.546	5.250	5.823	6.322	6.795
2.50%	1.564	2.339	3.106	3.862	4.605	5.323	5.898	6.417	6.909
5.00%	1.573	2.353	3.128	3.895	4.646	5.378	5.960	6.498	6.997
95.00%	1.645	2.475	3.312	4.161	5.033	5.846	6.526	7.187	7.835
97.50%	1.650	2.483	3.326	4.183	5.068	5.886	6.576	7.248	7.912
99.00%	1.654	2.492	3.341	4.207	5.106	5.931	6.628	7.310	7.991
99.50%	1.657	2.497	3.350	4.224	5.132	5.967	6.662	7.359	8.057

B. Quantiles of the slope coefficients βm for a sample size of 1000 observations

Quantile	β_2	β_3	β_4	β_5	β_6	β_7	β_8	β_9	β_{10}
0.50%	1.566	2.342	3.113	3.874	4.628	5.366	6.078	6.700	7.217
1.00%	1.571	2.351	3.124	3.892	4.652	5.395	6.115	6.746	7.271
2.50%	1.578	2.362	3.143	3.917	4.685	5.436	6.173	6.804	7.349
5.00%	1.584	2.373	3.158	3.938	4.710	5.475	6.221	6.855	7.412
95.00%	1.634	2.456	3.281	4.112	4.951	5.806	6.660	7.331	7.985
97.50%	1.638	2.462	3.291	4.124	4.970	5.835	6.691	7.374	8.035
99.00%	1.642	2.468	3.299	4.140	4.992	5.871	6.731	7.420	8.093
99.50%	1.645	2.472	3.305	4.149	5.006	5.891	6.759	7.453	8.133

C. Quantiles of the slope coefficients βm for a sample size of 2500 observations

Quantile	β_2	β_3	β_4	β_5	β_6	β_7	β_8	β_9	β_{10}
0.50%	1.584	2.373	3.158	3.938	4.715	5.486	6.242	6.982	7.697
1.00%	1.587	2.377	3.164	3.948	4.727	5.502	6.265	7.011	7.730
2.50%	1.591	2.384	3.174	3.962	4.746	5.525	6.294	7.054	7.784
5.00%	1.595	2.390	3.183	3.974	4.762	5.546	6.323	7.087	7.825
95.00%	1.626	2.441	3.258	4.078	4.899	5.727	6.563	7.418	8.191
97.50%	1.628	2.445	3.264	4.085	4.911	5.741	6.586	7.449	8.225
99.00%	1.631	2.449	3.270	4.094	4.925	5.759	6.612	7.486	8.266
99.50%	1.633	2.453	3.275	4.101	4.932	5.770	6.626	7.513	8.291

Note: "m" denotes an embedding dimension. Based on 20,000 replications. Source: Kočenda, E. and Briatka, L. (2005). Optimal range for the iid test based on integration across the correlation integral. Econometric Reviews, 24(3), 265–296. © Taylor&Francis.

REFERENCES

AGARWAL, R. P. (2000): *Difference Equations and Inequality: Theory, Methods, and Applications.* 2nd ed. New York: Dekker.

AKAIKE, H. (1978): *Information Theory and the Extension of the Maximum Likelihood Principle.* 2nd International Symposium in Information Theory, Petrov, B. N., and Csaki, F. (Eds.), Budapest.

ALBA, J. D., AND PAPELL, D. H. (2007): Purchasing power parity and country characteristics: Evidence from panel data tests. *Journal of Development Economics*, 83(1), pp. 240–251.

ANDREWS, D. W. K. (1993): Test for Parameter Instability and Structural Change with Unknown Change Point. *Econometrica*, 61, pp. 821–856.

ANDREWS, D. W. K., AND PLOBERGER, W. (1994): Optimal Tests When a Nuisance Parameter is Present Only Under the Alternative. *Econometrica*, 62, pp. 1383–1414.

ANTZOULATOS, A. A., AND YANG, Y. (1996): Exchange Rate Pass-Through in U.S. Manufacturing Industries: A Demand-Side Story. *International Trade Journal*, 10(3), pp. 325–352.

BABETSKAIA-KUKHARCHUK, O., BABETSKII, J., PODPIERA, J. (2008): Convergence in Exchange Rates: The Markets' View on CE-4 Joining EMU. *Applied Economic Letters*, 15(5), pp. 385–390.

BABETSKII, J., AND ÉGERT, B. (2005): Equilibrium Exchange Rate in the Czech Republic: How Good is the Czech BEER? *Czech Journal of Economics and Finance*, 55(5–6), pp. 232–252.

BAI, J. (1999): Likelihood Ratio Tests for Multiple Structural Change. *Journal of Econometrics*, 91, pp. 299–323.

BAI, J., AND PERRON, P. (1998): Estimating and Testing Linear Models with Multiple Structural Changes. *Econometrica*, 66, pp. 47–78.

BAI, J., AND PERRON, P. (2003A): Computation and Analysis of Multiple Structural Change Models. *Journal of Applied Econometrics*, 18, pp. 1–22.

BAI, J., AND PERRON, P. (2003B): Critical Values for Multiple Structural Change Tests. *The Econometrics Journal*, 6, pp. 72–78.

BAI, J., AND PERRON, P. (2006): Multiple Structural Change Models: A Simulation Analysis. In: Corbea, D., Durlauf, S. N., Hansen, B. E. (Eds.), *Econometric Theory and Practice: Frontiers of Analysis and Applied Research*, pp. 212–240, Cambridge University Press.

BANERJEE, A., LUMSDAINE, R. L., STOCK, J. H. (1992): Recursive and Sequential Tests of the Unit-Root and Trend-Break Hypotheses: Theory and International Evidence. *Journal of Business and Economic Statistics*, 10(3), pp. 271–87.

BANERJEE, A., AND URGA, G. (EDS.) (2005): Modelling Structural Breaks. *Journal of Econometrics*, 129(1–2), pp. 1–374.

BARRO, R. J. (1991): Economic Growth in Cross-section of Countries. *Quarterly Journal of Economics*, 106, pp. 407–443.

BARRO, R. J., AND SALA-I-MARTIN, X. (1991): Convergence Across States and Regions. *Brookings Papers on Economic Activity*, 1, pp. 107–182.

BARRO, R. J., AND SALA-I-MARTIN, X. (1992): Convergence. *Journal of Political Economy*, 100, pp. 223–251.

BARUNÍK, J., KOČENDA, E., AND VÁCHA, L. (2015): Gold, Oil, and Stocks: Dynamic Correlations. *International Review of Economics and Finance*, doi: 10.1016/j.iref.2015.08.006.

BAUMOL, W. J. (1986): Productivity Growth, Convergence, and Welfare: What the Long-run Data Show. *American Economic Review*, 76, pp. 1072–1085.

BAUMÖHL, E., LYÓCSA, Š., VÝROST, T. (2011): Shift Contagion with Endogenously Detected Volatility Breaks: The Case of CEE Stock Markets. *Applied Economics Letters*, 18(12), pp. 1103–1109.

BAUMÖHL, E., AND VÝROST, T. (2010): Stock Market Integration: Granger Causality Testing with respect to Nonsynchronous Trading Effects. *Czech Journal of Economics and Finance*, 60(5), pp. 414–425.

BAUWENS, L., LAURENT, S., ROMBOUTS, J. V. K. (2006): Multivariate GARCH Models: A Survey. *Journal of Applied Econometrics*, 21(1), pp. 79–109.

BEKAERT, G., AND HARVEY, C. L. (1997): Emerging Equity Market Volatility. *Journal of Financial Economics*, 43, pp. 29–77.

BEKŐ, J. (2003): Causality between Exports and Economic Growth: Empirical Estimates for Slovenia. *Prague Economic Papers*, 12(2), pp. 169–186.

BEN-DAVID, D. (1993): Equalizing Exchange: Trade Liberalization and Income Convergence. *QUARTERLY JOURNAL OF ECONOMICS*, 108, PP. 653–679.

BEN-DAVID, D. (1996): Trade Convergence Among Countries. *Journal of International Economics*, 40, pp. 279–298.

BEN-DAVID, D., AND PAPELL, D. H. (1997): International Trade and Structural Change. *Journal of International Economics*, 43(3–4), pp. 513–523.

BEN-DAVID, D., AND PAPELL, D. H. (1998): Slowdowns and Meltdowns: Postwar Growth Evidence from 74 Countries. *Review of Economics and Statistics*, 80(4), pp. 561–571.

BERA, A. K., AND HIGGINS, M. L. (1993): ARCH Models: Properties, Estimation and Testing. *Journal of Economic Surveys*, 7(4), pp. 305–366.

BERNARD, A. B., AND DURLAUF, S. N. (1996): Interpreting Tests of the Convergence Hypothesis. *Journal of Econometrics*, 71, pp. 161–173.

BERNDT, E. K., HALL, B. H., HALL, R. E., HAUSMAN, J. A. (1974): Estimation and Inference in Nonlinear Structural Models. *Annals of Economic and Social Measurement*, 3/4, pp. 653–665.

BLANCHARD, O., AND QUAH, D. (1989): The Dynamic Effects of Aggregate Demand and Supply Disturbances. *American Economic Review*, 79, pp. 655–673.

BLANCHARD, O., AND SIMON, J. (2001): The Long and Large Decline in US Output Volatility. *Brookings Papers on Economic Activity*, 1, pp. 135–164.

BOLLERSLEV, T. (1986): Generalized Autoregressive Conditional Heteroskedasticity. *Journal of Econometrics*, 31, pp. 307–327.

BOLLERSLEV, T. (2001): Financial econometrics: Past Developments and Future Challenges. *Journal of Econometrics*, 100(1), pp. 41–51.

BOLLERSLEV, T., CHOU, R. Y., KRONER, K. F. (1992): ARCH Modeling in Finance: A Review of the Theory and Empirical Evidence. *Journal of Econometrics*, 52(1–2), pp. 5–59.

BOLLERSLEV, T., AND ENGLE, R. F. (1993): Common Persistence in Conditional Variances. *Econometrica*, 61, pp. 167–186.

BOLLERSLEV, T., ENGLE, R. F., NELSON, D. (1994): ARCH Models. In: Engle, R. F., McFadden, D. (Eds.), *Handbook of econometrics*, 4. *Handbooks in Economics*, 2. Amsterdam; London and New York: Elsevier, North-Holland, pp. 2959–3038.

BOX, G., AND JENKINS, G. (1976): Time Series Analysis, Forecasting, and Control. San Francisco, California: Holden day.

BOX, G., AND PIERCE, D. (1970): Distribution of Autocorrelations in Autoregressive Moving Average Time Series Models. *Journal of the American Statistical Association*, 65, pp. 1509–1526.

BOX, G., AND TIAO, G. C. (1975): Intervention Analysis with Applications to Economic and Environmental Problems. *Journal of the American Statistical Association*, 70, pp. 70–79.

BRADA, J. C. (1998): Introduction: Exchange Rates, Capital Flows, and Commercial Policies in Transition Economies. *Journal of Comparative Economics*, 26(4), pp. 613–620.

BREUER, J. B., MCNOWN, R., WALLACE, M. (2002): Series-specific Unit Root Tests With Panel Data. *Oxford Bulletin of Economics and Statistics*, 64(5), pp. 527–546.

BRIATKA, L. (2006): How Big is Big Enough? Justifying Results of the iid Test Based on the Correlation Integral in the Non-Normal World. *CERGE-EI WP* No. 308.

BROCK, W. A., DECHERT, W. D., SCHEINKMAN, J. A. (1987): A Test for Independence Based on the Correlation Dimension. University of Wisconsin at Madison, *Department of Economics Working Paper*, SSRI 8702.

BROCK, W. A., HSIEH, D. A., LEBARON, B. (1991): *Nonlinear Dynamics, Chaos, and Iinstability: Statistical Theory and Economic Evidence*. Third Edition. The MIT Press: Cambridge, Massachusetts.

BROCK, W. A., DECHERT, W. D., SCHEINKMAN, J. A., LEBARON, B. (1996): A Test for Independence Based on the Correlation Dimension. *Econometric Reviews*, 15(3), pp. 197–235.

BUBÁK, V., KOČENDA, E., ŽIKEŠ, F., (2011): Volatility Transmission in Emerging European Foreign Exchange Markets. *Journal of Banking and Finance*, 35(11), pp. 2829–2841.

BULÍŘ, A. (2005): Liberalized Markets Have More Stable Exchange Rates: Short-run Evidence from Four Transition Countries. *Czech Journal of Economics and Finance*, 55(5–6), pp. 206–231.

BYSTROM, H. N. E. (2004): Orthogonal GARCH and Covariance Matrix Forecasting: The Nordic Stock Markets during the Asian Financial Crisis 1997–1998. *European Journal of Finance*, 10(1), pp. 44–67.

CAI, J. (1994): Markov Model of Switching-Regime ARCH. *Journal of Business and Economic Statistics*, 12(3), pp. 309–316.

CAMARERO, M., CARRION-I-SILVESTRE, J. L., TAMARIT, C. (2005): Unemployment Dynamics and NAIRU Estimates for Accession Countries: A Univariate Approach. *Journal of Comparative Economics*, 33, pp. 584–603.

CAMPBELL, J. Y., AND PERRON, P. (1991): Pitfalls and Opportunities: What Macroeconomists Should Know about Unit Roots. In: Blanchard, O. J., and Fischer, S. (Eds.), *NBER Macroeconomics Annual 1991*, pp. 141–201. Cambridge, MA/London: MIT Press.

CAPPIELLO, L., ENGLE, R., SHEPPARD, K., (2006): Asymmetric Dynamics in the Correlations of Global Equity and Bond Returns. *Journal of Financial Econometrics*, 4(4), pp. 537–572.

CARLINO, G. A., AND MILLS, L. O. (1993): Are US Regional Incomes Converging? *Journal of Monetary Economics*, 32, pp. 335–346.

CHAUDHURI, K., AND WU, Y. (2003): Random Walk versus Breaking Trend in Stock Prices: Evidence from Emerging Markets. *Journal of Banking and Finance*, 27, pp. 575–592.

CHOI, I. (2001): Unit Root Tests for Panel Data. *Journal of International Money and Finance*, 20, pp. 249–272.

CHU, C. S. J., AND WHITE, H. A. (1992): Direct Test for Changing Trend. *Journal of Business and Economic Statistics*, 10(3), pp. 289–299.

CLARE, A., O'BRIEN, R., THOMAS, S., WICKENS, M. (1998): Macroeconomic Shocks and the CAPM: Evidence from the UK Stockmarket. *International Journal of Finance and Economics*, 3(2), pp. 111–126.

COGLEY, T., AND NASON, J. M. (1995): Effects of the Hodrick-Prescott Filter on Trend and Difference Stationary Time Series: Implications for Business Cycles Research. *Journal of Economic Dynamics and Control*, 19, pp. 253–278.

COLLINGS, B. J. (1987): Compound Random Number Generators. *Journal of the American Statistical Association*, 82, Theory and Methods, pp. 525–527.

CRESPO-CUARESMA, J., AND WÓJCIK, C. (2006): Measuring Monetary Independence: Evidence from a Group of New EU Member Countries. *Journal of Comparative Economics*, 34, pp. 24–43.

CUÑADO, J., AND MCADAM, P. (2006): Real Convergence in Some Central and Eastern European Countries. *Applied Economics*, 38(20), pp. 2433–2441.

ČERNÝ, A. (2008): Stock Market Integration and the Speed of Information Transmission. *Czech Journal of Economics and Finance*, 58(1–2), pp. 2–20.

ČERNÝ, A., AND KOBLAS, M. (2004): Stock Market Integration and the Speed of Information Transmission: The Role of Data Frequency in Cointegration and Granger Causality Tests. *Journal of International Business and Economics*, 1(1), pp. 110–120.

DAVID, S., AND VAŠÍČEK, O. (2004): A macroeconomic Model and Stability Analysis by Parameters. *International Advances in Economic Research*, 10(4), pp. 297–312.

DECHERT, W. (1994): The Correlation Integral and the Independence of Gaussian and Related Processes. *SSRI Working Paper*, 9412, University of Wisconsin at Madison.

DERVIZ, A. (2002): The Uncovered Parity Properties of the Czech Koruna. *Prague Economic Papers*, 11(1), pp. 17–37.

DIBOOGLU, S., AND KUTAN, A. M. (2001): Sources of Real Exchange Rate Fluctuations in Transition Economies: The Case of Poland and Hungary. *Journal of Comparative Economics*, 29, pp. 257–275.

DICKEY, D. A., BELL, W., MILLER, R. (1986): Unit Roots in Time Series Models: Tests and Implications. *American Statistician*, 40, pp. 12–26.

DICKEY, D. A., AND FULLER, W. A. (1979): Distribution of the Estimators for Autoregressive Time Series with a Unit Root. *Journal of the American Statistical Association*, 74, pp. 427–431.

DICKEY, D. A., AND FULLER, W. A. (1981): Likelihood Ratio Statistics for Autoregressive Time Series with a Unit Root. *Econometrica*, 49(4), pp. 1057–1072.

DICKEY, D. A., AND PANTULA, S. (1987): Determining the Order of Differencing in Autoregressive Processes. *Journal of Business and Economic Statistics*, 15, pp. 455–461.

DIEBOLD, F., AND NERLOVE, M. (1990): Unit Roots in Economic Time Series: A Selective Survey. In George Rhodes Jr., and Thomas Fomby (Eds.), *Advances in Econometrics: A Research Annual*, vol. 8 (Co-integration, Spurious Regressions, and Unit Roots), JAI Press, Greenwich, Connecticut, pp. 3–69.

DIJK, D. VAN, MUNANDAR, H., HAFNER, C. M. (2011): The Euro Introduction and Non-Euro Currencies. *Applied Financial Economics*, 21(1–2), pp. 95–116.

DIKS, C. (2004): The Correlation Dimension of Returns with Stochastic Volatility. *Quantitative Finance*, 4, pp. 45–54.

DUFOUR, J.-M., AND GHYSELS, E. (EDS.) (1996): Recent Developments in the Econometrics of Structural Change. *Journal of Econometrics*, 70(1), pp. 1–8.

EDISON, H. J., AND FISHER, E. O'N. (1991): A Long-run View of the European Monetary System. *Journal of International Money and Finance*, 10(1), pp. 53–70.

ÉGERT, B., JIMÉNEZ-RODRÍGUEZ, R., KOČENDA, E., MORALES-ZUMAQUERO, A. (2006): Structural Changes in Transition Economies: Breaking the News or Breaking the Ice? *Economic Change and Restructuring*, 39(1–2), pp. 85–103..

ÉGERT, B., AND KOČENDA, E. (2007): Interdependence between Eastern and Western European Stock Markets: Evidence from Intraday Data. *Economic Systems*, 31(2), pp. 184–203.

ÉGERT, B., AND KOČENDA, E. (2011): Time-Varying Synchronization of the European Stock Markets. *Empirical Economics*, 40(2), pp. 393–407.

ÉGERT, B., AND KOČENDA, E. (2014): The impact of macro news and central bank communication on emerging European forex markets. *Economic Systems*, 38(1), pp. 73–88.

ELBOURNE, A., AND DE HAAN, J. (2006): Financial Structure and Monetary Policy Transmission in Transition Countries. *Journal of Comparative Economics*, 34(1), pp. 1–23.

ENDERS, W. (2009): *Applied Econometric Time Series*. Third Edition. New York: John Wiley&Sons.

ENGLE, R. F. (1982): Autoregressive Conditional Heteroskedasticity with Estimates of the Variance of U.K. Inflation. *Econometrica*, 50, pp. 987–1008.

ENGLE, R. F. (2002): Dynamic Conditional Correlation – A Simple Class of Multivariate GARCH Models. *Journal of Business and Economic Statistics*, 20, pp. 339–350.

ENGLE, R. F., AND BOLLERSLEV, T. (1986): Modelling the Persistence of Conditional Variances. *Econometric Reviews*, 5, pp. 1–50.

ENGLE, R. F., AND GRANGER, C. W. J. (1987): Co-integration and Error Correction: Representation, Estimation, and Testing. *Econometrica*, 55(2), pp. 251–276.

ENGLE, R. F., AND KRONER, K. F. (1995): Multivariate Simultaneous Generalized ARCH. *Econometric Theory*, 11(1), pp. 122–150.

ENGLE, R. F., AND LEE, G. J. (1999): A Permanent and Transitory Component Model of Stock Return Volatility. In: Engle, R. F., and White, H. (Eds.), *Cointegration, Causality, and Forecasting: A Festschrift in Honor of Clive W.J. Granger*, pp. 475–497, Oxford: Oxford University Press.

ENGLE, C., AND RODRIGUES, A. P. (1989): Test of International CAPM with Time-varying Covariances. *Journal of Applied Econometrics*, 4(2), pp. 119–138.

ENGLE, R. F., AND SHEPPARD, K. (2001): Theoretical and Empirical Properties of Dynamic Conditional Correlation Multivariate GARCH. *NBER Working Paper*, 8554.

ENGLE, R. F., LILIEN, D. M., ROBBINS, R. P. (1987): Estimating Time Varying Risk Premia in the Term Structure: the ARCH-M model. *Econometrica*, 55, pp. 391–408.

EWING, B. T., AND WUNNAVA, P. V. (2001): Unit Roots and Structural Breaks in North American Unemployment Rates. *North American Journal of Economics and Finance*, 12(3), pp. 273–282.

FERIDUN, M. (2006): An Investigation of the German Dominance Hypothesis in the Context of Eastern Enlargement of the EU. *Prague Economic Papers*, 15(2), pp. 172–182.

FESTIĆ, M. (2006): Procyclicality of Financial and Real Sector in Transition Economies. *Prague Economic Papers*, 15(4), pp. 315–349.

FESTIĆ, M., KAVKLER, A., REPINA, S. (2011): The Macroeconomic Sources of Systemic Risk in the Banking Sectors of Five New EU Member States. *Journal of Banking and Finance*, 35(2), pp. 310–322.

FIDRMUC, J., AND TICHIT, A. (2009): Mind the break! Accounting for changing patterns of growth during transition. *Economic Systems*, 33(2), pp. 138–154.

FISHMAN, G. S., AND MOORE, L. R. (1982): A Statistical Evaluation of Multiplicative Congruential Random Number Generators with Modulus 231-1. *Journal of the American Statistical Association*, 77, Theory and Methods, pp. 129–136.

FRIEDMAN, M. (1992): Do Old Fallacies Ever Die? *Journal of Economic Literature*, 30, pp. 2129–2132.

FU, R., AND PAGANI, M. (2012): On the cointegration of international stock indices. *Journal of Economics and Finance*, 36(2), pp. 463–480.

FUKAČ, M. (2005): Do Inflation Expectations Surveys Yield Macroeconomically Relevant Information? *Czech Journal of Economics and Finance*, 55(7–8), pp. 344–362.

FULLER, W. A. (1976): *Introduction to Statistical Time Series*. New York: John Wiley&Sons.

GERDTHAM, U.-G., AND LÖTHGREN, M. (2002): New Panel Results on Cointegration of International Health Expenditure and GDP. *Applied Economicss*, 34, pp. 1679–1686.

GERŠL, A. (2005): Testing the effectiveness of the Czech National Bank's foreign-exchange interventions. *Czech Journal of Economics and Finance*, 55(9–10), pp. 398–415.

GERŠL, A., AND HOLUB, T. (2006): Foreign Exchange Interventions Under Inflation Targeting: The Czech Experience. *Contemporary Economic Policy*, 24(4), pp. 475–491.

GHAZAL, G. A. (1994): Moments of the Ratio of two Dependent Quadratic Forms. *Statistics and Probability Letters*, 20, pp. 313–319.

GILMAN, M., AND NAKOV, A. (2004): Granger Causality of the Inflation-Growth Mirror in Accession Countries. *The Economics of Transition*, 12 (4), pp. 653–681.

GJIKA, D., AND HORVÁTH, R. (2013): Stock market comovements in Central Europe: Evidence from the asymmetric DCC model Original Research Article. *Economic Modelling*, 33, pp. 55–64.

GLOSTEN, L. R., JAGANNATHAN, R., RUNKLE, D. E. (1993): On the Relation Between the Expected Value and the Volatility of the Nominal Excess Return on Stock. *Journal of Finance*, 48, pp. 1779–1801.

GOLDBERG, S. (1986): *Introduction to Difference Equations, with Illustrative Examples from Economics, Psychology, and Sociology*. New York: Dover.

GRANGER, C. W. J. (1969): Investigating Causal Relationships by Econometric Models and Cross-Spectral Methods. *Econometrica*, 37(3), pp. 424–438.

GRANGER, C. W. J. (1981): Some Properties of Time Series Data and their Use in Economic Model Specification. *Journal of Econometrics*, pp. 121–130.

GRANGER, C. W. J. (1983): Co-integrated Variables and Error-Correction Models. *UCSD Discussion paper*, 83–13a.

GRANGER, C. W. J., AND WEISS, A. A. (1983): Time Series Analysis of Error-Correcting Models. In: Studies in Econometrics, Time Series, and Multivariate Statistics, New York: Academic Press, pp. 255–278.

GRASSBERGER, P., AND PROCACCIA, I. (1983): Measuring the Strangeness of Strange Attractors. *Physica 9D*, pp. 189–208.

GREENE, W. H. (2008): *Econometric Analysis*. Seventh Edition. Prentice Hall.

GURGUL, H., MAJDOSZ, P., MESTEL, R. (2006): Implications of Dividend Announcements for the Stock Prices and Trading Volumes of DAX Companies. *Czech Journal of Economics and Finance*, 56(1–2), pp. 58–67.

HADRI, K. (1999): Testing for Stationarity in Heterogeneous Panel Data with Serially Correlated Errors. *University of Liverpool Research Papers in Economics, Finance and Accounting*.

HADRI, K. (2000): Testing for Stationarity in Heterogeneous Panel Data. *Econometrics Journal*, 3(2), pp. 148–161.

HADRI, K., AND LARSSON, R. (2005): Testing for Stationarity in Heterogeneous Panel Data where the Time Dimension is Finite. *Econometrics Journal*, 8(1), pp. 55–69.

HANNAN, E. J., AND QUINN, B. G. (1979): The Determination of the Order of an Autoregression. *Journal of the Royal Statistical Society*, B, 41, pp. 190–195.

HAMILTON, J. D., AND SUSMEL, R. (1994): Autoregressive Conditional Heteroskedasticity and Changes in Regime. *Journal of Econometrics*, 64, pp. 307–333.

HANOUSEK, J., AND FILER, R. (2000): The Relationship between Economic Factors and Equity Markets in Central Europe. *Economics of Transition*, 8(3), pp. 623–638.

HANOUSEK, J., AND KOČENDA, E. (1998): Monetární vazby na českém mezibankovním trhu (Czech Money Market: Emerging Links among Interest Rates): *Czech Journal of Economics and Finance*, 48(2), pp. 99–109.

HANOUSEK, J., KOČENDA, E. (2011A): Public Investments and Fiscal Performance in New EU Member States. *Fiscal Studies*, 32(1), pp. 43–72.

HANOUSEK, J., KOČENDA, E. (2011B): Foreign News and Spillovers in Emerging European Stock Markets. *Review of International Economics*, 19(1), pp. 170–188.

HANOUSEK, J., KOČENDA, E, KUTAN, A.M. (2009): The Reaction of Asset Prices to Macroeconomic Announcements in New EU Markets: Evidence from Intraday Data. *Journal of Financial Stability*, 5(2), pp. 199–219.

HAYO, B., AND KUTAN, A. M. (2005): The Impact of News, Oil Prices and Global Market Developments on Russian Financial Markets. *The Economics of Transition*, 13, pp. 373–393.

HENRY, J., AND MCADAM, P. (2001): A Retrospective Structural Break Analysis of the French German Interest Rate Differential in the Run-Up to EMU. *International Finance Review*, 2, pp. 21–49.

HODRICK, R. J., AND PRESCOTT, E. C. (1997): Postwar U.S. Business Cycles: An Empirical Investigation. *Journal of Money, Credit and Banking*, 29(1), pp. 1–16.

HOLMES, M. J., OTERO, J. (2010): On the Stationarity of Current Account Deficits in the European Union. *Review of International Economics*, 18(4), pp. 730–740.

HORSKÁ, H. (2002): Inflation Targeting in Poland (a comparison with the Czech Republic): *Prague Economic Papers*, 11(3), pp. 237–254.

HORVÁTH, R., AND PETROVSKI, D. (2013): International stock market integration: Central and South Eastern Europe compared. *Economic Systems*, 37(1), pp. 81–91.

HOSKING, J. R. M. (1981): Fractional Differencing. *Biometrika*, 68, pp. 165–176.

HSIEH, D. A. (1991): Chaos and Nonlinear Dynamics: Application to Financial Markets. *Journal of Finance*, 46, pp. 1839–1877.

HSIEH, D. A., AND LEBARON, B. (1993): The BDS Test. Chapter 2, in Brock, W. A., Hsieh, D. A., LeBaron, B., *Nonlinear Dynamics, Chaos, and Instability: Statistical Theory and Economic Evidence*. Third edition. MIT Press, Cambridge, Massachusetts.

HSING, Y. (2004): Impacts of Macroeconomic Policies on Output in the Czech Republic: An Application of Romer's IS-MP-IA Model. *Prague Economic Papers*, 13(4), pp. 339–346.

HSING, Y. (2005): Effects of Macroeconomic Policies and Stock Market Performance on the Estonian Economy. *Prague Economic Papers*, 14(2), pp. 109–116.

HURNÍK, J., AND NAVRÁTIL, D. (2005): Labor Market Performance and Macroeconomic Policy: The Time Varying NAIRU in the CR. *Czech Journal of Economics and Finance*, 55(1–2), pp. 25–39.

HUŠEK, R., AND FORMÁNEK, T. (2005): Estimation of the Czech Republic Sacrifice Ratio for the Transition Period. *Prague Economic Papers*, 14(1), pp. 51–63.

HUTSON, E., AND KEARNEY, C. (2005): Merger Arbitrage and the Interaction between Target and Bidder Stocks during Takeover Bids. *Research in International Business and Finance*, 19(1), pp. 1–26.

HYLLEBERG, S. R., ENGLE, R. F., GRANGER, C. W. J., YOO, B. (1990): Seasonal integration and cointegration. *Journal of Econometrics*, 44, pp. 215–238.

IM, K. S., PESARAN, M. H., SHIN, Y. (2003): Testing for Unit Roots in Heterogeneous Panels. *Journal of Econometrics*, 115(1), pp. 53–74.

INCLÁN, C., AND TIAO, G. C. (1994): Use of Cumulative Sums of Squares for Retrospective Detection of Changes of Variance. *Journal of the American Statistical Association*, 89(427), pp. 913–923.

JOHANSEN, S. (1988): Statistical Analysis of Cointegration Vectors. *Journal of Economic Dynamics and Control*, 12, pp. 231–254.

JOHANSEN, S. (1991): Estimation and Hypothesis Testing of Cointegration Vectors in Gaussian Vector Autoregressive Models. *Econometrica*, 59(6), pp. 1551–1580.

JOHANSEN, S., AND JUSELIUS, K. (1990): Maximum Likelihood Estimation and Inference on Cointegration – with Applications to the Demand for Money. *Oxford Bulletin of Economics and Statistics*, 52(2), pp. 169–210.

JOHANSEN, S., AND JUSELIUS, K. (1992): Testing Structural Hypotheses in a Multivariate Cointegration Analysis of the PPP and the UIP for UK. *Journal of Econometrics*, 53, pp. 211–244.

KAPOUNEK, S., AND LACINA, L. (2011): Inflation Perceptions and Anticipations in the Old Eurozone Member States. *Prague Economic Papers*, 11(2), pp. 120–139.

KEARNEY, C., AND MUCKLEY, C. (2008): Can the Traditional Asian US Dollar Peg Exchange Rate Regime Be Extended to Include the Japanese Yen? *International Review of Financial Analysis*, 17(5), pp. 870–885.

KEJRIWAL, M., AND PERRON, P. (2010): Testing for Multiple Structural Changes in Cointegrated Regression Models. *Journal of Business & Economic Statistics*, 28(4), pp. 503–522.

KIM, C. J., AND NELSON, C. R. (1999): Has the U.S. Economy Become More Stable? A Bayesian Approach Based on a Markov-Switching Model of the Business Cycle. *Review of Economics and Statistics*, 81(4), pp. 608–616.

KIM, S., AND TSURUMI, H. (2000): Korean Currency Crisis and Regime Change: A Multivariate GARCH Model with Bayesian Approach. *Asia Pacific Financial Markets*, 7(1), pp. 31–44.

KMENTA, J. (1986): *Elements of Econometrics*, Second Edition. New York: Macmillan Publishing Company.

KOČENDA, E. (1996): Volatility of a Seemingly Fixed Exchange Rate. *Eastern European Economics*, 34(6), pp. 37–67.

KOČENDA, E. (1998): Altered Band and Exchange Volatility. *Economics of Transition*, 6(1), pp. 173–181.

KOČENDA, E. (2001A): Macroeconomic Convergence in Transition Economies. *Journal of Comparative Economics*, 29, pp. 1–23.

KOČENDA, E. (2001B): An Alternative to the BDS test: Integration Across the Correlation Integral. *Econometric Reviews*, 20(3), pp. 337–351.

KOČENDA, E. (2005): Beware of Breaks in Exchange Rates: Evidence from European Transition Countries. *Economic Systems*, 29(3), pp. 307–324.

KOČENDA, E., AND BRIATKA, L. (2005): Optimal Range for the iid Test Based on Integration across the Correlation Integral. *Econometric Reviews*, 24(3), pp. 265–296.

KOČENDA, E., KUTAN, A., YIGIT, T. (2006): Pilgrims to the Eurozone: How Far, How Fast? *Economic Systems*, 30(4), pp. 311–327.

KOČENDA, E, KUTAN, A. M., YIGIT, T. M. (2008): Fiscal Convergence in the European Union. *North-American Journal of Economics and Finance*, 19(3), pp. 319–330.

KOČENDA, E., MAUREL, M., SCHNABL, G. (2013): Short- and Long-Term Growth Effects of Exchange Rate Adjustment. *Review of International Economics*, 21(1), pp. 137–150.

KOČENDA, E., AND PAPELL, D. H. (1997): Inflation Convergence within the European Union: A Panel Data Analysis. *International Journal of Finance and Economics*, 2(3), pp. 189–198.

KOČENDA, E., AND VALACHY, J. (2006): Exchange Rate Volatility and Regime Change: Visegrad Comparison. *Journal of Comparative Economics*, 34(4), pp. 727–753.

KOMÁREK, L., AND MELECKÝ, M. (2003): Currency Substitution in a Transitional Economy with an Application to the Czech Republic. *Eastern European Economics*, 41(4), pp. 72–99.

KRISHNAMURTHI, L., NARAYAN, J., RAJ, S. P. (1989): Intervention Analysis Using Control Series and Exogenous Variables in a Transfer Function Model: A Case Study. *International Journal of Forecasting*, 5(1), pp. 21–27.

KROLZIG, H. M. (2001): Business Cycle Measurement in the Presence of Structural Change: International Evidence. *International Journal of Forecasting*, 17(3), pp. 349–368.

KUTAN, A., AND YIGIT, T. (2004): Nominal and Real Stochastic Convergence of Transition Economies. *Journal of Comparative Economics*, 32, pp. 23–36.

KUTAN, A., AND YIGIT, T. (2005): Nominal and Real Stochastic Convergence: Are the New EU Members Ready to Join the Euro Zone? *Journal of Comparative Economics*, 33(2), pp. 387–400.

KWIATKOWSKI, D., PHILLIPS, P., SCHMIDT, P., SHIN, Y. (1992): Testing the Null Hypothesis of Stationarity against the Alternative of a Unit Root. *Journal of Econometrics*, 54, pp. 159–178.

LEDOIT, O., SANTA-CLARA, P., WOLF, M. (2003): Flexible Multivariate GARCH Modeling with an Application to International Stock Markets. *The Review of Economics and Statistics*, 85(3), pp. 735–747.

LEE, K., PESARAN, M. H., SMITH, R. (1997): Growth and Convergence in Multi-Country Empirical Stochastic Solow Model. Journal of Applied Econometrics, 12(4), pp. 357–392.

LEÓN-LEDESMA, M. A., AND MCADAM, P. (2004): Unemployment, Hysteresis and Transition. *Scottish Journal of Political Economy*, 51(3), pp. 377–401.

LEVIN, A., AND LIN, C.-F. (1992): Unit Root Tests in Panel Data: Asymptotic and Finite-Sample Properties. University of California at San Diego, *Economics Working Paper Series*, 92–23, Department of Economics, UC San Diego.

LEVIN, A., LIN, C.-F., CHU, C.-S.-J. (2002): Unit Root Tests in panel data: Asymptotic and Finite-Sample Properties. *Journal of Econometrics*, 108(1), pp. 1–24.

LINTNER, J. (1965): The Valuation of Risk Assets and the Selection of Risky Investment in Stock Portfolios and Capital Budgets. *Review of Economics and Statistics*, 47, pp. 13–37.

LJUNG, G., AND BOX, G. (1978): On a Measure of Lack of Fit in Time Series Models. *Biometrica*, 65, pp. 297–303.

LYÓCSA, Š., BAUMÖHL, E., VÝROST, T. (2011A): The Stock Markets and Real Economic Activity: New Evidence from CEE. *Eastern European Economics*, 49(4), pp. 6–23.

LYÓCSA, Š., BAUMÖHL, E., VÝROST, T. (2011B): Volatility Regimes in Macroeconomic Time Series: The Case of the Visegrad Group. *Czech Journal of Economics and Finance*, 61(6), pp. 530–544.

MACKINNON, J. G. (1991): A Critical Values for Cointegration Tests. In: Engle, R. F., and Granger, C. W. J. (Eds.), *Long-Run Economic Relationships: Readings in Cointegration*, Oxford University Press, New York, pp. 266–276.

MADDALA, G. S., AND WU, S. (1999): A Comparative Study of Unit Root Tests with Panel Data and a New Simple Test. *Oxford Bulletin of Economics and Statistics*, Special Issue 61, pp. 631–652.

MADDISON, A. (1991): *Dynamic Forces in capitalist development*. Oxford University Press, Oxford.

MANDELBROT, B. (1963): The variation of Certain Speculative Prices. *The Journal of Business*, 36, pp. 394–419.

MARQUARDT, D. (1963): An Algorithm for Least-Squares Estimation of Nonlinear Parameters. *SIAM Journal of Applied Mathematics*, 11, pp. 431–441.

MCCOSKEY, S., AND KAO, C. (1998): A Residual-Based Test of the Null of Cointegration in Panel Data. *Econometric Reviews*, 17, pp. 57–84.

MCKENZIE, M. D., AND KIM, S.-J. (2007): Evidence of an Asymmetry in the Relationship Between Volatility and Autocorrelation. *International Review of Financial Analysis*, 16(1), pp. 22–40.

MILLS, T. C., AND MARKELLOS, R. N. (2008): *The Econometric Modelling of Financial Time Series*, 3rd edition. Cambridge University Press.

MILLS, T. C. (2003): *Modelling Trends and Cycles in Economic Time Series*. Palgrave Macmillan, Houndmills, United Kingdom.

MILLS, T. C., AND WANG, P. (2003): Have Output Growth Rates Stabilised? Evidence from the G-7 Economies. *Scottish Journal of Political Economy*, 50(3), pp. 232–246.

MOORE, T., AND PENTECOST, E. J. (2006): An Investigation into the Sources of Fluctuation in Real and Nominal Wage Rates in Eight EU Countries: A Structural VAR Approach. *Journal of Comparative Economics*, 34(2), pp. 357–376.

MOSIN, J. (1966): Equilibrium in a Capital Asset Market. *Econometrica*, 34, pp. 768–783.

NELSON, C. R., AND PLOSSER, C. I. (1982): Trends and Random Walks in Macroeconomic Time Series: Some Evidence and Implications. *Journal of Monetary Economics*, 10, pp. 130–162.

NELSON, D. B. (1990): ARCH Models as Diffusion Approximations. *Journal of Econometrics*, 45, pp. 7–38.

NELSON, D. B. (1991): Conditional Heteroskedasticity in Asset Returns: A New Approach. *Econometrica*, 59, pp. 347–370.

NEWEY, W., AND WEST, K. (1987): A Simple, Positive Semi-definite, Heteroskedasticity and Autocorrelation Consistent Covariance Matrix. *Econometrica*, 55(3), pp. 703–708.

NG, S., AND PERRON, P. (1995): Unit Root Tests in ARMA Models with Data-Dependent Methods of the Selection of the Truncation Lag. *Journal of the American Statistical Association*, 90, pp. 268–281.

OPLOTNIK, Ž. (2003): Bank of Slovenia Adjustment Policy to Surges in Capital Flows. *Prague Economic Papers*, 12(3), pp. 217–232.

ORLOWSKI, L. T. (2003): Monetary Convergence and Risk Premiums in the EU Accession Countries. *Open Economies Review*, 14, pp. 251–267.

ORLOWSKI, L. T. (2004): Money Rules for Monetary Convergence to the Euro. *Journal of Policy Modelling*, 26 (7), pp. 817–837.

OZMEN, E., AND PARMAKSIZ, K. (2003A): Policy Regime Change and the Feldstein-Horioka Puzzle: The UK evidence. *Journal of Policy Modeling*, 25(2), pp. 137–149.

OZMEN, E., AND PARMAKSIZ, K. (2003B): Exchange Rate Regimes and the Feldstein-Horioka Puzzle: The French Evidence. *Applied Economics*, 35(2), pp. 217–222.

PAGAN, A. R., AND SCHWERT, G. W. (1990): Alternative Models of Conditional Stock Volatility. *Journal of Econometrics*, 45, pp. 267–290.

PAPELL, D. H., MURRAY, C. J., GHIBLAWI, H. (2000): The Structure of Unemployment. *Review of Economics and Statistics*, 82(2), pp. 309–315.

PARK, J. Y., AND CHOI, B. (1988): A New Approach to Testing for a Unit Root. Department of Economics, *Cornell University Working Paper* 88–23.

PATTERSON, K. (2000): *An Introduction to Applied Econometrics: A Time Series Approach*. Palgrave, Houndmills, United Kingdom.

PEARL, J. (2000): *Causality: Models, Reasoning, and Inference*. Cambridge UniversityPress.

PEDRONI, P. (1999): Critical Values for Cointegration Tests in Heterogeneous Panel with Multiple Regressors. *Oxford Bulletin of Economics and Statistics*, 61, pp. 653–670.

PEDRONI, P. (2004): Panel Cointegration: Asymptotic and Finite Sample Properties of Pooled Time Series Tests with an Application to the PPP Hypothesis. *Econometric Theory*, 3, pp. 579–625.

PERRON, P. (1989): The Great Crash, the Oil Price Shock, and the Unit Root Hypothesis. *Econometrica*, 57(6), pp. 1361–1401.

PERRON, P., AND QU, Z. (2007): Estimating and Testing Multiple Structural Changes in Multivariate Regressions. *Econometrica*, 75(2), pp. 459–502

PERRON, P., AND VOGELSANG, T. J. (1992): Nonstationarity and Level Shifts with an Application to Purchasing Power Parity. *Journal of Business and Economic Statistics*, 10, pp. 301–320.

PESARAN, M. H, SHIN, Y., SMITH, R. J. (2001): Bounds Testing Approaches to the Analysis of Level Relationships. *Journal of Applied Econometrics*, 16(3), pp. 289–326.

PHILLIPS, P. (1987): Time Series Regression with a Unit Root. *Econometrica*, 55(2), pp. 277–301.

PHILLIPS, P., AND PERRON, P. (1988): Testing for a Unit Root in Time Series Regression. *Biometrica*, 75, pp. 335–346.

PHILLIPS, P., AND OULIARIS, S. (1990): Asymptotic Properties of Residual Based Tests for Cointegration. *Econometrica*, 58, pp. 165–193.

PODPIERA, R. (2001): Interactions between Markets and Dually Listed Stocks: The Case of the Czech Republic. *Czech Journal of Economics and Finance*, 51(3), pp. 166–181.

POGHOSYAN, T., KOČENDA, E., ZEMČÍK, P. (2008): Modeling Foreign Exchange Risk Premium in Armenia. *Emerging Markets Finance and Trade*, 44(1), pp. 41–61.

QUAH, D. (1992): The Relative Importance of Permanent and Transitory Components: Identification and Some Theoretical Bounds. *Econometrica*, 60(1), pp. 107–118.

QUAH, D. (1993): Galton's Fallacy and Tests of the Convergence Hypothesis. *Scandinavian Journal of Economics*, 95, pp. 427–443.

QUAH, D. (1994): Exploiting Cross Section Variation for Unit Root Inference in Dynamic Data. *Economics Letters*, 44(1–2), pp. 9–19.

QUAH, D. (1996): Empirics for Economic Growth and Convergence. *European Economic Review*, 40(6), pp. 1353–1375.

ROCKINGER, M., AND URGA, G. (2001): A Time-Varying Parameter Model to Test for Predictability and Integration in the Stock Markets of Transition Economies. *Journal of Business and Economic Statistics*, 19(1), pp. 73–84.

SANSÓ, A., ARRAGÓ, V., CARRION, J. L. (2004): Testing for change in the unconditional variance of financial time series. *Revista de Economiá Financiera*, 4, 32–53.

SAYGINSOY, Ö., AND VOGELSANG, T.J. (2011): Testing For a Shift in Trend at an Unknown Date: A Fixed-*b* Analysis of Heteroskedasticity Autocorrelation Robust OLS-Based Tests. *Econometric Theory*, 27(05), pp. 992–1025.

SCHWARZ, G. (1978): Estimating the Dimension of a Model. *Annals of Statistics*, 6, pp. 461–464.

SCHWERT, W. (1989): Tests for Unit Roots: A Monte Carlo Investigation, *Journal of Business and Economic Statistics*, 7(2), pp. 147–159.

SENSIER, M., AND VAN DIJK, D. J. (2004): Testing for Volatility Changes in U.S. Macroeconomic Time Series. *The Review of Economics and Statistics*, 86(3), pp. 833–839.

SHARPE, W. (1964): Capital Asset Prices: A Theory of Capital Market Equilibrium Under Condition of Risk. *Journal of Finance*, 19, pp. 425–442.

SIMS, CH. (1980): Macroeconomics and Reality. *Econometrica*, 48, pp. 1–49.

SPEIGHT, A. E. H., AND McMILLAN, D. G. (2001): Cointegration and Predictability in Prereform East European Black-Market Exchange Rates. *Applied Economics Letters*, 8(12), pp. 755–759.

STAVÁREK, D. (2005): Stock Prices and Exchange Rates in the EU and the USA: Evidence of their Mutual Interactions. *Czech Journal of Economics and Finance*, 55(5–6), pp. 141–161.

STAVREV, E. (2006): Driving Forces of Inflation in New EU Countries. *Czech Journal of Economics and Finance*, 56(5–6), pp. 246–256.

STOCK, J. H., AND WATSON, M. W. (1993): A Simple Estimator of Cointegrating Vectors in Higher Order Integrated Systems. *Econometrica*, 61(4), pp. 783–820.

STOCK, J. H., AND WATSON, M. W. (1996): Evidence and Structural Instability in Macroeconomic Time Series Relations. *Journal of Business and Economic Statistics*, 14(1), pp. 11–30.

STRAUSS, J., AND YIGIT, T. M. (2003): Shortfalls of Panel Unit Root Testing. *Economics Letters*, 81(3), pp. 309–313.

SYRIOPOULOS, T. (2006): Risk and Return Implications from Investing in Emerging European Stock Markets. *Journal of International Financial Markets, Institutions and Money*, 16(3), pp. 283–299.

THEILER, J., AND LOOKMAN, T. (1993): Statistical Error in a Chord Estimator of Correlation Dimension: The 'Rule of Five'. *International Journal of Bifurcations and Chaos*, 3, pp. 765–771.

TODA, H. Y., AND YAMAMOTO, T. (1995): Statistical inference in vector autoregressions with possibly integrated processes. *Journal of Econometrics*, 66(1–2), pp. 225–250.

TOMLJANOVICH, M., AND VOGELSANG, T. J. (2002): Are US Regional Incomes Converging? Using New Econometric Methods to Examine Old Issues. *Empirical Economics*, 27, pp. 49–62.

UCTUM, M., THURSTON, T., UCTUM, R. (2006): Public Debt, the Unit Root Hypothesis and Structural Breaks: A Multi-Country Analysis. *Economica*, 73, pp. 129–156.

VOGELSANG, T. J. (1997): Wald-type Tests for Detecting Breaks in the Trend Function of a Dynamic Time Series. *Econometric Theory*, 13, pp. 818–849.

VOGELSANG, T. J. (1998): Trend Function Hypothesis Testing in the Presence of Serial Correlation. *Econometrica*, 66, pp. 123–148.

VOGELSANG, T. J. (1999): Testing for a Shift in Trend when Serial Correlation is of Unknown Form. *Tinbergen Institute Discussion Paper*, 99–016/4.

VOGELSANG, T., AND PERRON, P. (1998): Additional Tests for a Unit Root Allowing the Possibility of Breaks in the Trend Function. *International Economic Review*, 39, pp. 1073–1100.

VOŠVRDA, M., AND ŽIKEŠ, F. (2004): An Application of the GARCH-*t* Model on Central European Stock Returns. *Prague Economic Papers*, 13(1), pp. 26–39.

WANG, J., AND ZIVOT, E. (2000): A Bayesian Time Series Model of Multiple Structural Changes in Level, Trend and Variance. *Journal of Business and Economics*, 18, pp. 374–386.

WESTERLUND, J. (2005): A Panel CUSUM Test of the Null of Cointegration. *Oxford Bulletin of Economics and Statistics*, 62, pp. 231–262.

WESTERLUND, J. (2007): Testing for Error Correction in Panel Data. *Oxford Bulletin of Economics and Statistics*, 69, pp. 709–748.

WU, Y. (1997): The Trend Behavior of Real Exchange Rates: Evidence from OECD Countries. *Weltwirtschaftliches Archiv*, 133(2), pp. 282–296.

WU, J. L., TSAI, L. J., CHEN, S. L. (2004): Are Real Exchange Rates Non-Stationary? The Pacific Basin Perspective. *Journal of Asian Economics*, 15(2), pp. 425–438.

YALCIN, Y., AND YUCEL, E. M. (2006): The Day-of-the-Week Effect on Stock-Market Volatility and Return: Evidence from Emerging Markets. *Czech Journal of Economics and Finance*, 56(5–6), pp. 258–278.

ZAKOIAN, J.-M. (1994): Threshold heteroskedastic models. *Journal of Economic Dynamics and Control*, 18(5), pp. 931–955.

ZETTELMEYER, J. (2004): The Impact of Monetary Policy on the Exchange Rate: Evidence from Three Small Open Economies. *Journal of Monetary Economics*, 51, pp. 635–652.

ZIVOT, E., AND ANDREWS, D. (1992): Further Evidence on the Great Crash, the Oil Price Shock, and the Unit Root Hypothesis. *Journal of Business and Economic Statistics*, pp. 251–270.

ŽIKEŠ, F., AND BUBÁK, V. (2006A): Seasonality and Non-Trading Effect on Central European Stock Markets. *Czech Journal of Economics and Finance*, 56(1–2), pp. 69–79.

ŽIKEŠ, F., AND BUBÁK, V. (2006B): Trading Intensity and Intraday Volatility on the Prague Stock Exchange: Evidence from an Autoregressive Conditional Duration Model. *Czech Journal of Economics and Finance*, 56(5–6), pp. 223–244.

INDEX